CROSSCURRENTS *Modern Critiques*

CROSSCURRENTS *Modern Critiques*
Harry T. Moore, *General Editor*

Edward A. Bloom and Lillian D. Bloom

Willa Cather's
GIFT OF SYMPATHY

WITH A PREFACE BY
Harry T. Moore

Carbondale

SOUTHERN ILLINOIS UNIVERSITY PRESS

For F.B. and B.B.

FIRST PUBLISHED, FEBRUARY 1962
SECOND PRINTING, SEPTEMBER 1962
ARCTURUS BOOKS EDITION, FEBRUARY 1964

Copyright © 1962 by Southern Illinois University Press
All rights reserved
Library of Congress Catalog Card Number 62–7231
Printed in the United States of America
Designed by Andor Braun

ALTHOUGH Willa Cather was born in Virginia, she spent most of her girlhood and some of her young womanhood on the Nebraska prairies in the 1880's and 90's. In her subsequent writings, she captured the spirit of that time and place as no one else has captured it, and any future attempts to do so will have the handicap of being synthetic.

Nebraska had been opened to homesteaders in 1863: Willa Cather knew the first generation of them. She knew those of American stock, such as her own family, and those of foreign birth, such as the Pavelkas from Bohemia, whom she portrayed as the Shimerdas in My Ántonia. After attending the state university at Lincoln, then a prairie town, Miss Cather was a teacher and journalist in Pittsburgh and New York. Eventually she broke away from a highly successful career on the staff of McClure's to become a novelist. Some of her books reflect her extensive travels in the United States, Canada, and Europe, but her best work remains rooted in her Nebraska experience.

A Lost Lady was so intrinsically Nebraskan that Miss Cather found she couldn't change the locale of the main action to Colorado when she wanted to disguise the story in order to avoid hurting the feelings of friends of its leading characters, the late Governor and Mrs. Garber of Nebraska. The Professor's House is for the most part set in a small college, something like the University of Nebraska in Willa Cather's student days; she places it vaguely on the shores of Lake Michigan, but in this case a generalized Midwestern scene was sufficient to contrast with the sharply detailed New Mexico sequence. What she was essentially doing in this novel was examining the decay of American values. She believed that the deterioration set in about 1922—an ironic year to select, for Miss Cather was a Republican, and in 1922 Warren G. Harding's cronies were running wild. In any event, after that time most of Willa Cather's work focused, not always with complete artistic success, upon what seemed to her a better-ordered past.

The approach to Willa Cather by Edward A. and Lillian D. Bloom in the present volume is through a study of her "gift of sympathy," which they have skillfully related to this author's thematic interests and her technical proficiency. They deal not only with the fiction and the small body of poetry, but also with the essays, which are full of theoretical and factual statements that form an important commentary on Miss Cather's ideas as they were worked out in her writings. The present book is thus a highly valuable examination of this author and of an important part of modern American literary expression.

HARRY T. MOORE

Southern Illinois University
May 12, 1961

CONTENTS

INTRODUCTION

IN THE FOLLOWING PAGES we have attempted to analyze and illuminate the art of Willa Cather. Our major concern, of course, has been with the novels. But since Miss Cather tended to present variations on relatively few themes in her short stories, in her novellas, and even in her literary essays, as well as in her novels, we have gone to all of her printed writings which are germane to the scope of this book. And since Miss Cather's moral, philosophical, and critical attitudes are virtually all of a piece with her esthetic practice, we have explored her nonfictional utterances and have attempted to bring them into conjunction with her fiction.

Like many others of Miss Cather's large audience, we began reading her novels with no motivation except to derive pleasure. Not only did we discover an abundance of enjoyment, but we soon found ourselves tempted to go back and reread—many times. Each reading became a fresh experience; familiar details became clearer, and springs hitherto unnoticed kept welling to the surface. By her own admission a practitioner of simplicity in art, Miss Cather affords the pleasures of uninvolved narration and yet embroiders and augments her stories with subtle layers of related meanings. Gradually, we felt that we were discovering a richness of esthetic and idea in her novels which no single or superficial reading could possibly reveal.

It is the essence of Willa Cather's art and mind as they seem to us which we have wished to set forth. Fundamentally, we have concluded that she was interested in three major themes: the spirit of the frontier in both modern and ancient times; the threat to that spirit in the encroachments of materialism and selfish acquisitiveness; and the nature of the artist. Our chief materials, as we have said, have been the written works which she produced over a period of almost fifty years. Not all of them, of course, are equally pertinent, and a few have no direct bearing upon the major themes as we understand them. For that reason we have stressed certain works while concerning ourselves with others only casually. The latter include *Alexander's Bridge, Lucy Gayheart,* and *My Mortal Enemy.*

To present a meaningful critical view of Willa Cather, we have organized our chapters as demonstrations of the principal thematic concerns and of the narrative techniques which she employed in their development. Additionally—that is to say, in the explication of these matters—we have devoted chapters to Miss Cather's literary criticism and her moral or philosophical enunciations. To synthesize her attitudes and working habits, we have analyzed her most famous novel, *Death Comes for the Archbishop.* And by way of conclusion, we have attempted to identify her with the great tradition of nineteenth-century American fiction, as well as with certain aspects of literature common to her own era.

The seeds of *Willa Cather's Gift of Sympathy* have been germinating for several years. Our earliest ventures may be found in articles which we wrote for periodicals, and in which we had not yet anticipated the problems of book publication. We are grateful for the opportunity we have had to hear editorial and critical reaction to the earlier essays, to reassure ourselves that our approach was sound, and to amplify, alter, or omit details and evaluations. We wish to acknowledge in at least this small measure the responsiveness of the editors of *American Literature, University of Toronto Quarterly,* and *Twentieth-Century Literature.* We wish also to express our thanks to Hyatt H. Waggoner, who read our book in manuscript and generously gave us the benefit of his knowledge of American literature. But responsibility for the presentation of fact and opinion is finally and fully ours.

A writer as celebrated as Willa Cather must be the subject of many books and essays, all of which we have read with degrees of appreciation and reward. The only justification for a new study of Miss Cather, however, is that it attempt to take a direction which others have not taken. Such has been our aim throughout this volume. Yet certain books have proved indispensable because of their necessary biographical details or insights of a personal nature which are not revealed directly in Willa Cather's fiction. These are the biographies by E. K. Brown (completed by Leon Edel), *Willa Cather* (New York, 1953), and Edith Lewis, *Willa Cather Living* (New York, 1953); also the volume by Mildred Bennett, *The World of Willa Cather* (New York, 1951).

For permission to quote extensively from the following works, we are grateful to Houghton Mifflin Company: *Alexander's Bridge, O Pioneers!, The Song of the Lark,* and *My Ántonia.* We are also indebted to Alfred A. Knopf and the estate of Willa Cather for permission to quote from the following: *One of Ours, A Lost Lady, The Professor's House, My Mor-*

*tal Enemy, Death Comes for the Archbishop, Shadows
on the Rock, Lucy Gayheart, Sapphira and the Slave
Girl, Youth and the Bright Medusa, Obscure Des-
tinies, The Old Beauty and Others, Not Under Forty,*
and *Willa Cather on Writing.*

Willa Cather's
GIFT OF SYMPATHY

IF, AS IS OFTEN PROPOSED, an author's work must be examined in the light of personal traditions—the heritage of family and place, inborn attitudes and environment—then it must be noted that Willa Cather was a Southerner by birth, a Midwesterner by adoption, and a cosmopolitan by instinct. These complexities were augmented by the aristocratic, pioneer, religious, and humanitarian sympathies of her private life. Such diverse strains might also be expected to reveal themselves artistically in a broad variety of themes and situations, for the serious artist has a penchant—conscious or unconscious—for interpreting life within the ready frame of his own sensitized experiences.

But Willa Cather, as an artist both keen and serious, must prove a disappointment to those who would interpret her fiction predominantly from the pattern of her biography. While such a testing of development is justifiable for the study of many writers, it must when applied to Miss Cather be regarded as biographical fallacy. All the elements of her personality and environment are indeed to be found in her fiction, but the complexities have been reduced to intelligent simplicity and the potential variety has been compressed into a relatively few themes and situations. An almost too simplified answer resides in these fortuitous circumstances: She left her Virginia home while yet a child, too young to absorb deeply the Southern tradition. She grew up in the Midwest, where she acquired attitudes which might be termed native. But she achieved esthetic, emotional, and intellectual maturity in a cosmopolitan atmosphere and society away from the Midwest. All this diversity blended into a rich amalgamation of experience and sympathy; regional proscription grew into universal breadth. Lateral, individualized events were transversed by a generic consciousness and conscience.

Of the influences which shaped the creative genius of this novelist her Southern background is perhaps the least notable. Life on the family farm "Willowshade," near a village called Back Creek, was happily tranquil for a child not yet ten years old, but when she moved to Nebraska with her parents she was only temporarily distressed by the change. At the outset, after the static complacency of Virginia, she was undoubtedly sensitive to the brawling confusion of pioneer life. And it would be natural that she miss familiar childhood scenes. Yet she not only soon became absorbed in her new existence, but she also reacted against the old. The atmosphere of the Midwest, despite certain tacitly acknowledged social barriers between the immigrants and the native settlers, seemed more relaxed and congenial to Willa Cather than the binding artificiality of the South. We are informed by Edith Lewis, a companion of long standing, that as Miss Cather acquired perspective, she realized compliance with sentimental expectations of conduct separated one from the spontaneous truths of experience, but resistance—particularly in the South—branded one as a social rebel.

Even as a young girl she enjoyed a pronounced individualism that might have made her socially intolerable had she remained in Virginia. Once she told Miss Lewis "of an old judge who came to call at Willowshade, and who began stroking her curls and talking to her in the playful platitudes one addressed to little girls —and of how she horrified her mother by breaking out suddenly: 'I'se a dang'ous nigger, I is!' It was an attempt to break through the smooth, unreal conventions about little girls—the only way that occurred to her at the moment." The anecdote suggests something of Miss Cather's later creative independence and of her attraction to the organic vitality of a pioneer community.

Although there is no reason to believe that her reaction to the South was founded upon anything more than a philosophical or sociological bias, her disaffection was sufficiently active for a long time to deter substantial imaginative use of her childhood memories. It is true that she incorporated some of her reminiscences in the poems "The Swedish Mother" and "Poor Marty," and as a university student she wrote the romantic short story "A Night at Greenway Court," which is set in eighteenth-century Winchester, Virginia. These, however, are not works we particularly care to remember. When she finally turned her energies to the composition of a novel about the South, she had passed the crest of her creative powers. Her own advancing years and the deaths of her parents, according to Miss Lewis, renewed for her the associations which impelled her to undertake *Sapphira and the Slave Girl*. Literary friends, furthermore, had long been urging her to recapture the legends and scenes which were a part of her heritage. In 1938 Willa Cather visited Winchester for the first time since 1883. The events of *Sapphira*, which was to be her final novel (1940), take place in 1856.

Like a resurrection of the past, the scenes of her childhood were refreshed with warmly nostalgic remembrances. "Every Virginian," she wrote in *Sapphira*, "remembers those locusts which grow along the highways: their cloud-shaped masses of blue-green foliage and heavy drooping clusters of cream-white flowers like pea blossoms. Excepting the very old trees, the giants, the locusts look yielding and languid, like the mountain boy lounging against the counter when he goes to the country store." But emotions such as these, called up as they might be in any sensitive person after long absence, were only partial compensation. There was, in fact, another side of the South that held no pleasure for her. Myra Henshawe of *My Mortal Enemy* at one point bursts forth unaccountably: "The palavery kind of Southerners; all that slushy gush on the surface, and no sensibilities whatever—a race without consonants and without delicacy." True, Myra is laboring under a stress of illness, poverty, and frustration that drives her into an unreasonable tirade, and her remarks must be weighed.

In the more controlled atmosphere of *Sapphira*, however, what Miss Cather had remembered of the South—long before her return—shapes the dominant mood into one of disapprobation and this cannot be dismissed as a passing thought. If *Sapphira* may be regarded as representative of the author's attitude, then she never ceased to feel, as Miss Lewis says, "something smothering in the polite, rigid social conventions of that Southern society." Provincialism, an irrevocable barrier between outsider and native, was not easily disavowed. In the opening pages of the novel, Miss Cather sets forth the conflict of "not belonging," of being acceptable only to one's kind. "Trusted, but scarcely liked," Sapphira's husband was never allowed to forget that he was an outsider. "He was silent and uncommunicative (a trait they didn't like), and his lack of a Southern accent amounted almost to a foreign accent." Speaking in the idiom and accents of his own region "was not, on Back Creek, a friendly way of talking." Such social fixity, much more stringent than that of the West in which she grew up, and breeding special moral values which were a confusion or inversion of her own, could elicit from Miss Cather nothing but displeasure. No wonder, then, that almost until the end of her career she had chosen to ignore the South, which connoted for her static acceptance, and to seek her dominant themes in settings where dynamism—whether of positive growth or negative materialism—was still the order.

One may speculate that had she remained in the South she could not have attained full self-discovery, and that in moving to the Midwest she began awakening to herself and humanity. But the transformation was to be one with esthetic as well as ethical implications, both imaginatively and morally rooted. As such it depended on steadily intensive growth rather than on a sudden flowering. She came to Nebraska at the right time and at the right age to participate in the new culture then forming as a hybrid of many old cultures. She absorbed the simple joys of a new land and was inspired by the admirable qualities of emigrant peoples—Bohemians, Swedes, and the like. Miss Lewis tells us that even as a child Willa Cather viewed the Midwestern frontier "not as pure landscape, but filled with human significance, lightened or darkened by the play of human feeling." The excitement of youthful responsiveness to nature mingled with an unformulated but satisfying concept of man's place in the universal scheme. Curious and filled with the zest of living, she gained from these seminal experiences an enlargement of vision which was to give meaning to her mature years and which was to enrich her early pioneer novels.

But it would be erroneous to assume that Miss

Cather took a romantic attitude toward the farmers who were her neighbors and beheld them in an aura of Rousseauian simplicity as rustic noblemen. Even in her principal frontier novels, where she asserts affirmative conclusions, she is willing to represent the hard lives of the Nebraska farmers. Never bitter like Hamlin Garland, because she acknowledges rewarding tranquillity, she does not gloss over the pain of back-breaking toil and poverty. But if, in those novels whose cycle begins with O Pioneers!, she subordinates the hardships of the individual to his victory over the land, she was not always so hopeful. As early as 1900, only four years after she left her Nebraska home, she described in the short story "Eric Hermannson's Soul" the immigrants on the Divide as "poor exiles of all nations." They were "men with whom the world had dealt hardly; the failures of all countries, men sobered by toil and saddened by exile, who had been driven to fight for the dominion of an untoward soil, to sow where others should gather, the advance-guard of a mighty civilization to be." Of the title character she wrote: "Toil and isolation had sobered him, and he grew more and more like the clods among whom he labored." Five years later, in "The Wagner Matinee," Miss Cather again uncompromisingly indicted the toll exacted by the land. Still too close to her subject, in point of time and geography and personal involvement, to achieve the esthetic mellowness which was to distinguish many of her novels, she stated her outraged concern in unequivocal terms. Reacting against the environment she was eventually to exalt, she felt with special acuteness the hurt of immediate exacerbation because she was not yet capable of detaching herself from primary, superficial impressions.

Another reaction of a totally different kind is apparent in her first novel, Alexander's Bridge, where, despite nebulous suggestions, she rejects prairie life as inappropriate to her fictive interests. Alexander himself, Western in his origins, had the physical attributes usually associated with the legendary heroes of the frontier. Like his forefathers, he matched his strength with that of nature, daringly bridging the rivers of the North American continent. But the heroic undertones of Alexander's character remain undeveloped presentiments, obscured by the indirection of a Jamesian style and the author's fresh recollection of a trip to London.

It is probably well that Miss Cather wrote this novel, for its appearance in cold type became a constant reproach for faults which she consciously thereafter sought to avoid. Honest critic of herself that she always was, she soon recognized the shallow conception and execution of *Alexander's Bridge*. Once she discovered its inadequacies, she did not delude herself. Rather, she admitted that it was a book not born of herself but an anomalous creation made out of the fusion of her imaginings with those imposed upon her by the literary fashions and influences of her day.

A lesser writer might not "have recovered from the editorial point of view" which she ascribed to herself at this time. As it was, in 1911, only a few months after concluding *Alexander's Bridge*, she composed a novella called "The Bohemian Girl," her first attempt to write at length and with qualified sympathy of life on the Divide. The story is told from the point of view of Nils, who is returning at the outset of the narration to his Midwestern home after an absence of twelve years, approximately the length of time Willa Cather had spent in Pittsburgh and New York. The importance of "The Bohemian Girl" to her development is considerable. Hesitant by comparison with the proliferous novels which treat her reaction to the prairie, the early story nonetheless usefully concretizes her contempt for the second-generation pioneers, the grasping and complacent men who were at best, as she put it, merely a "tame lot."

But while she was engaged in finding fault with obvious defections, she was also undergoing a philosophical metamorphosis. In the all-encompassing annals of human history, she realized, the aridity of the second generation would be less significant than the positive accomplishments of their fathers. Thus she was coming to an appreciation of the true pioneers, those who wrested from the wilderness a civilization for themselves. It was a sympathetic understanding, as she herself says, which comes only with time and distance.

Her suspicions of *Alexander's Bridge*, probably incipient during the writing of "The Bohemian Girl," became a distasteful reality to her when in the spring of 1912 she made a prolonged stay in Arizona and New Mexico, then still relatively untrammeled frontier country. This unsophisticated country, so reminiscent of her own youthful haunts, possessed the vitality of a spiritual hunger which transmitted itself to her and which ultimately could not be denied the literary expression of her genius. Here it occurred to Miss Cather, as it did to Thea Kronborg on first exposure to the Southwest, that "She had always been a little drudge, hurrying from one task to another—as if it mattered. . . . Her mind was like a ragbag into which she had been frantically thrusting whatever she could grab. And here she must throw this lumber away." And in the Southwest "the things that were really hers separated themselves from the rest. Her ideas simplified, became sharper and clearer. She felt united and strong." Likewise purified by her stay in the Southwest, Miss Cather produced the first of her frontier novels, *O Pioneers!*

Her critical reaction to her Midwestern background underwent several changes. When she first left Red Cloud in 1896, she must have felt as the young Thomas Hart Benton did when he departed from the Midwest for Paris and New York. With him she must have scorned the Midwest's worshipful cult of the useful and the immediately practical, and must have detested its inability to make the artist feel comfortable even in his own home town. Indeed, like many of the Midwestern artists who in the Nineties escaped from prairie towns to Chicago and New York, Miss Cather was repelled by the provincial "hostility of comfortable, self-satisfied people toward any serious effort." Her own literary analogues for this kind of repressive thinking are to be found in such works as "The Sculptor's Funeral," *The Song of the Lark*, and *Lucy Gayheart*, in all of which the artist is obliged to escape small town conformity in order to bring about the flowering of his talent. But this was for the most part a temporarily inflated reaction, stimulated no doubt by Miss Cather's youthful introduction to the cosmopolitanism and sophistication of large Eastern cities and to the age-old, tradition-rich culture of Europe. In time, the vigor of this reaction lessened, became softened, and was gently transformed into the maturity of attitude, critical though it be, found in all of her pioneer novels of the Midwest.

As would be expected of any young writer, then, Willa Cather made a few false starts: first, she had deceived herself about the true meaning of the Midwest, as she was later to understand it; and then she had made the even more serious error of rejecting the Midwest and its culture as literary material. From these early errors of judgment, however, she recovered as though in response to a bracing tonic. To restore to her conscious sympathies attitudes which she had repressed, and to return from artificiality which had become offensive to her artistic integrity was indeed a triumph of self-recognition as well as of artistic maturity.

Redeemed and reinvigorated, Willa Cather for the remainder of her active career dedicated her talents to a sympathetic depiction of familiar experiences, scenes, and people. Yet she is not a regional novelist in the sense of being a chauvinistic apologist or even critic of the Midwest. The familiar and the sympathetic were rather emblematic of a much larger cosmopolitan, generic outlook. The problems of spiritual growth and material decline have implications in her novels as ancient as the history of man. Whether she writes of relative contemporaneity or the historical past, of immigrants in Nebraska or ancient Indians in New Mexico or colonists in French Canada, they all have for her the shared experiences of struggle, achievement, and even decline. The stories have the grace and art of individualized events, but the themes are coalesced in the cosmopolitanism of her instincts and her awareness that, despite variations, man's ethos is basically changeless. In the first novels, then, she may write from the nostalgia of recalled experience, but their meaning is as much informed by a sense of traditional values and moral continuity as, let us say, either of her "historical" novels. As the never-terminable record of human contest, both immediate and distant, retrospective but never topical, history is the essence which clothes her major novels.

ii

Writing purposefully in each of her novels of the frontier, Willa Cather directed her talents to the exposition of one lofty theme and always arrived at her ultimate moralistic goal. Affirmatively, she lauds man's ineluctable pilgrimage toward an ethical ideal; or, when the struggle has not been maintained, she sadly recognizes the frustrating conditions that circumvent his attainment of that end. Toward the fulfillment of her aim she concretizes the elder Dumas' artistic principle, which she quoted in *The Song of the Lark* and "The Novel Démeublé," that "to make a drama, a man needed one passion, and four walls." Never profligate of her resources, Miss Cather knew that the intensive exploration of limited themes and magnitude of purpose are inseparable. The author may never satisfy himself that he has met the demands prompted by his inner vision, but he has no choice other than to work ceaselessly toward their resolution. He is virtually obsessed, captive of an idea that has " 'teased' the mind for years." Yet his preoccupation is rationally as well as emotionally directed, esthetically causative. As I. A. Richards has described the relationship between thematic density and artistic accomplishment, "when a writer has found a theme or image which fixes a point of relative stability in the drift of experience, it is not to be expected that he will avoid it. Such themes are a means of orientation." Born of instinct, nurtured by experience, the themes which "teased" Miss Cather gave her steadfast authority to advance her large aims.

Part of the novelist's art, as Miss Cather practiced it, is to associate with each tale an axiomatic moral purpose. Toward this end, therefore, she imposes on her characters and situations a heavy dual responsibility. Externally, they must convey narrative movement and credibility; but simultaneously and with seeming inevitability they must project the inner truth of their actions. Each of her frontier novels becomes in whole or in part an allegory built upon one dominating theme, although the allegory need not be construed as an arbitrary, static diagram of point-to-point equations. They are allegories in the sense that each literal narrative depends for its essential meaning upon a secondary level of interpretation. In the usual manner of allegorists from Dante and Spenser to Franz Kafka, Miss Cather univocalizes particular levels of her stories. Although the result of combined levels is an inner complexity, the exterior impression is one of simplicity. Miss Cather's characters tend to offer flat surfaces, rather than depths of personality; her situations are generally free of psychological complexity. Like two other notable allegorists, Hawthorne and Melville, Miss Cather is interested more immediately in the broad outline of human destiny than in any motivation fostered by private oddities. Similarly, Henry James—particularly in such novels as *The Wings of the Dove* and *The Golden Bowl*—was preoccupied with moral values and the meaning of inner reality.

Like her distinguished predecessors, Miss Cather is predisposed to sacrifice animation and sharply delineated personality to innate meaning. This suggests, perhaps, why her allegorical figures are apparently vague when compared with the people drawn by such realistic novelists as Henry Fielding or Jane Austen. To be sure, Willa Cather's persons and places are more than convenient vehicles for ideas presented in her particular form of the novel. But from the beginning the idea is the thing and, therefore, once the reader has grasped the intellectual motif, all the other elements fall into perceptible patterns.

Regarded in their totality, Miss Cather's novels of the frontier comprise an allegory of quest—the individual's seeking and finding a direction of life. Immaterial in origin, the quest is ever liberated from all external prompting. The pioneer's yearning is indeed so fused to the anima that it becomes a creative power rich in imagination and spiritual values. Desire, as Miss

Cather insists in *The Professor's House,* "is the magical element" in the creative process. And earlier, in *The Song of the Lark,* she had maintained, "nothing is far and nothing is near, if one desires. . . . There is only one big thing—desire." Because the search for an ideal is synonymous with innate groping for perfectibility, it has great moral value; and because in Miss Cather's philosophy the mere desire for an ideal is in itself an act of creation, the conceptual instinct has esthetic significance. Exalting an indivisible union of the moral and the esthetic, she summed up her attitude in *The Song of the Lark* through the idea that "artistic growth is, more than it is anything else, a refining of the sense of truthfulness." Visionaries and mystics, those characters in her frontier novels dedicated to this notion, heed only that something within themselves which they intuit as their real lives and consciousness. Guided by this inner reality, they abandon the fixed conventions of civilized society, wandering forth, orphan souls seeking an ideal—a divine presence in the early novels or a Christian God in the later. Pagan or Christian, this ineffable being is a powerfully felt presence but unfettered by substance. While the ideal is apprehended through heightened perception, it can have meaning only through the physical tests of fortitude, persistence, and survival. Thus interpreted, the ideal is not tangential to but harmonious with the problems of everyday existence.

As long as Miss Cather's major concern was the degrees of affinity between frontiersmen and their adopted environments, she made little, if any, point of the countries from which they came and the reasons for their exodus. In *Death Comes for the Archbishop* she broadened her interest; but it was only in *Shadows on the Rock* that she analyzed the original society rejected by her pioneers in their hope of finding a refuge in the wilderness. Before these novels, she had merely suggested her feelings in such terms as "old" and "sad" for European countries which sent their pioneers into the American wilderness. Never in the early novels had she attempted to recreate or even explain the physical nature of the European homelands. In *Shadows on the Rock*, however, she projected a series of vivid contrasts, playing off the new against the old. Her picture of seventeenth-century France is that of a dying civilization. Her critical delineation is of a country steeped in evil and cruelty, heedless of individual justice, and hospitable to the pleasures of the few. Monsieur Auclair typifies for all times and in varying intensity the pioneer torn between his love for the familiar and his despair over inequity. Like most of Miss Cather's European immigrants, Auclair was "a creature of habit and derived an actual pleasure from doing things exactly as he had always done them." Ambivalently, however, Auclair's "mind was free," a contradiction that gradually impressed upon his consciousness the image of a country vast and free. "He fell into the habit of looking to Canada as a possible refuge, an escape from the evils one suffered at home, and of wishing he could go there." Absorption in and by the familiar was precious to Auclair but never so precious as his intellectual freedom. And in this sense the seventeenth-century Frenchman enjoys a kinship with the nineteenth-century immigrants; self-liberation was their common goal.

Miss Cather provides similar motivations for pioneers who are native Americans. In *Sapphira and the Slave Girl*, which has no seeming connections with her early frontier novels, Miss Cather devotes herself to depicting a barren social order. Because of its rigidity and static quality, this Southern culture could no longer harbor the idealist and consequently furnished the Midwestern frontier with many of its hardiest pioneers. The Southern background which Miss Cather is describing is that of herself and of the Burdens, although in reality the events of *Sapphira* predate by about thirty years the novelist's own departure to the Midwest. The chronological difference, however, is relatively unimportant, for Miss Cather had linked the events of her childhood to those of an unchanging South.

The personal feeling already alluded to, strongly a part of Miss Cather's youthful attitudes, remained with her all her life and found its literary expression in *Sapphira*. She dramatized her continuing rebellion against the inflexibility of Southern social custom in the novel's opening scene at Sapphira's breakfast table. Here the sense of imposed decorum neutralizes a vainly expected intimacy between husband and wife. Here, too, is a society which refuses to sanction any kind of social refraction. Sapphira regarded her daughter Rachel as being "difficult" because she was "rebellious toward the fixed ways which satisfied other folk." The slaves also pay the homage of custom to social intransigence. Till, Sapphira's loyal slave, repudiates her runaway daughter Nancy, who had violated what seemed to be a law of both society and God. Nancy's guilt, according to Till, was leaving her "natural place in the world." The moral cowardice fed by such organized rigor is typified through the character of the miller, who while privately detesting slavery is afraid to take an overt stand against a socially acknowledged institution.

Martin, on the other hand, the symbol of Southern masculine society, contains within himself not only the essence of the area's amorality, but before the novel is finished, he with his disfiguring blue tooth, "an ignominious brand," becomes one of the emblems of a festering decay that was slowly spreading out over the entire region. And slavery, the great passive force in the novel, represses and imprisons not only the Negroes but the very people who give it its greatest support. An ominous shadow, its presence exacts acceptance.

This, then, suggests the background of Miss Cather's pioneers, Europeans and Americans alike. Enervated by the spiritual vacuum of their native environments, her pioneers can yet muster sufficient strength to set forth on an odyssey which transcends both time and place. From beginning to end in her frontier novels, no matter how disparate her characters may be in time and culture, she joins them in a common aspiration that wipes out finite considerations. She consistently emphasizes their attraction to nature—sometimes sentimental, always devotional—which gives them mystic insight into divine causes. In *O Pioneers!* she compresses this notion brilliantly. With all of her primitive simplicity and her unmotivated goodness, Alexandra can respond to nature with the fervor of piety. As she looks across the long-swelling Divide, she radiates a secret joy which eludes her brother Emil. "For the first time, perhaps, since that land emerged from the waters of geologic ages, a human face was set toward it with love and yearning." Inarticulate, she is imbued with the spirit which Miss Cather must describe for her. "It seemed beautiful to her, rich and strong and glorious. Her eyes drank in the breadth of it, until her tears blinded her." The author passes from Alexandra's rapturous absorption to her own eloquent exposition. "Then the Genius of the Divide, the great, free spirit which breathes across it, must have bent lower than it ever bent to a human will before. The history of every country begins in the heart of a man or a woman."

Even as the westward movement continued from the plains of Nebraska to those of Colorado, so Miss

Cather makes the setting of *The Song of the Lark* coincide with this shifting temper. In this novel, to be sure, the frontier has already become somewhat spent by the materialistic provincialism which is everywhere prevalent. Nevertheless, the essence of the shrinking frontier still corresponds to the spiritual groping of a few of its inhabitants. Thus to Thea the great flat plains, which still retained their virgin pioneer strength, seemed youthful and hospitable to the "refugees from old, sad countries." Artistically sensitive, as Alexandra is not, she feels her spirit being liberated by the endless prairie, freed of physical limitations. Not even fences could shut in one's thoughts "as mountains and forests can." The flat land reaching out to the sun, thrilling to the songs of the larks, had a newness for Thea as though it were her own discovery. "It was hard to tell about it, for it had nothing to do with words; it was like the light of the desert at noon, or the smell of sagebrush after rain; intangible but powerful." Thea felt a personal relationship with the land, a strengthening friendship of a "naïve, generous country that gave one its joyous force, its large-hearted, child-like power to love, just as it gave one its coarse, brilliant flowers."

Despite her early concentration upon the Midwestern prairie, Miss Cather in time realized that this was but one frontier and the nineteenth-century immigrants but a single representation of the pioneer spirit. Her expanding interest opened her eyes and her sympathetic mind to a comparable spiritual motivation which had sustained the cliff dwellers in the fulfillment of their primitive culture. Their houses of hewn rock, Miss Cather reflected in *The Song of the Lark*, were the shelters where "A dream had been dreamed . . . long ago, in the night of ages, and the wind had whispered some promise to the sadness of the savage." The rock in which these primitives dwelt she translated (in

Death Comes for the Archbishop) into a symbol of innate longing, for "The rock, when one came to think of it, was the utmost expression of human need; even mere feeling yearned for it; it was the highest comparison of loyalty in love and friendship." For the primitive cliff dweller or any other beleaguered people, aboriginal or civilized, the rock becomes a concept of divinity, the fortress of the weak against the strong.

Spiritual desire, again, spurred on the pioneer French of Willa Cather's seventeenth-century Canadian novel, *Shadows on the Rock*. Hopefully seeking, like the cliff dwellers, they found their rock and built a refined citadel in the midst of barbarism. What indefinable longing, Father Saint-Cyr pondered, was answered thousands of miles away from homeland and tradition? Why should the rock of Quebec draw adventurers to it with magnetic force? "Why should this particular cliff in the wilderness be echoing tonight with French songs, answering to the French tongue?" Rational explanations were wanting, but the priest was reminded of forbiddingly naked islands in the Gulf of the St. Lawrence to which the sea birds came instinctively each year. There they laid their eggs and protected their young in comfortless caves and hollows. And they flocked noisily, drenched by the spray, their strident clamors sounding against the desolate winds. The headland of Quebec, it seemed to the mystically attuned Saint-Cyr, "was scarcely more than that; a crag where for some reason human beings built themselves nests in the rock, and held fast."

The same inexplicable need brought the Catholic missionaries of *Death Comes for the Archbishop* to the great Southwest. In this unbounded area of the Ur-Americas, where primitive Christianity and paganism were really not markedly disparate, the reverend fathers nevertheless were able to witness an inner ex-

uberance that absorbed the best elements of Christianity. It is this kind of environment that can cause Father
Latour to reject the sophisticated refinements of his
past and submit himself gladly to the, for him, more
meaningful piety of the desert country. Brought up
in gentility, he can forego the graces of Old-World
culture because they are pale by comparison with the
pious mood of this vitalizing land. His pleasure is perhaps even tinged with hedonism, but the zest which
he has gained from the Southwest gives him an infinitely more profound valuation of his faith, an immediate relation to his God which strengthens his
priestly office. "He had noticed that this particular
quality in the air of new countries vanished after they
were tamed by man and made to bear harvests." The
air of the once open range of Texas and Kansas which
he had known "had quite lost that lightness, that dry
aromatic odour. The moisture of plowed land, the
heaviness of labour and growth and grain-bearing,
utterly destroyed it; one could breathe that only on the
bright edges of the world, on the great grass plains or
the sagebrush desert." Latour had come back to breathe
in this mysterious fragrance for the days that remained
to him. "Something soft and wild and free, something
that whispered to the ear on the pillow, lightened the
heart, softly, softly picked the lock, slid the bolts, and
released the prisoned spirit of man into the wind, into
the blue and gold, into the morning, into the
morning!"

Willa Cather's conception of spiritual desire is thus
for the most part associated with her rendering of the
frontier. Congruent with her ethos, she rejects any consideration of the frontier which tends to exploit popular legend or perpetuate negative conclusions. Hers is
not the Wild West of melodramatic adventure and
outlawry and violent, man-made justice. Nor is it the

plaything of socio-economic forces. Deviations from legal order rarely are represented, even as the minor spice of narrative action; and while deterministic problems are a part of the growing pioneer cycle, they are always peripheral to the central issues. As a positive energy, her frontier inspires idealistic quests, spiritual struggles, and religious awareness. It is, in short, as much a philosophical attitude as it is a physical reality.

Just as Miss Cather's idea of the frontier is one of subtle fusion of the real and the ideal, so her handling of the spiritual quest is a blend of the material and the intangible. The quest, always against the odds of monumental physical struggle, is inextricably linked with a seemingly cruel, insensitive nature. It is this aspect of the seeking that Miss Cather treats most capably, applying her artistic insight and skill to the paradox involved in the struggle itself. Whether immigrant pioneers or erudite Frenchmen, her principal characters have been long sheltered by fixed social traditions. Suddenly they find themselves in conflict with a primeval force infinitely older than the traditions themselves. The irony implicit in the paradox is enforced by the realism with which the struggle is described. Artistically skeptical of physical concreteness, Miss Cather generally limits realistic details to the description of the struggle. Actually, the realism is intrinsic to the situation itself. Her pioneers fight to master a language, to conquer the soil, to hold their land, and to build an ethic. Abandoning their earlier unsatisfactory environment with its decadent mores, they bring only their yearning, their religion, and the best of their culture into the wilderness to prepare themselves for a newly purposeful life. And as the novelist points out in *Shadows on the Rock*: "*Inferretque deos Latio*. When an adventurer carries his gods with him into a remote and savage country, the colony he founds will, from the beginning, have graces, traditions, riches of the mind and spirit."

So endowed with absolute idealism, the pioneer spirit was innately victorious, filled with the dream of youth; and "To fulfill the dreams of one's youth," Father Vaillant prophesied in the *Archbishop*, "That is the best that can happen to a man." Ideals, as Miss Cather said in *One of Ours*, "were not archaic things, beautiful and impotent; they were the real sources of power among men." This notion occurs again and again in the pioneer novels. She maintains in *O Pioneers!*, for instance, that "A pioneer should have imagination, should be able to enjoy the idea of things more than the things themselves." And similarly, Professor St. Peter of *The Professor's House* felt that "A man can do anything if he wishes to enough. . . . If there were an instrument by which to measure desire, one could foretell achievement." To Captain Forrester of *A Lost Lady*, the dream, that is the idealization, was at its inception "an accomplished fact." The hardships which the pioneer endures and the struggles in which he participates are merely a difficult test. After long strife he seems to advance in his intuitive search, arriving at a triumph that for him is ultimate proof of the rightness of his way.

Human experience is a graph of rising and falling events, corresponding to man's fortunes and misfortunes. And man, Willa Cather believed, is responsible for his own moments of rise and decline. Once he begins to lose sight of ideals and to give precedence to material gains, he nullifies his hard-won progress. The frontiersman or pioneer—the term is of little consequence—is represented fictionally as the creature of his own desires for good or evil. In recording his adventures, Miss Cather habitually stresses inner strength and weakness and the decay that results once he succumbs to material desire. The wish for good demands particular conviction if the pioneer is to withstand the enfeebling pressures of a materialistic society. Good intentions alone are insufficient; the man of true spirit must supplement purpose with active striving. Miss Cather's essential concern here is a traditional one, the romantic appeal for constant struggle toward perfectibility. As Goethe had written over a century before in *Faust:* "A good man with his groping intuitions still knows the path that is true and fit."

From this kind of recognition Miss Cather turns to a philosophical interpretation of life as a gigantic tug of war in a conflict between the ideal and the material. The theme which she develops throughout her novels is devastatingly plausible, for in this tension materialism inevitably seems to exhibit the superior strength. More hopeful in her fiction than in her private life, Willa Cather searches beyond contemporary society, looking for analogues of man's trials in other eras. Always her conclusion is the same and implacable. Cyclically, even as the evils of material progress flower noxiously from yearning and desire, good must come ultimately from the temporary condition of evil.

Unlike many of the other novelists of her generation who professed either dispassionate or satirical observations of mankind, Willa Cather records her theme with delicate subjective adumbrations. Here she is in the tradition well established in the nineteenth century by Hawthorne and James, and carried forward by E. M. Forster and Virginia Woolf in the twentieth. Rejecting her generation's fondness for muscular realism, Miss Cather in her essay "The Novel Démeublé" also shuns one of its offshoots, enumerative exactitude. "There is a popular superstition," she says, "that 'realism' asserts itself in the cataloguing of a great number of material objects, in explaining mechanical processes, the methods of operating manufactories and trades, and in minutely and unsparingly describing physical sensations." But realism, she insists, is more than anything else the position the writer takes toward his materials, "a vague indication of the sympathy and candour with which he accepts, rather than chooses, his theme." She objects, then, to the merciless uninterpretative reports on the condition of mankind— mere photographic observations. Her intention, to modify physical probability with moral necessity, brings her to an artistic theory much akin to Hawthorne's when he proposed in his preface to *The House of Seven Gables* a distinction between "Romance" and "Novel." But she is perhaps even closer to Henry James' distinction between the realistic and the romantic. Of the first, he held that there are things, presumably of fact, which "we cannot possibly *not* know, sooner or later, in one way or another." Opposed to these matters of fact or of realistically direct perception we find those elusive, intangible, "romantic" qualities which can never be known any way but indirectly, even "with all the facilities in the world, all the wealth and all the courage and all the wit and all the adventure." These are "the things that can reach us only through the beautiful circuit and subterfuge of our thought and desire." These twin ideas, thought and desire, are undeniably basic to the motivation underscoring Miss Cather's works. Despite the usual danger of conventional tags and diversity of terms, it is apparent enough that all three novelists— Hawthorne, James, and Cather—were defending that aspect of romanticism sometimes called moral realism. The moral realist is less concerned with his knowledge that there are moral principles than he is with governing himself according to these principles, no matter what inconsistencies or difficulties they may entail.

iii

For the narrative elaboration of her theme, Miss Cather turns to those symbolic devices which best give concrete substance to the moral idea. The fundamental understanding of her work is, indeed, dependent upon an understanding of her meaningful employment of a set of symbols, all of which are segments of the total theme. Each symbol is a part of but inseparable from the whole. In this connection, Coleridge's famous dictum may be usefully applied to Miss Cather's symbolism: "A symbol . . . is characterized by a translucence of the special in the individual or of the general in the especial or of the universal in the general. Above all by the translucence of the eternal through and in the temporal. It always partakes of the reality which it renders intelligible; and while it enunciates the whole, abides itself as a living part in that unity; of which it is the representation."

Tested by this criterion, Miss Cather's symbols actualize ideas, giving them strength and magnitude and reality. Her symbols are so tightly coordinated with the ideas they project that no one of them may be divorced or altered without inestimable damage to the whole. This inalienability becomes evident in the systematic, chronological study of her writings. The idea is the reality, the reality is the idea. Hers are symbols of necessity, their origins resting in significant designs of universal human experience. That is to say, they are not essentially private symbols like those, for instance, of Mallarmé, Baudelaire, Verlaine, and the other French *symbolistes*, whom Miss Cather admired but did not care to imitate. Nor is an unrelated esthetic of art for art's sake—isolated from inner meaning—for her ever a measure of artistic skill. The esthetic she always associated with her moral purpose, and this she must exemplify through the use of crystalline, objective symbols.

Willa Cather's principal symbol is the vast panorama of an untamed land. But it is a functionally complex symbol, accommodating several thematic levels, all inherently united. Note, for instance, that she sees the land as a meeting place for her idealistic pioneers, who find here both common cause and spiritual sanctuary. Yet she is impressed that the land or nature is an overwhelming force, often capable of exacting rigorous submission even while it may offer protection. But above all, she ever reminds us that the land is the manifestation of a divine, supersensible force.

Miss Cather's attitude toward the land is one of almost pious exaltation, for she sees it as a place of communion for idealistic pioneers. So viewed, it is the consecrated, tangible evidence of a superior authority and is large with the might of that force. It is then mandatory for the pioneer, according to Miss Cather's theosophy, to recognize this authority; for in order to obey it he must in some way identify it. The order and harmony apparent everywhere in the land are instrumental to his recognition. The pioneer sees the earth as the spirit of a forbidding but not necessarily orthodox deity, jealously enforcing the harmony which becomes the measure of his own well-being. Savagely beautiful, the land is anthropomorphized so that human attributes, at once fiercely active and melancholy, inhere in it. Such is the essence of this force as the novelist describes it in O *Pioneers!* After the false security of summer, the winter is especially ominous, making the prairie a frozen threat. "The homesteads were few and far apart; here and there a windmill gaunt against the sky, a sod house crouching in a hollow. But the great fact was the land itself, which seemed to overwhelm the little beginnings of human society that struggled in its sombre wastes." The hardness of the land is an embittering reminder "that men were too weak to make any mark here." Resentful of human incursions, "the land wanted to be let alone, to preserve its own fierce strength, its peculiar, savage kind of beauty, its uninterrupted mournfulness." To some, "It is like an iron country, and the spirit is oppressed by its rigor and melancholy. One could easily believe that in that dead landscape the germs of life and fruitfulness were extinct forever."

As Miss Cather depicts this aspect of the land, it is not hard for her to move from human to animal metaphor, for like a beast the land is fundamentally hostile to encroachments upon its solitude. And like any untamed being, it resists civilizing influences until the benefits of these influences are proved. With an imperfect understanding of his adversary, man struggles while nature withdraws her support, "in the season in which [she] recuperates, in which she sinks to sleep between the fruitfulness of autumn and the passion of spring." John Bergson felt that the land was "still a wild thing that had its ugly moods; and no one knew when they were likely to come, or why. Mischance hung over it. Its Genius was unfriendly to man."

But it must be observed that Bergson's vain resistance is a fault that lies within himself. Unlike his daughter Alexandra, he has been unable to identify himself with the land, to understand that to survive he must bend his own will and derive joy from the act of submission. Nature for all its apparent cruelty is the force that will temper the pioneer and bring him, as a result of his acquiescence, to his ultimate peace.

The seasons are merely tests of individual determination imposed by a divine power upon man so that man himself can prove his worth.

The pervasive religious temper of the land manifest throughout the frontier novels grows out of Miss Cather's deliberate attempt to parallel the pioneer's mission with the introspective search of the Old Testament. The entire frontier tradition with which she deals is molded in the cast of a stern element. Simplicity and goodness are drawn from harsh nature through an awareness of but also a faith in some divine supervision. Like the ancient wandering tribes of Israel, Willa Cather's pioneers have gone forth into the wilderness, searching for an ideal and a sanctuary from a troubled existence. And there in the wilderness they often find their sanctuary. Their rewards may be summed up in the words of the Psalmist: "The work of righteousness shall be peace; and the effect of righteousness quietness and confidence forever. Great peace have they that love Thy law, O God; and there is no stumbling for them."

For the righteous pioneer, there was always a refuge. The symbol is elemental. In *O Pioneers!* and *My Ántonia* it is the land itself. But frequently the symbol is intensified and made more specific. In *The Song of the Lark, The Professor's House, Death Comes for the Archbishop,* and *Shadows on the Rock,* the concentrated symbol becomes a rock, the altar of devotion, rising out of the land. But at the same time the rock must be regarded as a warning against acquisitive desire. Finally, in a profoundly mystical way, it is the culmination of the quest. This is the lesson that makes itself clear through the Catholic eyes of a Bishop Latour or of the people of seventeenth-century Canada. And again it is the lesson to be sought by those people who seek a spiritual belief—unimpaired by creed—in an absolute. This is the revelation that comes to a Thea Kronborg and a Tom Outland.

Man's relationship to nature, in Miss Cather's frontier, is enigmatic. His microcosmic world is both juxtaposed to and absorbed in the universal scheme of creation while the macrocosm, the essence of an omnipresent divinity, looms as protection and threat. But the threat need trouble only those who neglect homage to a superior will. Shelter rather than harm will be the reward of those who have heeded the lesson of a supernal order and are sincerely reverent in their acknowledgment. Nature as barrier or refuge is always the *idée fixe* in the pioneer's life. In the immutable scheme of things, nature may at times seem to be subdued, but it would be a fatal error to assume that her conquest is permanent. Nature is ultimately the controlling energy. To crystallize man's relationship to his environment, Miss Cather frequently portrays him on a reduced scale while projecting the phenomena of nature in heroic magnitude.

Her most effective presentation of this disparity may be found in a lyric passage in *My Ántonia*. Describing a brilliant sunset in a cloudless Nebraska sky, she makes us suddenly aware of a huge black image on the blazing red face of the sun. "On some upland farm a plough had been left standing in the field. The sun was sinking just behind it. Magnified across the distance by the horizontal light, it stood out against the sun, was exactly contained within the circle of the disc; the handles, the tongue, the share—black against the molten red. There it was, heroic in size, a picture writing on the sun." Then, even in the awed moments of describing the miracle, the vision disappeared from the sinking sun. "The fields below us were dark, the sky was growing pale, and the forgotten plough had sunk back to its own littleness somewhere on the prairie."

The effectiveness of this device does not lie in its novelty, for other writers have attempted comparable projections. In *The Prairie*, for instance, James Fenimore Cooper magnified a human figure to colossal proportions against a setting sun. Another time he caused an executioner's rope to cut a huge black line across the face of a full moon. But Cooper's purpose was to create melodramatic, suspenseful effects, and his only apparent regard was for the immediate, sensational response. Miss Cather, on the other hand, is attempting to detach the reader only momentarily from physical reality. For a breathless instant she establishes an illusion of human splendor; but it is only an illusion, serving to impress on us more strongly than ever the amplified infinity of nature.

The pioneer is cast in an ironically uneven fight against the deified land, from which he may profit only through the insight of spiritual submission rather than through animal strength. A willingness to submit spells in effect the fulfillment of the individual's destiny. As proof of this concept, Miss Cather has drawn at least two portraits of characters submerged and destroyed by the land to which they failed to reconcile themselves. These are the portraits of Bergson in *O Pioneers!* and Shimerda in *My Ántonia*. Both men, already old when they came to the Middlewestern prairie, clung tenaciously to the habits, traditions, and motivations of their European environments. They were either unwilling or unable to modify beliefs which had virtually been fixed and adapt them to problems occasioned by their new circumstances. For example, "John Bergson had the Old-World belief that land, in itself, is desirable. But this land was an

enigma. It was like a horse that no one knows how to
break to harness, that runs wild and kicks things to
pieces." Thwarted by this attitude, John Bergson's
desire for the land turns to hatred and rebellion. And
so he dies destroyed by the land which he once coveted
ardently. His daughter, however, by her own admission
looks to the land only with "love and understanding,"
waiting *passively* and *submissively* for the land to redeem her faith.

Miss Cather finds submission a virtue, restlessness
and indecision its opposite. Reminiscent of the classical traditions of Roman Stoicism and Judaeo-Christian
theology—though she appears closer to the first—she
implies in her philosophy a quietude characterized by
a mood of fatalistic assent. Alexandra and Ántonia,
both called fatalists, maintain an impervious calm and
subordinate their personalities to that of the land in a
salutary way. Claude Wheeler in *One of Ours*, on the
other hand, indulges in a sentimental and quasi-philosophical fatalism, attributing all the events in his life
to a destiny which he simultaneously condemns and
exalts. Auclair in *Shadows on the Rock* sees all of
human life governed by a principle over which one has
no control and which he identifies with "fate" or with
"destiny."

At the same time it must be observed that there is
no contention between the notion of fatalism on the
one hand and that of desire on the other. As Miss
Cather makes explicit in *Shadows on the Rock*, the
thought pattern of one's life is indeed shaped by an
uncontrollable destiny, but within the limits of that
destiny one has the power of volition. Man has the
faculty to shape the single day, the single event. "One
made a climate within a climate; one made the days,—
the complexion, the special flavour, the special happiness of each day as it passed; one made life." So, in a

moment of mystic clarity, Thea realizes that her life
is at the mercy of "blind chance," but that within this
microcosmic fatalism she has the force "to take it in
her own hands"; better to lose everything than irreso-
lutely "draw the plough." This is a concept which has
been accepted by contemporary spokesmen of Judaeo-
Christian belief and given similar interpretation. As
the mystic Martin Buber has synthesized the premise,
"destiny is not a dome pressed tightly down on the
world of men; no one meets it but he who went out
from freedom. . . . He who goes out to it with concentrated being and risen power to enter into relation
becomes aware of freedom. And to be freed from
belief that there is no freedom is indeed to be free."

Certainly Miss Cather's fictive philosophy is not
one of despair, even when her artistic obligations lead
her into delineations of misfortune. She believed, as
the Stoics did, that hard circumstances may have salutary effects. According to Seneca: " 'No man . . . seems
to me more unhappy than one who has never met
with adversity' for such a man has never had an opportunity to test himself." But, again, Miss Cather's own
Christian tradition also supports this view of man's
need to test his spiritual resolution. Like Faulkner in
"The Bear," for instance, she valued the courage and
humility by which individuals learn to assess themselves. With hopeful anticipation, the author of *O Pioneers!* wrote that "down under the frozen crusts, at
the roots of the trees, the secret of life was still safe,
warm as the blood in one's heart; and the spring would
come again! Oh, it would come again!"

While submissive devotion offers unique satisfaction
to those who meet the test, no one—and this includes
Willa Cather—would expect the pioneers to suffer the
rigors of the elements for spiritual satisfaction alone.
That is to say, these people are not anchorites; they

are men with strongly developed notions of family responsibility, and material reward must be one of the fruits of submission. But it must be admitted that Miss Cather at times is so absorbed by this concept of submission that she almost forgets earnest reality must be served as well as abstract purity. She is sometimes lulled by the world she herself has fabricated in which the dream and the myth override the claims of everyday necessity. As though to propitiate the gods of grubby existence, she seems to say there is something genii-like in the land and at the appropriate time it will respond to man's desire with a shower of riches. The land, she says at one point in O Pioneers!, "pretended to be poor because nobody knew how to work it right; and then, all at once, it worked itself. It woke up out of its sleep and stretched itself, and it was so big, so rich, that we suddenly found we were rich, just from sitting still."

This, of course, is metaphorical exaggeration, but Miss Cather's enthusiasm is undeniable. She has, however, another attitude toward man in relation to the wealth of the land, one suggesting that the material good derived from patient acquiescence is only temporary. "The land belongs to the future. . . . I might as well try to will the sunset over there to my brother's children. We come and go, but the land is always here. And the people who love it and understand it are the people who own it—for a little while."

The natural order and harmony of the pioneer's world, for Miss Cather a conclusive and definite proof of a supernal will, is based on an ancient thesis which she may well have drawn from classical Stoicism or the Bible. Whether in the orderly arrangement of forests, prairies or mountains, or of the constellations overhead, the regularity that betokens the perfect workings of a divine power is ever apparent. For Miss

Cather, as for Cicero and Seneca and the Psalmist as well as for innumerable Christian thinkers, contemplation of the celestial bodies leads to the full perception of a divine spirit and the magnificence of its work. The instrument of her belief in *O Pioneers!* is Alexandra, who "always loved to watch [the stars], to think of their vastness and distance, and of their ordered march. It fortified her to reflect upon the great operations of nature, and when she thought of the law that lay behind them, she felt a sense of personal security." The idea is repeated similarly in *One of Ours:* "Claude walked . . . under the frosty brilliance of the winter stars. As he looked up at them, he felt more than ever that they must have something to do with the fate of nations, and with the incomprehensible things that were happening in the world. In the ordered universe there must be some mind that read the riddle of this one unhappy planet, that knew what was forming in the dark eclipse of this hour."

The successful pioneer must not only pay abstract homage to the natural order as the law of a superior force, but he must also seek to reaffirm it in his everyday life. This was an idea that Miss Cather held dear even as early as the short story "The Enchanted Bluff." In describing the Norwegian pioneer district of Nebraska, she was attracted to the orderly farm lands "where there was nothing wilful or unmanageable in the landscape." And Alexandra's meticulous government of her farm is esteemed as her unconscious oblation. Prim order is manifest everywhere, in the fencing, the windbreaks, even in the shade trees and the row of white beehives. The symmetry of the farm bespeaks Alexandra's rapport with a larger harmony. "You feel that, properly, Alexandra's house is the big out-of-doors, and that it is in the soil that she expresses herself best."

Ultimately, all distinction vanishes between the pioneer spirit and the land; one merges into the other and each is an extension of the other. By this measure, Alexandra, who is the essence of the pioneer spirit, and the land, which is the symbol of the conclusive quest, coalesce their identities. "There were certain days in her life, outwardly uneventful, which Alexandra remembered as peculiarly happy; days when she was close to the flat, fallow world about her, and felt, as it were, in her own body the joyous germination in the soil." The sense of unity is perhaps best epitomized by Jim Burden in *My Ántonia*, who feels "that is happiness; to be dissolved into something complete and great. When it comes to one, it comes as naturally as sleep."*

iv

The land, Miss Cather's chief symbol for objectifying the spiritual quest, is realistic evidence of man's ability to thrust himself into an alien wilderness, to abandon his old modes of living and thinking, and to seek a course of moral good. With its paradoxical union of violent force and fruitful beneficence, summation of an absolute peace which follows purposeful struggle, the land is part of an experience that at some time has been common to all peoples. Yet as a symbol it does not completely satisfy Miss Cather; she gropes for new devices to express the same idea and finds that the pioneer spirit of the ancient past correspondingly leads to an answer. Hence, she lessens her emphasis on the perfections of the land in novels other than *O Pioneers!* and *My Ántonia* and draws her analogues of the immutable ideal from history. Yet, while minimizing the symbol of the land or reducing it to relative

* These words, fittingly, have been engraved on Willa Cather's tombstone in the Jaffrey, New Hampshire, cemetery.

obscurity in many of her novels or even allowing it to appear only by suggestion, she never allows it to vanish completely. The magnet of the land draws her people in *The Song of the Lark, One of Ours, A Lost Lady, Death Comes for the Archbishop,* and *Shadows on the Rock.* Actually, the land and the historical absolute (or ideal, since the two terms are synonymous in Miss Cather's ethic) are parallel for her in symbolic meaning; both become the artistically manageable representation of the primal quest.

Through imaginative reconstruction of prerecorded history, probing the arcana of Indian relics in the Southwest, Miss Cather began to amplify her concept of the eternal ideal. Placing modern people among the vestiges of a long silent order, she discovered a spiritual continuity whose aura conveyed intimations of immortality. In effect, she was equating the past with the present, attempting to prove that the one really durable monument is the spirit. Awareness of this truth becomes central to the exploratory short story "The Enchanted Bluff" and the more serious novelistic efforts of *The Song of the Lark, The Professor's House,* and *Death Comes for the Archbishop,* in which identification with the struggles of those old inhabitants of the mesas and cliffs becomes a restorative. Even a robust individual like Ray Kennedy, friend of Thea, deeply "felt the hardness of the human struggle or the sadness of history . . . among those ruins" of the cliff dwellers. But he also felt there an obligation to do his best. And from those same ruins, Thea acquired a sense of the past and was imbued with "older and higher obligations" than she had had before. There "her power to think seemed converted into a power of sustained sensation." Tom Outland, of *The Professor's House,* envisaged the cliff dwellers as "a strong and aspiring people . . . with a feeling for design," and he felt that their survival through relics was something of a miracle. The desire they experienced, as St. Peter summed it up, was beyond earthly possessions or even needs; "they lived for something more than food and shelter."

The symbol of the historical ideal is more complex than that of the land. It is an abstraction which Miss Cather employs to modify another abstraction—man's spiritual adventure. Her use of an abstract symbol is a seeming contradiction in terms, but any misinterpretation is readily clarified by analysis of her second major symbol. This may be stated as the novelist's subjective rendering of a primitive people whose culture survives only as meager archeological remains in the mesas and canyons of the Southwest. Effective in part because of its complexity, the symbol is not merely a sign or "picture writing"; nor is it merely an idea. The symbol operates as an indivisible combination of both, drawing its strength from the special complex of emotional attitudes which Miss Cather brings to it. Casual analysis would suggest a paradox in the symbol itself because she turns to an elemental society for the lesson that she would teach to her advanced contemporaries. In all actuality, however, this is no paradox; for while the cliff dwellers may be primitive in calendar time, they are enlightened in degree of culture or civilization. Their culture is comparable in Miss Cather's eyes with the best in all cultures and timeless in spirit. The idea becomes clear upon comparison with Miss Cather's earlier symbol of the land, in her use of which she concluded that the ethically best man is he who lives closest to nature. She turns then to the cliff dwellers and finds that their ethical goodness stems, in accentuated significance, from spiritual proximity to nature.

Miss Cather, whose historical sense was largely

directed toward the study of early conflicts between idealism and materialism, would have rejected any hint that she used the symbol of the historical ideal as a romantic or vague reference to the past for its own sake. "There was nothing of the antiquarian in her," explains Edith Lewis; "she did not care for old things [or historical situations] because they were old or curious or rare—she cared for them only as they expressed the human spirit and human lot on earth." The historical ideal as a conceptual link between man's enduring quest and the timeless victory of good is most effectively set forth in *The Song of the Lark, The Professor's House* and *Death Comes for the Archbishop*; in these novels Miss Cather adapts the culture of the cliff dwellers and their descendants, the pueblo Indians, to her theory of the absolute and finds it propitious.

Like the pioneer tales in her novels of the West, the legends of the cliff dwellers exemplify man's struggle for an absolute. During their search for this perfection, the cliff dwellers fought grimly for existence, harried by the rigors of nature and the persecutions of the Spaniards or other Indians. Theirs, too, was actually the eternal struggle of idealism against materialism. Through the vision of Father Duquesne, in *The Professor's House*, Miss Cather recreates the life and death of an isolated tribe, decent and religious, respectful of their dead, sentimental about kin and home. But the very civilization they laboriously built up, strong in tradition and domestic comforts, probably proved their undoing. Attention to refinements distracted them from the dangerous exigencies of a savage world in which they had formed their island. Father Duquesne reflected that these people must have been destroyed in their summer camp "by some roving Indian tribe without culture or domestic virtues" for their possessions or "from mere love of slaughter. I feel sure that these brutal invaders never even learned of the existence of this mesa, honeycombed with habitations. If they had come here, they would have destroyed. They killed and went their way."

The cliff dwellers, then, are Miss Cather's emblems of the victory of good through the perpetuation of their cultural remains (it is noteworthy that she does not allow the marauders to invade the stronghold and the remains are truly undefiled) and the condemnation by history of their oppressors.

The philosophical truths of the past as they offer a solution to present existence are understood by people of transcendent imagination and deep-rooted spiritual values. As the land offers a way of ethical life to those with genuine humility that comes with a sympathetic understanding of a superior force, so a knowledge of the historical ideal offers strength to those who can convert their knowledge to true understanding. Motivated by this consistent thesis, Miss Cather activates her symbolism of the historical ideal and gives it immediate application through visionaries or people with acute inward perception. Thea Kronborg and Tom Outland, for instance, are spiritualized introverts able to profit from the lesson of the past. Tom's mystic reaction to the remains of the cliff dwellers is illustrative of this gain. The mesa somehow helped him to unify and resolve his inner problems. "For me," he says, "the mesa was no longer an adventure but a religious emotion. . . . Every morning, when the sun's rays first hit the mesa top, while the rest of the world was in shadow, I wakened with the feeling that I had found everything, instead of having lost everything. Nothing tired me. Up there alone, a close neighbour to the sun, I seemed to get the solar energy in some direct way. And at night, when I watched it drop down behind the edge of the plain below me, I used to feel that I couldn't have borne another hour of that consuming light, that I was full to the brim, and needed dark and sleep."

Father Latour, likewise, is introspective and capable of deep understanding, though he already has the strength of a dogmatic, yet nonetheless intensely personal, religious experience. Having discovered the goal of his quest in Catholicism, he can yet understand the inspiration of a comparable if pagan philosophy. All these dreamers are admirable instruments for the development of Miss Cather's symbolism because they are responsive to the mystic associations of a buried past to which a realist would be impervious.

For those near mystics who, unlike Father Latour, are still groping for philosophical values, the lesson of the cliff dwellers becomes a rock as firm as the Biblical concept of God. Thea and Tom are visionaries, in Miss Cather's sense, who have not yet successfully translated their visions into action. They need a sanctuary—a respite from the present—even as the pioneers of the West required an inward haven. But Miss Cather's dreamers are not escapists in the esthetic connotation of the term. Each for some reason needs a justification for being and, symbolically, the rediscovered culture of the old Indians provides that justification. Thea Kronborg is an artist chafing against material restraints. In her conflict she needs the strength she finds among the ghosts of a triumphant ideal which has resisted materialism even at the cost of its own existence. Once understanding that, she dedicates herself in action to the same ideal, saluting "Endeavor, achievement, desire, glorious striving of human art!" Exalted by her insight, she rejoices that even as a vanished race the cliff dwellers have gained their immortality; for "along the trails, in the stream, under the spreading cactus, there still glittered in the sun the bits of their frail clay vessels, fragments of their desire." Similarly, Tom Outland, tortured by the conflict between the acceptance or renunciation of material values, joins himself finally to the *modus vivendi* of the cliff dwellers, translating their standards and course of action into his own.

The vestiges of the ancient cliff dwellers combine for Thea and Tom both spiritual and physical certainty. From antiquity they extract the will to take their active place in the present, not the longing to seal themselves hermetically in the void of a romantic past. Miss Cather is not reluctant to explain what is to be learned from an examination of those ancient lives. For them, she reasons, existence was a primal struggle against barbarism and irreverence. Their search for spiritual good, such as would bring them to their final goal of an untroubled peace, was their ideal quest; and it was one which Miss Cather frequently urges moderns to imitate. Again in the words of Father Duquesne, she testifies to this longing: "Like you, I feel a reverence for this place. Wherever humanity has made that hardest of all starts and lifted itself out of mere brutality, is a sacred spot. Your people were cut off here without the influence of example or emulation, with no incentive but some natural yearning for order and security. They built themselves into this mesa and humanized it." It is at this point that Miss Cather's occasional homiletic leanings become most pronounced. So intent does she become in teaching her lesson that she seems at times almost to forget the outward trappings of her story and to concern herself most deeply with the justification of her particular moral belief. But when she turns to didactic statement, she does not long forget her narrative function; ultimately the artist supersedes the teacher and the lesson becomes an inevitable part of the story.

"IN NEBRASKA," SHE WROTE IN 1923 at the height of her career, "as in so many other States, we must face the fact that the splendid story of the pioneers is finished, and that no new story worthy to take its place has yet begun." Something of this same position is expressed in *One of Ours* when she says, "The statue of Kit Carson on horseback, down in the Square, pointed westward; but there was no West, in that sense, any more"—only a sky shutting down over the world like a lid. Behind these two observations is a dualistic premise affecting her frontier novels. First, she believes that through all the ages the pioneer principle has been the only valid test of man's spirituality. Second, she believes that antispiritual forces have always warred against pure idealism and that these forces have ultimately been destroyed, because the measure of endurance is conviction. As we have already seen, Miss Cather's firm reliance upon historical analogy or precedent is rooted in the latter melioristic idea. As she absorbed into her own work the experiences of many frontiers, she saw true idealism overrun and temporarily defeated by "machine-made materialism," her term for modern progress. But, happily, she observed idealism renewing itself in subsequent eras, revitalized and strengthened; and she was convinced for a long time that conflict of this nature has always been elemental in man's perpetual groping for perfectibility. When in 1923 she wrote her essay "Nebraska," she was already looking to the quondam Midwestern frontier, then being vitiated by a mechanistic culture and philosophy, for the very seeds of revolt that would break up "the hard molds of American provincialism" and "challenge the pale proprieties, the insincere, conventional optimism of our art and thought."

Without making the distinction in so many words, she found tradition and conformity to be two very different things. Tradition, as she appears to see it, elicits from the individual an unconscious response to a continuing pattern of customs and beliefs which are salutary. If the individual is bound to this pattern, it is because of an innate volition. The earthly limits he necessarily sets upon himself are compensated by supraphysical freedom that is the ultimate reward. Conformity, on the other hand—that which she derogates specifically as "the hard molds of American provincialism"—is her version of Babbittry. This is adducible in the unconscious violation of one's free soul, the sacrifice of one's freedom to transient gain. It is the starvation of integrity in the individual to whom the desire to emulate his neighbor's fortunes and comforts becomes more relevant than the now muted urgings of personal conscience.

While symbolizing throughout her novels of the frontier the ideal theme of man's eternal quest for truth, Miss Cather conjunctively develops a set of symbolic references under the comprehensive name of "machine-made materialism" to represent her attack upon society's deliberate rejection of ideal values. Although the term itself is conceptual, certain visual or physical signs are implicit within it. The most important of these signs are, first, the ugly, devitalized communities which arose abortively out of the "wild land" and through which she protests against a form of esthetic degeneration; and, second, the characters— land grabbers, sons of pioneers, and amoral beings like the lost lady, Marian Forrester—who represent Miss Cather's displeasure with acquisitiveness and moral devaluation. Even in "Nebraska," where she uses the term "machine-made materialism" freely and in a philosophical sense, she is always thinking of the direct manifestations of this idea. In other words, "machine-made materialism" is not a mere phrase for her but the embodiment or the synthesis of idea plus various signs and subjective emotions. Although she does not transfer the term to her novels, she is obviously thinking of the tangible evils represented by that opprobrious tag. To assign a symbolically creative function to an abstract term is thoroughly consistent with her own practice of fusing the abstract and the concrete. As in the concept of the historical ideal, the term is capable of evoking a series of spatial and temporal images.

As an abstraction brought to narrative life, her protest against "machine-made materialism" rises above conceptual statement to symbolic dimension, but only after it is appropriately integrated with the other two dominating symbols—the land and the historical ideal. For her the land is both test and end of ethical striving; the historical ideal is the universal objective proof of man's response to that test. Inevitably, as she observed and recorded these beneficial values, she described the fading of pioneer strength in the West which she had also witnessed. From her vigorous examination of an encroaching degeneration, she concluded angrily that the basic corrosive force was "machine-made materialism." She was completely repelled by the resulting esteem for crippling secular mores and man's divorce from durable ennobling aspirations. The particular tokens of "machine-made materialism" became for her an epitome of evil, a refutation of moral and esthetic standards that she had always found to be the only valid principles of existence. In short, through specific signs of displeasure, Miss Cather solidified her protest. Within the texture of her novels, she made her symbols dramatically functional and simultaneously gave concrete reality to ideas or concepts.

Read in the sequence of their publication, except for the logical interchange of *One of Ours* (1922) and *A Lost Lady* (1923), the frontier novels of the Midwest demonstrate Willa Cather's conscious development of the three groups of ideas which take symbolic form—the land, the historical ideal, and "machine-made materialism." This development is of realistic significance, for in it the novelist represents the most important era of Midwestern expansion and decline, the last few decades of the nineteenth century. It is in these years that she places *O Pioneers!*, *The Song of the Lark*, *My Ántonia*, and *A Lost Lady*. Census figures, for example, show that the population of Nebraska in 1870 was only 123,000. *O Pioneers!* opens about 1880 when the settlement of Nebraska is still relatively sparse. As Miss Cather remarks in "Nebraska": "Even as late as 1885 the central part of the State, and everything to the westward, was, in the main, raw prairie. The cultivated fields and broken land seemed mere scratches in the brown, running steppe that never stopped until it broke against the foothills of the Rockies."

This is the hardly interrupted open land she described in *O Pioneers!*, where her reverential absorption in the prairie and its people left little to be noted of material values. By the time of the central action of *The Song of the Lark* and *My Ántonia* in the last decade of the nineteenth century, the population of Nebraska had risen to more than one million, and towns were becoming increasingly numerous. In these two novels, Miss Cather's symbolism is infected by the drab, ugly Western towns to such a degree that she forcefully disapproves of the new materialism which is rapidly supplanting the old esthetic and moral ideals. The chief period of A *Lost Lady*, thematically the last in her series of Midwestern frontier novels, represents the complete and tragic decline of the West as a victim of the new order, moral and esthetic and economic. Miss Cather's penultimate fictive commentary upon the triumph of Western materialism over idealism, *One of Ours*—set a generation later than A *Lost Lady*, during the first World War—is her seemingly conclusive proof that the land can no longer harbor its former supersensible vitality.

Despite a persistent dismay, she never ceased to hope that the signs of festering were but tokens of a temporary phenomenon, and her comment in "Nebraska" is filled wtih the hope that fills all her novels. "Surely the materialism and showy extravagance of this hour are a passing phase! They will mean no more in half a century from now than will the 'hard times' of twenty-five years ago—which are already forgotten." Looking back, she indeed saw a temporary recess of "materialism and showy extravagance" caused by the "wave of generous idealism, noble seriousness which swept over the State of Nebraska in 1917 and in 1918." And even if such nobility did not last, it nevertheless gave, she hoped, a presage of what was to come.

Responsibility, as it becomes fixed in Willa Cather's ethos, is such a personal commitment that it often does not lend itself to rational interpretation. The rarefied climate of spiritual aspiration is, of course, wholly admirable as a matter for philosophical discourse; and even a material-minded audience can draw intellectual satisfaction from another's strivings. Very frequently, it thus becomes evident, the dispassionate reader must be willing to waive the rationale of his own existence in order to achieve a sympathetic understanding of Miss Cather's purpose. But only an author as emotionally compelling as Miss Cather can elicit such receptiveness and make the reader feel ultimately that, after all, the abstraction touches him in a practical as well as symbolic way. A significant part of her compulsion inheres in her sensitivity to the necessary relationship between ideal and pragmatic reality. The moral and esthetic goals whose abandonment by society she deplores are her idealizations of a desire growing out of a particular negative fact. It is this fact —the frustration and debasement of inner principle— that is chargeable against society for the decline of the West. Now, although she considers deterministic forces as merely factitious tests of the human dilemma, she is willing to concede—indeed, *must* concede for her worldly audience—that these are among the practical realities of frontier existence; but she never slips so far away from her idealized speculation as to dissociate "real" from ideal cause and effect.

Part of her accusation against society, then, occurs on the socio-economic level, since she is concerned with inequalities arising from exploitation and from man's inhumanity to man. This accusation is the result of surprisingly realistic thinking, because her attitudes are supported by the actual course of Western expansion. When the free land was all distributed, the spontaneous initiative of the small landholders vanished; affluent interests assumed control, dominating the Western economy and replacing with hard, impersonal efficiency the former enthusiasm of the struggling farmers who took a personal pride in the development of the land. The region became, to apply Frederick Jackson Turner's phrase, a debtor West, building upon borrowed capital and ultimately causing the defeat of visionary pioneers like Captain Forrester of *A Lost Lady*. The frontiersmen were the true dreamers of the nation who suffered for their impracticality by falling victim to the land boomers. These often unprincipled individuals, such as the incredible Wick Cutter of *My Ántonia* and the villain of the early short story "El Dorado," thrived on their high rates of interest, or like Cutter's satanic descendant Ivy Peters of *A Lost Lady* had monopolistic aims. To intensify the evil of their callings, Miss Cather made them not only financial sharks but moral degenerates. Out of their usurious practices grew a monomania that could be satisfied only by the authority of total possessiveness. Their hunger for wealth was complemented by physical lust. Whatever they touched they corrupted or destroyed.

Neither knowledge of the economic pressures disfiguring the pure cause of the frontier nor indignation over their widespread acceptance could induce Miss Cather to protest, except rarely, in the direct manner of such realistic observers as Joseph Kirkland, Hamlin Garland, or Henry George. On one occasion, to be sure, she does have Claude Wheeler speak with the pseudo voice of a later Henry George; the hero of *One of Ours* deplores the power of his monopolistic father, philosophizing that "he would rather go out into the world and earn his bread among strangers than sweat under this half-responsibility for acres and crops that were not his own. He knew that his father was sometimes called a 'land hog' by the country people, and he himself had begun to feel that it was not right they should have so much land,—to farm, or to rent, or to leave idle, as they chose. It was strange that in all the centuries the world had been going, the question of property had not been better adjusted. The people who had it were slaves to it, and the people who didn't have it were slaves to them."

Two generations earlier Henry George, in blaming poverty upon material progress, had demanded the destruction of land monopolies and the equal distribution of the land. But Miss Cather, who seldom treats an economic problem without translating it into terms of esthetic morality, was content to leave vociferous protests to the reformers whose enthusiasm she did not pretend to share. The land depression of 1893–97 (which her own family barely survived) became for her—perhaps in comfortable retrospect—a testing period of pioneer strength.

Characteristically, she does not confront the depression squarely as a crisis affecting numerous specific lives. Rather, she takes a somewhat Olympian, abstract view of a broad situation, remaining judicially aloof as she measures philosophical determinants. She assumes as a commonplace of general experience that the "years of trial," as she calls the period of depression, "had a salutary effect upon the new State" of Nebraska. During these years, the settlers of genuine purpose demonstrated the strength of their resistance to adversity, while "the drifting malcontents who are ever seeking a land where man does not live by the sweat of his brow" sought less rigorous conditions. She inferred an inevitable justice from the failures of superfluous banks and the grief that befell the "money lenders who drove hard bargains with desperate men." The moral is plain enough to her: "The strongest stock survived, and within ten years those who had weathered the storm came into their reward." And the reward, we need hardly guess, was not only financial stability but the sanctification of inner peace.

Willa Cather's response to the gradual conversion of faith and an idea into visible results is thus divided between approval and reproach. Although she can never celebrate a positive doctrine of material reward as wholeheartedly as she does that of the innate quest, she can justify at least one aspect of civilized progress. She finds it admirable that farmers have acquired genuinely necessary comforts and labor-saving devices, a partial reward for unremitting pioneer effort. Along with their successful adaptation to the land, the pioneers have achieved the abatement of physical hardship. Perhaps the tangible bounties that are among the results of their struggle are of secondary importance as compared with spiritual rewards, but they nonetheless bring their particular satisfactions. This is certainly apparent to Jim Burden of *My Ántonia*, who grows up in a dynamically changing country where the old pasture land is giving way to orderly, cultivated fields and the red of the prairie grass is vanishing among the greens and yellows of fertile crops. He sees also a certain physical repose reflected in the substantial wooden houses which have replaced dreary caves and sheds of sod. To Jim, "all this meant happy children, contented women, and men who saw their lives coming to a fortunate issue. . . . The changes seemed beautiful and harmonious . . . it was like watching the growth of a great man or a great idea." While she derives generous pleasure from this amply deserved comfort and tranquillity, Miss Cather at the same time (in "Nebraska") sees and condemns "the other side of the medal, stamped with the ugly crest of materialism, which has set its seal upon all of our most productive commonwealths."

In "Nebraska," where she analyzes this situation, she concludes that taste, manners, and moral sense have been corrupted by such narcotic pleasures as motion pictures and bad fiction and by a superabundance of prosperity. And these are among the weakening influences which have accelerated the decline of second-generation pioneers, as in *One of Ours* and *A Lost Lady*. Reproachful of the spurious values prompting the behavior of her contemporaries, she looks back nostalgically in "Nebraska" to heroic endurance and achievements which make current defections seem all the more censurable. "The generation that subdued the wild land and broke up the virgin prairie is passing, but it is still there, a group of rugged figures in the background which inspire respect, compel admiration." Theirs was a moral triumph, wrested as it was from adverse circumstances in a testing of human character. Theirs was the pride of individual accomplishment. Without justifying the thwarted incentives of their children, "the generation now in middle life," Miss Cather can nevertheless understand their drive. Brought up in hardship, they reached out instinctively—as soon as they could buy them—for material comforts, which she regrets must be both expensive and ugly. "Their fathers came into a wilderness and had to make everything, had to be as ingenious as shipwrecked sailors. The generation now in the driver's seat hates to make anything, wants to live and die in an automobile, scudding past those acres where the old men used to follow the long corn-rows up and down. They want to buy everything ready made: clothes, food, education, music, pleasure." These are facts Miss Cather has reluctantly come to understand if not to become resigned to.

But she is also troubled that the third generation— "the full-blooded, joyous one just coming over the hill"—may be delayed in living up to the promise she has for it. "Will it believe that to live easily is to live happily?" While she is hopeful that this is the generation which will revert to the lessons of its forebears, the rhetorical question carries a concern for the immediate future. She prophesies that the "showy extravagance of this hour" is a passing mood. But she is impatient for the resurrection and she is mistrustful of even the transient deterrent. Here is the concretion of Willa Cather's literary case against materialism, and here also is the clue to one of the thematic directions she takes in her series of Western frontier novels.

Although *O Pioneers!* is the first significant revelation of her frontier attitudes, the lesser, apprentice writings incorporate some of those which are relevant to the problem of materialism—the death of the spirit. In the early (1897) short story "A Resurrection," for instance, she considers the Nebraska community of Brownville, which had been "shorn of its glory and importance by the railroad maneuvers that had left everybody poor." Filled with empty buildings and aimless boys and men, "the village became a little Pompeii buried in bonded indebtedness. The sturdy pioneers moved away and the 'river rats' drifted in," indifferent to tradition or natural beauty.

One of her important though little known germinal explorations of provincial deterioration is in "The Bohemian Girl," which was published in 1912 in *McClure's,* the year before *O Pioneers!* appeared. Of the Ericsons, the prosperous, greedy, smug second-generation group who provide the central interest in the story, Miss Cather ironically wrote, "There never was such a family for having nothing ever happen to them but dinner and threshing." Even this early in her career Miss Cather had established an active prejudice against such unimaginative callow acceptance. Like a foreshadowing of numerous future protagonists—for instance, Carl of *O Pioneers!,* Jim Burden of *My Ántonia,* and Claude Wheeler of *One of Ours*—Nils leaves his family and neighbors because he is repelled by their pettiness and grasping. This story is further significant in that it contains one of Miss Cather's first portraits of the typical descendants of pioneers, a portrait which she was to develop later with greater fullness in *O Pioneers!* and *One of Ours*. Olaf, the essence of animal stolidity, sums up in his personality and appearance everything Miss Cather came to regard as a violation of the original frontier spirit. Slow to respond, whether in speech or action, "Olaf was a big, heavy Norwegian" whose face was the clue to his insensitivity. It was "devoid of any expression, betraying his fifty years as little as it betrayed anything else, and powerful by reason of its very stolidness. . . . The one thing . . . always felt in Olaf was a heavy stubbornness, like the unyielding stickiness of wet loam against the plow." For her Olaf is but one of many of those farmers whose values represent a complete denial of the creative spirit, whose attitudes mark the resistance to that which does not have immediate utility, and perhaps above all, whose behavior epitomizes a narrow insistence upon self-aggrandizement.

Any attempt to understand her view of the frontier's destructive element must begin with "The Bohemian Girl," tentative and groping though this early account may be. Not until the composition of *My Ántonia*, as a matter of fact, does Miss Cather seriously develop her attitudes toward materialism. But even in *O Pioneers!*, as in "The Bohemian Girl," there are at least presentiments of a doctrine which was to emerge as the fully conceived symbol of "machine-made materialism" in later novels. Although the solid goodness of Alexandra is designed to expatiate the essential theme of pioneer idealism, there is another lesser though salient motif. It acts as a foil to the first and reveals a condition of potential degeneration.

The moral strength of Alexandra is contrasted with the deficiencies of her brothers, Oscar and Lou, the embodiment of those real-life Nebraskans "scudding past those acres where the old men used to follow the long corn-rows up and down." Through their venality and bad taste, the novelist synthesizes those traits she believes contribute most heavily to the negation of pure quest. Mercenary and dependent, the brothers have an instinctive fear of financial insecurity rooted in the memories of impoverished childhood. Sharing the impulses of too many of their contemporaries, they have turned the excessive prosperity of their later years to avarice, and if they ever had incipient refinement or sensitivity they have effectively smothered them in grossness. Deriving neither solace nor inspiration from their pioneer environment, they absorb only those experiences which they can find in plodding, back-breaking routine. "Like most of their neighbours," observes Miss Cather, "they were meant to follow in paths already marked out for them, not to break trails in a new country." Virtually bovine in their dulled attitudes, they are able to survive mainly because there is no longer any necessity for a dynamic creative impulse. They need merely comply with patterns of conformity that have grown out of earlier creative effort. But their kind of enervated compliance is in effect a rejection of the frontier principle. As Miss Cather states in *O Pioneers!*, "A pioneer should have imagination, should be able to enjoy the idea of things more than the things themselves." Their very divorce from the imaginative insight that makes Alexandra a true pioneer invests Oscar and Lou with a reverence for mediocrity. Indifferent to permanent values, they stupefy themselves with the immediate reality of drudging habit and erratic fussiness.

Oscar, who represents one aspect of commonplace

existence, was endowed with a physical strength which
he abused. He was "the sort of man you could attach
to a corn-sheller as you would an engine. He would
turn it all day, without hurrying, without slowing
down." But he was effectively insulated against all
creative thought or, indeed, any kind of intellectual
activity. Unthinking habit so possessed him that he
would follow a set procedure without regard to efficiency. "He felt that there was a sovereign virtue in
mere bodily toil, and he rather liked to do things in
the hardest way. If a field had once been in corn, he
couldn't bear to put it into wheat. He liked to begin
his corn-planting at the same time every year, whether
the season were backward or forward." If the seasons
failed him, his own regularity was a reproof to the
irregularity of the weather. "When the wheat crop
failed, he threshed the straw at a dead loss to demonstrate how little grain there was, and thus prove his
case against Providence." Unlike Oscar, Lou was a
projector, bustling over unimportant details, planning
large ones, and seldom managing to give his immediate
attention to more than relative trivia. He was proud of
the farm, always desirous of keeping it trim. But in
his enthusiasm for neatness he might readily neglect
the most pressing business of daily routine until he
was forced to frantic exertion. "In the middle of the
wheat harvest, when the grain was overripe and every
hand was needed, he would stop to mend fences or to
patch the harness; then dash down to the field and
overwork, and be laid up in bed for a week. The two
boys balanced each other." The harshness of this dual
portrait serves to accent Willa Cather's contempt for
meaningless detail and at the same time, by implication, her passion for the innately valuable.

By the time *The Song of the Lark* and *My Ántonia*
were written, the symbolic representations of "ma-

chine-made materialism" were elaborated and given augmented significance. In these two novels Miss Cather brings into sharpened focus her disapproval of those forces of Western exploitation. The most direct evidence is the appearance of small towns which have sprung up all over the prairie and which fictionally become the target of her detestation, providing her with a symbol of devastating force. These communities are for Willa Cather a clearly revealed denial of the idealism which emanated from the untamed land. Separately or combined, the prairie towns seem to epitomize the unfortunately materialistic compulsion that brought about their founding. That is, she deliberately ignores the protective and social needs which bring men together in communities, and she ascribes their origins chiefly to a base hope for the material gain to be derived from pooled effort. Many social historians and novelists would doubtless attack the limitations inherent in this view. And Miss Cather herself, who was thoroughly steeped in the knowledge of communal trends, would probably admit her special pleading. But it was a pleading devoted to an eminent cause and she declined the obligations of reportorial exactitude.

Fully aware of the omitted details, she could justify her willful restriction precisely because she was a novelist and not a reporter. Perhaps one reason she did not remain in newspaper work was her unwillingness to be an impartial observer. As a case in point, when in 1894 the *Nebraska State Journal* assigned her to gather material for an article about Brownville, she intentionally exaggerated the town's deterioration. Nor is there any record that she felt remorse over the inhabitants' discomfiture. She was always made uncomfortable and disconcerted by the ugliness and meanness and conformity of provincial settlements. These negative traits spell the loss of creative imagination, and creative imagination she deems an inseparable part of the pioneer spirit. Her sympathies are fully with Crazy Ivar, the not-so-crazy hermit of O *Pioneers!*, when he complains, "The way here is for all to do alike."

Miss Cather's towns—for the most part inhabited by people infected with a virus of moral disintegration and esthetic perversion—share a surprising affinity with those of authors so distant in temperament from her as Sinclair Lewis, Sherwood Anderson, and Edgar Lee Masters. Despite her townsmen's pioneer heritage, most of them have grown into parochial attitudes, such as the stultifying desire to find "a soft place." Miss Cather's fictive discontent is in this respect an emotional expression of sociological findings that progress in the small towns of the prairie was generally to be regarded as growth in material things. This desire for ease was what drove the children of pioneers to the towns in the first place. Once settled there, she points out in *The Song of the Lark*, they gave way in their desire for ease to the "sole ambition [of getting] something for nothing."

Such a repudiation of useful initiative made the small towns hostile to any kind of creative activity that did not produce results in dollars and cents. Conformity became the watchword and those who did not conform were destroyed either figuratively or literally. The small towns of the Middle West were activated by the quasi-philosophical premise that common sense resided in the minds of the majority. From this kind of dubious reasoning, consequently, there developed an attitude which James Bryce has called "the fatalism of the multitude" and which is evidenced in the provincial code of behavior.

Even as early as 1902 Miss Cather was able to consider this notion as a truism. In "The Treasure of the

Far Island" she creates the character of a lawyer, sensitive and formerly distinguished, who because he cannot adjust to the arbitrary standards of the small town is driven to alcoholism. She describes him as the pathetic victim of an intractable order in which refinement must be stamped out as uselessly weak. Clinging vainly to what remains in him of culture, he is "one of those brilliant wrecks sometimes found in small towns, who, when he was so drunk he could not walk, used to lie back in his office chair and read Shakespeare by the hour to a little barefoot boy." The lawyer of this little known short story is, of course, the archetype of her much more celebrated figure, the sculptor, whose tragedy was "the yearning of a boy, cast ashore upon a desert of newness and ugliness and sordidness, for all that is chastened and old, and noble with traditions."

The pressures of conformity have reduced the small town to "the fear of the tongue," as Miss Cather terms it in *The Song of the Lark*. The townsmen cannot help feeling themselves the objects of their fellows' prying eyes and gossip, and they retaliate in kind. Their interests are never shaped by influences lying outside of their proscribed lives, nor are these interests ever determined by inner needs. They live in a moral and intellectual vacuum whose focus of meaning is the town itself. And since this kind of narrow proximity invites carping censure, the townsmen refuse to find "attractive" anything "in its natural state—indeed scarcely anything was decent until it was clothed by the opinion of some authority." Characters such as Anna and Mrs. Archie in *The Song of the Lark* have their primary function in substantiating this thesis. Of Anna, Miss Cather says that her "nature was conventional, like her face." For the trivial reason that she considered her position as a minister's daughter socially important, she tried to act her part by reading "sentimental religious story-books" and by emulating "the spiritual struggles and magnanimous behavior of their persecuted heroines." Anna was so incapable of thought that everything virtually had to be interpreted for her; "her notions about the smallest and most commonplace things were gleaned from the Denver papers, the church weeklies, from sermons and from Sunday School addresses." These were opinions which their dull readers subsequently categorized "like a book of popular quotations . . . totally unrelated to the emergencies of human life."

Of Mrs. Archie, an emblem of the trifling ignobility even more than the conventionality of the small town, Miss Cather says: "Such little mean natures are among the darkest and most baffling of created things. There is no law by which they can be explained. The ordinary incentives of pain and pleasure do not account for their behavior. They live like insects, absorbed in petty activities that seem to have nothing to do with any genial aspect of human life." Embittered by her recognition of futile wasted lives, Miss Cather speaks out more vehemently than is her custom. Angered in a similar way, Jim Burden on many a night wandered distractedly "up and down those long, cold streets, scowling at the little, sleeping houses on either side, with their storm-windows and covered back porches," flimsy evidences of tasteless mass production. "Yet for all their frailness, how much jealousy and envy and unhappiness some of them managed to contain. The life that went on in them seemed to be made up of evasions and negations; shifts to save cooking, to save washing and cleaning, devices to propitiate the tongue of gossip." Living behind those thin walls was like living in a tyranny of enforced yea-saying. People became furtive and repressed, afraid to give any outward show of singularity. "The growing piles of ashes and cinders in the back yards were the only evidence that the wasteful, consuming process of life went on at all." Again, the tragic reminder that to fit oneself into the unyielding mold of provincialism is to destroy the spirit.

While Miss Cather was certainly not a realist in the sense that she reproduced photographic details, she nevertheless was close enough to ordinary experience to actualize the various ramifications of the caste system inherent in the small town structure. Attitudes fostered by middle-class conventionalism were of course predominant. Miss Cather knew, for instance, that certain standards for religious and marital alliances were virtually obligatory among members of the prevailing group. Respectability, which was a middle-class byword, entailed association with some major Protestant sect overtly dedicated to stern religious conformity. Narrow-minded, as drawn by Miss Cather, her typical middle class is represented by such people as Anna and Mrs. Archie in *The Song of the Lark,* and by the bankers and other substantial citizens of *My Ántonia,* who look with condescending horror upon any alliance between their sons and the immigrant hired girls who earn their own living. Even the young men of the town, under the contented ministrations of their parents, are contaminated by this righteous parochialism. And if they are occasionally made uncomfortable by their infection, they stolidly prefer it to any disruption of an established social order. "The Black Hawk boys looked forward to marrying Black Hawk girls, and living in a brand-new little house with best chairs that must not be sat upon, and hand-painted china that must not be used." When, as young men will do, they glanced up from their ledgers or bank cages to follow the sensuous charms of Lena

Lingard or Tiny Soderball, they did not long permit themselves the luxury of natural admiration. They quickly recalled themselves to caste and duty, imbued with the admonitions of their elders.

As Miss Cather ironically generalized: "The country girls were considered a menace to the social order. Their beauty shone out too boldly against a conventional background. But anxious mothers need have felt no alarm. They mistook the mettle of their sons. The respect for respectability was stronger than any desire in Black Hawk youth." Although Miss Cather herself would have been one of the young women eligible for marriage into this stratum, she preferred the ways of Lena and Tiny and fled with them from such armored emotion.

There would also be found in a typical small town an upper-class group of "respectable" people, such, for instance, as Captain and Mrs. Forrester of *A Lost Lady*, who failed to see a violation of morality in their pursuit and practice of daily pleasures. Finally, the stratification would leave room for a "lower" class— Catholics, foreigners, and laborers who necessarily moved outside of the dominant pattern. This group is represented by the fun-loving Mexicans in *The Song of the Lark* and the hired girls in *My Ántonia*.

Along with these broad social classes still other groups existed which were comprised of those regarded as social anomalies, and who as such were neither to be accepted nor rejected—merely tolerated—by the prevailing groups. These were the old people and the unmarried women, the latter habitually referred to as spinsters. In *Alexander's Bridge*, antecedent to her fictive interest in the West, Miss Cather makes passing reference to the position held by elderly people in Midwestern society; and in "Old Mrs. Harris" she dramatizes their plight. A recent social historian, Lewis E.

Atherton, has analyzed the situation in this way: "Middle Border ideals of progress held that everything old was inferior. In seeking 'advantages' for their children and in emphasizing *growth* in size and numbers, the pioneers themselves had disdained the past. Why, then, should a new generation, swollen with conceit over its advanced civilization, do more than humor the elderly." Spinsters likewise held an ambiguous position, for it was an accepted tradition of the social structure that all women marry. That social structure made little provision for an unmarried woman except as an unpaid servant and as the focus for the carping anger of her family. For this reason, perhaps, Miss Cather treats compassionately the celibate Aunt Tillie in *The Song of the Lark*.

Willa Cather detested these generally accepted social divisions, and she resented the parvenu attitudes which decreed that some people are socially more or less desirable than others. Painful though she found the condition, however, she knew that it was too firmly set by obdurate custom to admit of noteworthy change at any foreseeable time. From her readings and experience she could but conclude that the class laminae of village life, intensified as they were, had existed even earlier during the pioneer phase of Midwestern development. If Miss Cather's analysis in "Nebraska" may be accepted, then the American pioneers forced an unnatural rift between themselves and their European neighbors as a result of their snobbery or just plain lack of curiosity.

Feeling an unjustifiable superiority because their own European roots were so dimly distant and because they cherished their insularity, which they confused with security, they completely failed to understand these newer immigrants. The profit they could and should have derived from the assimilation of older traditions they denied themselves because of their guarded isolation. As Miss Cather saw these early settlers of the Midwest—whether they came from New England or the South—they were kindly and helpful to their foreign neighbors whenever there was sickness or trouble. But their assistance might be regarded as "cold beneficence" (to borrow Coleridge's phrase), dictated by impersonal, normative standards rather than by spontaneous fellowship.

Creating an example of this order in *My Ántonia,* Miss Cather shows how the Burdens respond to the misfortunes of one of their foreign neighbors. They were most helpful to the destitute, bereaved family of Shimerda after his suicide, but the Burdens' humaneness is uncomfortably tempered by an aloof, patronizing attitude. In "Nebraska" she expressed her confidence that "Knut Hamsun might have worked a year for any one of our Southern farmers, and his employers would never have discovered that there was anything unusual about the Norwegian." Similarly, a New England settler might have been aware of intelligence in his hired hand, but he would have been suspicious of it; and the shiftless family from West Virginia would have felt disgraced if one of them had married the nephew of a professor at the University of Upsala.

Those undemocratic and tacitly enforced social barriers, laughable and yet pathetic in the petty stupidity which erected them, became crystallized for Miss Cather in the small town. In *My Ántonia,* the daughters of Black Hawk merchants "had a confident, unenquiring belief that they were 'refined,' " and that they were assuredly superior to such immigrant Midwesterners as Lena Lingard or Tiny Soderball or Ántonia. This crudely naïve feeling was part of a general adult misapprehension that "all foreigners were ignorant people who couldn't speak English." Native forms, no matter how gross, were regarded as preferable to the most sophisticated of European cultures. Regional chauvinism simply did not allow for the incorporation of new or different values. The unfamiliar was always regarded as the alien.

Drab, uncharitable, and unlovely though Miss Cather's townspeople are, they can as individuals do no real harm except to themselves. There can be no denying that they represent a cumulative influence which in its massing of conventional prejudices is abrasive and even debilitating. But their negativism is never of a willful kind. Their failure comes from reliance upon organized thinking and conduct. But even though Miss Cather used these townspeople as contrasts to the pioneers, she came to realize that they were not true foils. In order to give more dramatic force to the pioneer situation, she therefore began to envision characters whose deliberate, self-motivated evil would be a contrast to the pioneer's unpremeditated goodness, whose destructiveness would threaten the pioneer's creativeness, and whose greed would be a contrast to the pioneer's generosity. These new characters—Wick Cutter and Ivy Peters—were slow in evolution, the result of time and esthetic experimentation.

The townspeople and their country replicas—such as the Bergson boys, Oscar and Lou—typify the fearful little men of no initiative or imagination who cling to the safety of routine which will, they hope, protect them from indebtedness and its dreaded legal token, the mortgage. Bitterly real enough among the vicissitudes of this country's landholders, the mortgage was a favorite, heavy-handed literary device turned to obvious use by such Western spokesmen as Hamlin Garland and Joseph Kirkland. As early as 1901 Miss

Cather began to fictionalize—and rather badly at that —the problem of the mortgage and its effects upon both the victim and the holder. The result was "El Dorado: A Kansas Recessional," a highly melodramatic short story whose tone is synthesized in its subtitle.

In the pioneer novels the mortgage appears first in *O Pioneers!* merely as a kind of massive abstraction, detached from any active human agency. Not until *My Ántonia* do we see a usurer, the specific human emblem of rapacious greed, exerting his force upon people like the Shimerdas. Here we may view the mortgage as a vicious example of man's avarice, the very essence of the new gross materialism that was sweeping the Midwestern frontier toward the end of the nineteenth century. To develop the idea of greed and to give it the force of a repellently evil symbol, Miss Cather depicts in unfortunately sensational terms "Wick Cutter, the merciless Black Hawk moneylender, a man of evil name throughout the county." Cutter's religious hypocrisy is typical of his treacherous nature. His physical appearance is parasitic and of a softness that belies the crabbed soul. His personality, as it is described by Miss Cather, is utterly loathsome.

A regular contributor to the town's Protestant churches, "for sentiment's sake," he admitted, he customarily bragged that he had been reared in a pious atmosphere. As an added, satirical reminder of his moral perversity, he bears the name of Wycliffe; the religious connotations are totally out of keeping with his rascality. "In every frontier settlement," we are informed, "there are men [like Cutter] who have come there to escape restraint." Curiously ambivalent in his righteousness, he gambled and was a bad loser. Yet he "boasted that he never drank anything stronger than sherry, and he said he got his start in life by saving the money that other young men spent for cigars." As a foreshadow of I. O. Snopes in Faulkner's *The Hamlet,* Cutter "was full of moral maxims for boys," sententiously familiar with "Poor Richard's Almanack," and he professed affection for "the good old times" and the simple life. Physically repulsive, he was nevertheless as vain of his appearance as a woman and often took mud baths at hot springs for the improvement of his skin. Cutter was persistently unfaithful to his wife, with whom his relations were understandably strained. Yet some kind of conventional propriety kept them together "in a fussy, scroll-work house, painted white and buried in thick evergreens, with a fussy white fence and barn. . . . He was so fastidious and prim about his place that a boy would go to a good deal of trouble to throw a dead cat into his back yard, or to dump a sackful of tin cans in his alley. It was a peculiar combination of old-maidishness and licentiousness that made Cutter seem so despicable." The gross embodiment of all the materialists who came to tear the vitality out of the original dream of the West, Cutter in his greed turns to irrationality and mania. Through his selfishness he destroys many of his debtors and ultimately destroys himself.

Although *A Lost Lady* follows *One of Ours* in order of publication, it is actually the culminating work in the sequence of frontier novels and therefore should be examined at this point. Set a full generation after *A Lost Lady, One of Ours* reveals not the processes of Western decay but what Miss Cather presents as the tragic consequences of an inevitable seriate degeneration. In *A Lost Lady,* the negativistic symbol of "machine-made materialism" appears in its final form, completely developed. All the other elements of the novel are pared down to allow the amplification of this one symbol; the total novel becomes a parable descriptive of the frontier's downfall through the atrophying force of misdirected progress.

An analysis of Willa Cather's concrete representations of venality makes it apparent that the theme of A *Lost Lady* is an integral part of the one great theme which runs through all of her novels relating to the frontier. The true pioneer spirit is subdued and falls before the encroachment of profligate materialism. Because man has failed to maintain rapport with the gods that he brought with him into the wilderness, he has lost his right to happiness. And yet, having sacrificed the old ideals in favor of the false new ones, the crass realist is himself lost in the welter of progress which results from the new. His abundant possessions are no assurance, Miss Cather emphasizes, of his right to earthly happiness. Again she implies the question that she asks in "Nebraska": Will the new generation "believe that to live easily is to live happily?"

In Ivy Peters, a second-generation pioneer, the novelist concentrates the cause for the decline of the true West, and in this sense she makes him an ominous symbol. He is a compound of all the aggressive yet enervating forces that drain the frontier spirit, and he is a deliberate sinner against both nature and man. His wanton mutilation of the woodpecker is an omen of the perverted and sadistic will that leads Ivy ultimately to the more sinister evil of ruthless exploitation. Symptomatic of Ivy's overpowering self-assertiveness and perversity, his motiveless crime against an innocent creature typifies the dominant strain of all his future actions. Not unlike the wanton destruction of animals by men in such classics as Coleridge's "The Rime of the Ancient Mariner" and Poe's "The Black Cat," Ivy Peters' crime is directed not only against a defenseless animal but against nature and God. The incident may be regarded as a parable of what happens to a free, living force when it collides with the crassness and reckless cruelty of the unregenerate will symbolized by Ivy Peters. The woodpecker, free and apparently secure, is suddenly attacked by Peters; becoming desperate in its confusion, it heeds the primal instinct which warns it to retreat to its customary perch. So the metaphorical frontier, attacked by the destructively materialistic acts of men like Ivy Peters, becomes equally desperate in its confusion and like the bird knows only defensive retreat.

But more important than its function as a parable is the credible foreshadowing imparted by this jejune assault to Ivy Peters' later acts of satanic pride. As a man capable of measuring right and wrong, he willfully violates the philosophical and theological conceptions of creation. This he does—like Satan and, to a lesser degree, like Adam and Eve—by making his personal whims and greed the sole motives of his actions. Desiring power, luxury, and complete fulfillment of his own convenience, he rejects all ideal values because they are not utilitarian. Willa Cather sees in him the incarnation of all the detestable ills of materialism, the violation of all the moral and esthetic principles that brought greatness to the West, for Ivy Peters nullifies the primal idealism which sustained the pioneers; he fosters the ugly utility which reinforces his debilitating schemes. Knowing the vicious consequences of his greed, he proceeds regardless of any hurt that he may inflict upon others.

He is especially debased because he makes no creative contribution to the land. He is willing to despoil it and its people without ever considering the satisfactions of abiding by an ideal. The tragedy of what he is doing is pointed up through a comparison between the old visionaries and this upstart opportunist. The dreamers who had settled the old West had been magnanimous but impractical adventurers. They had constituted "a courteous brotherhood, strong in attack but weak in defence, who could conquer but could not hold." Supplanting them now were unprincipled parvenus like Ivy Peters, "who had never dared anything, never risked anything. They would drink up the mirage, dispel the morning freshness, root out the great brooding spirit of freedom, the generous easy life of the great land-holders." Ivy and his kind would mangle the vastness and glory of pioneer enterprises, destroying and cutting up the land "into profitable bits, as the match factory splinters the primeval forest." What Ivy did when he drained the Forrester marsh becomes the measure of exploitation desired by "this generation of shrewd young men, trained to petty economies by hard times."

And yet neither Ivy Peters alone nor the negation he represents is responsible for the wasting away of a frontier. His active, obvious evil requires a kind of unwitting support from those who have become either too weak or too indifferent to resist the desiccation of a lofty ideal. In attacking the tangible defects of progress, Miss Cather is attacking those active wrongs typified by the career of Ivy Peters. Simultaneously, she presents the accessory causes of Western decay through the personification of two pioneer types. Captain Forrester is the tragic agent of a weakened morality which precludes his defense of that which he recognizes as just. At the same time, Marian Forrester is paralyzed by a residual inertness that simply prevents her from identifying right and wrong and from choosing between them. The captain and Mrs. Forrester, therefore, with their combined inability to act of their own accord, serve as partial foils to the unqualified evil of Peters.

The rise and fall of Captain Forrester parallel the rise and fall of the true West. The pathetic dream which is his career is sketched in the tones of a chiaroscuro, traceries of light and shadow playing back and forth on each other, rendering impressions of successes and failures. The luster of noble purpose and gentility is shaded and dimmed but never obliterated—if only to remain as nostalgic memory—by flaws of human error. Essentially of the pioneer caste, he saw the beginnings of the frontier, thrived and matured therein, and then fell before a cankerous reality. His physical deterioration is a metaphorical extension of the frontier's decay, sped by the inroads of opportunism. Miss Cather patterned his growing debility after the fading resistance to materialism that destroyed many pioneers of the captain's generation. "Once last winter he had been drinking with some old friends at the Antlers,—nothing unusual, just as he always did, as a man must be able to do,—but it was too much for him. When he came out to join me in the carriage," Marian Forrester said, "coming down that long walk, you know, he fell. There was no ice, he didn't slip. It was simply because he was unsteady. He had trouble getting up. I still shiver to think of it. To me, it was as if one of the mountains had fallen down." Captain Forrester is rescued from contempt because, despite his waning strength—a token of the West's depletion—he has retained his integrity. In at least one instance, as the only director of the failing bank to restore the depositors' funds, Captain Forrester stubbornly clings to the ideals of generosity and nobility that were the real glory of the Western dream. His only guilt is his failure to follow his vision, and his self-recognition invites our compassion. Thus, as a frustrated pioneer living to see the result of his own weakness, he takes on an intensified pathos.

His death elicits from Miss Cather the obvious symbolical comparison with the arrival of winter. After the funeral: "The grey day was darkening, and . . . swift squalls of snow were falling over the wide meadows between the hill and the town, and the creaking of the big cottonwoods about the house seemed to say that winter had come." An era had passed and the philistines had come to rule the land. It is, as Niel reflects, "the sunset of the pioneer." The nearly vanished glory of the West is like the remains of a buffalo hunter's fire somewhere on the prairie. Only the warm ground and the flattened grass tell the traveller that the hunter had been there. Now the path-breakers are old and weary. "It was already gone, that age; nothing could ever bring it back. The taste and smell and song of it, the visions those men had seen in the air and followed." But Niel has the incomparable memory of that age which he had seen reflected mystically in the faces of the old men.

The central figure of A Lost Lady is the captain's wife, Marian Forrester, the tragic heroine whose moral indifference places her at the core of a great transitional crisis. Like the frontier itself, she is receptive to the influence of the new order. Subject at the same time to the dying spiritual tradition of the frontier, she is incapable of active selection between the ideals that are falling behind her and the sham values forming around and before her. Thoroughly pliable under the experience of each day and bending to each aggressive idea, she at first waxes with the brightness of a joyous pioneer spirit. When she is possessed by the captain, the best (and the worst) in the pioneer ideal, Mrs. Forrester assumes all the characteristics of the pioneer. In so doing she reveals to the fullest her graciousness, strength, and vitality. When the pioneer spirit withdraws before the inevitable encroachment,

when the brightness of idealism changes to the dark-
ness of materialism, Marian Forrester's spontaneity
persists outwardly; but inwardly she like the frontier
darkens to become a penumbral figure. She is truly
a product of the time.

Mrs. Forrester is genuinely tragic because she drifts
away from the felicitous spirit of the pioneer and is
absorbed into the new evil order promulgated by men
like Ivy Peters. That she had violated "a moral scruple"
was a sin, to be sure. But in the opinion of her disillusioned champion Niel, she had added to this sin
one of a much deeper gravity. She had outraged "an
esthetic idea" in which resided the absolute values of
beauty and moral good. The tragedy is compounded
when beauty, physical or interior, is proved to be not
only a deception but a destroyer in itself. A youthful
romantic like Niel could not sympathize with a compromise that set aside a great concept in favor of the
momentary comfort or the hollow adulation. To a
young man the thought that life must have a termina-
tion is not very seriously taken, nor is the consequent
belief in the sacrifice of the physical self before an
altar of principle unreasonable. Because Niel insists on
viewing Mrs. Forrester as a beautiful abstraction, he
conjures up the sacrificial image that would perpetuate
for him an adored essence. Caught up in his own
youthful inexperience, it would seem, he can only
imagine Marian's enriched past, and can only much
later understand her inability to maintain or restore
the past. At the height of his disillusionment he is dis-
appointed in her, for "she was not willing to immolate
herself, like the widows of all these great men, and
die with the pioneer period to which she belonged;
. . . she preferred life on any terms." What he does
not recognize at that time is that she is moved capri-
ciously, the child of prevailing influences. Without

the forceful example of the pioneer spirit before her, she must herself become coarsened and accept the disastrous fruits of transient reality.

It was not until the death of Captain Forrester that the truth of Marian's personality became evident. For years her many friends had been inclined to regard the infirm captain as a burden that "dimmed her and kept her from being all that she might be." But, actually, it was she who was the unstable and unknown quantity. Without the captain "she was like a ship without ballast, driven hither and thither by every wind. She was flighty and perverse. She seemed to have lost her faculty of discrimination; her power of easily and graciously keeping everyone in his proper place." Mrs. Forrester's inability to choose typifies for Willa Cather the tragic apathy of all those pioneers who submit to materialism and its false values. Mrs. Forrester's surrender to Ivy Peters is but a physical manifestation of her final dissolution. Because the materiality of civilization is a destroying force for Miss Cather, Marian Forrester is destroyed, mourned only by those last few functionless idealists, the Western pioneers. So Niel Herbert "would like to call up the shade of the young Mrs. Forrester, as the witch of Endor called up Samuel's, and challenge it, demand the secret of that ardour; ask her whether she had really found some ever-blooming, ever-burning, ever-piercing joy, or whether it was all fine play-acting. Probably she had found no more than another; but she had always the power of suggesting things much lovelier than herself, as the perfume of a single flower may call up the whole sweetness of spring."

As her virtual aftermath of pioneer idealization, Miss Cather equates exploitation with enervating, consuming decadence once again in *One of Ours*. In this novel—more than in any of the others—the symbol of the machine carries ubiquitous importance. Young Ralph Wheeler was infatuated with machines for themselves, constantly improvising upon and improving them, crowding the cellar with machines which had outlived their usefulness. Claude, the hero of *One of Ours*, reflecting on these many discarded mechanical gadgets, realized that "machines . . . could not make pleasure, whatever else they could do. They could not make agreeable people, either."

As a matter of fact, in the portion of the novel dealing with Nebraska, the machine becomes a malevolent symbol, causing disaster to those who are not sympathetic to it. The domestic and emotional crisis of Claude's life is brought about by his inability to come to terms with mechanical progress. One day when he is working with a team of mules, a motor truck frightens the animals and Claude is thrown against a barbed-wire fence. In the convalescence which follows his injury, he responds to the kindness of Enid Royce, a loveless and frigid bigot; and mistaking kindness for love, he marries her. The marriage is based upon tenets as impersonal as the action of the truck which indirectly brought the couple together.

Although the entire incident may be regarded as an oblique token or product of the new mechanical culture, it is nevertheless a significant part of Miss Cather's total attitude and is certainly ancillary to her fictive development. The failure of Claude's marriage is further identified with the machine as Enid drives through the countryside in her black electric car distributing prohibition pamphlets, while Claude dines on lonely meals of canned salmon and broods through the empty evenings.

This, in short, is a mechanically determined society which has greater regard for the robot-like offerings of the age than for positive creative accomplishment. The nearly deified machine has been given a central position, to be passively questioned and vainly opposed by Claude Wheeler. He becomes an unfortunate anachronism unable to contend with the materialism of the present. A reflection of departed high-minded idealism, he is equally a tragic reminder of the implacable consequences of materialism. The tradition of materialism in which he has been reared has, ironically, depleted him. Repelled by the doctrine of getting ahead, he at the same time lacks the pioneers' strength to fight for an ideal (one that he does not really understand clearly). Claude and everyone else seemed to know there was something wrong with him. His parents were inclined to blame his uncertainty on religion, but for different reasons. "Mr. Wheeler was afraid he was one of those visionary fellows who make unnecessary difficulties for themselves and other people. Mrs. Wheeler thought the trouble with her son was that he had not yet found his Saviour." His brother Bayliss was convinced that Claude was "a moral rebel," that he was so uncommunicative because he was concealing radical notions. The neighbors liked Claude but in a tolerating way, laughing at him as one who was odd.

Claude himself "was aware that his energy, instead of accomplishing something, was spent in resisting unalterable conditions, and in unavailing efforts to subdue his own nature." That is, just when he had reconciled himself to the conformity expected of him, he would become animated with the hope of a meaningful destiny. He would be seized by "the conviction that there was something splendid about life, if he could but find it." But his life was made up of such erratic fumblings and he never did find himself as long as he remained a part of Nebraska. A wistful, attenuated romantic who is acutely sensitive to his own maladjustment, he has but two courses to follow. The first is to subordinate himself to the materialism of his own age, like so many weak pioneers before him. This he does with disastrous personal results. The second is to flee, not so much toward an ideal as away from repugnant standards, again like many unsuccessful pioneers. This too he does and dies, an escapist reaching out for an exalted cause which, paradoxically, he discovers in the destructive element of war.

Claude Wheeler accepted the violent transition to war because of his despairing recognition that the evils of the now established order could bring him only frustration, and because of his realization that "No battlefield or shattered country" would ever be "as ugly as this world would be if men like his brother Bayliss controlled it altogether." The ugliness wrought by men like Bayliss—the last in a long line of second-generation pioneers—caused Claude to envision in farming a symbol of modern futility.

In return for the superior grains and livestock the farmer took to market, "he got manufactured articles of poor quality; showy furniture that went to pieces, carpets and draperies that faded, clothes that made a handsome man look like a clown." The expensive machinery he was obliged to buy was of shoddy, short-lived construction. "A steam thrasher didn't last long; a horse outlived three automobiles." The pride farmers had once taken in the individuality of their property seemed to have vanished as they accumulated material goods. The trees they had once carefully planted were now being cut down. "Just why, nobody knew; they impoverished the land . . . they made the snow drift. . . . With prosperity came a kind of callousness; everybody wanted to destroy the old things they used to take pride in."

And the communal attitude was also changing.

Friendliness had given way to contention; lawsuits among neighbors were commonplace. Torn between extremes of stinginess and extravagance, the people "were always stirring up trouble. Evidently, it took more intelligence to spend money than to make it." Out of place in this kind of social and economic chaos, Claude was, furthermore, unable to adjust himself to what he considered the prevailing design of American life, in which "people were always buying and selling, building and pulling down." He felt the need for quietude and a revaluation of tradition that had been ignored in favor of material progress. "Life was so short that it meant nothing at all unless it was continually reinforced by something that endured; unless the shadows of individual existence came and went against a background that held together."

With the composition of *A Lost Lady* and *One of Ours*, Willa Cather must have realized that she had said everything that was meaningful to her about the rise and decline of the Western frontier. And yet she still felt an urgent need to communicate her interpretation of man's inner conflicts, his triumphs and his defeats. Having used up the West as a fitting locale in which these struggles had taken place, she turned to other locales, historically more remote but nonetheless in direct spiritual kinship with the frontier of the Midwest. Hence, she gave up the writing of novels set in the plain states of the late nineteenth and early twentieth centuries. Her direct observation formerly had been the source of her inspiration; history next became a similar tool. The result of her readings in history, softened and interpreted by personal experience and friendships, is abundantly evident in *Death Comes for the Archbishop* and *Shadows on the Rock*. But regardless of the difference in setting and time, these two historical novels, like all of her novels of the frontier, allegorize the individual's withdrawal from a "stupefied materialistic world" and his quest for a direction of life which will relate him most meaningfully to a higher order, either of an impersonal nonreligious power or of a highly personal, Christian God.

THE IDEALISM by which Willa Cather attempted to measure existence in general and to bring balance into her own life was not always sufficient to buoy her up. As she regretfully watched the contraction and gradual disappearance of the American frontier, she sustained herself for a time with the hope that new frontiers—intellectual if not physical—would ultimately replenish or at least replace the old values which had been permitted to dry up. She fought against the despair which might prove to be the death of this hope, but she was too much aware of daily circumstances to insulate herself indefinitely against reality that seemed so hard to her. Growing older—and more bitter and more dogmatic—she came to believe that the forces which destroyed the frontiers were part of the larger elements of a deteriorating American culture, indeed of a world culture. Personally, she felt that as an aftermath of the war the world had broken in two about 1922, with an unbridgeable moral and philosophical and artistic cleavage between the "backward-" and the "forward-goers," as she wrote in her introduction to *Not Under Forty*. This second group, dubiously significant by virtue of numbers and impressed by herd impulse into "progressive" action, has taken over the regulation of the new world. The new society is marked everywhere by dullness and dreariness at worst, and by stultifying conformity and efficient amorality at best. Repelled by smothering sameness and devalued indifference, Miss Cather endured the collapse of her cherished ideals in the only way she knew. And so for a period of almost thirty years she devoted her life to an intellectual detestation of a paralyzing, sick modernity and sought substitute values in a personally oriented study of history.

Her own definition of the past—as of many other concepts which she apprehended intuitively rather than rationally—is vague. For her it was not so much a chronological delimitation as it was the peculiarities of a society "whose manners, dress, conventions, loyalties, codes of honour, were different from anything existing in the world today." A society like this one would include individuals from disparate strata but of philosophically kindred attitudes, all of them desiring the resurrection or enrichment of tradition. Among them might be found the pioneers carving a world out of the wilderness, but also the sophisticated Madame Grout and Mrs. Fields, and the fictitious Gabrielle Longstreet representing the "security, the solid exterior, the exotic contradictions behind the screen; the deep, claret-coloured closing years of Victoria's reign."

Always subjective, Miss Cather's faith in tradition grew slowly from premonitory inklings to an agonized conviction which she synthesized more than any place else in *The Professor's House*. She remains artistically aloof, resisting any obvious interposition of her own personality. Yet Godfrey St. Peter's portrait is so intimately articulated that the professor's dilemma inevitably recalls Miss Cather's. Like his author, St. Peter is increasingly overwhelmed by the materialism of his environment, and in his mind he dwells for longer and longer intervals with the "sense of the past."

As she undertook her analysis of St. Peter's postwar world, she came to the acute realization that its standards of conduct and meaning were false contradictions of her own, that its so-called values were a profanation of tenets which she associated with her own indeterminate Golden Age. Increasingly, she resented the sense of acquisition, which was to her the principal characteristic of twentieth-century America and certainly a violation of the frontier and artistic principles which she revered. Sensitized to eminent purpose by his own historical researches, St. Peter experiences almost relief in the knowledge that Tom Outland, the modern projection of the pioneer type, escapes through death "the trap of worldly success." The anguish of personal loss is softened by the conviction that a man may endure nobly even in the remembrance of his uncorruptible ideals.

On the other hand, St. Peter feels alienated from his present-day society, which can best be symbolized by the outstretched hand, the demanded reward. Earlier, in *The Song of the Lark*, Miss Cather had distastefully considered "the general scramble of American life, where everyone comes to grab and take his chance." Later, in *The Professor's House*, St. Peter unhappily sees his own daughter Rosamond convert the "glittering idea" of Outland's genius into "chemicals and dollars and cents" as she indulges in a methodical and passionless "orgy of acquisition," very much "like Napoleon looting the Italian palaces."

But what made this covetousness particularly reprehensible for Miss Cather was that its exponents enjoyed added delight and complacency if their possessions came without effort. The desire to get something for nothing was, she felt, one of the most dominating and pernicious influences in American life. It is this disillusioned belief which underlies her portrait of

Mrs. Crane, who, snivelling and conniving and grasping, attempts to drain off some of the Outland fortune for her own use.

Detestable though she might find the grasping instinct of contemporary life, Willa Cather yet had room for a certain compassion toward these hoarders and spenders. But it is not a compassion to be confused with acceptance or even tolerance. Rather, it is a kind of pity which only a person of blameless conduct might extend to a weakling dying of vices he is incapable of controlling or succumbing to forces of irresistible magnitude. That is not to say that Miss Cather assumed a sanctimonious air; but she did ameliorate her contempt through a wisdom which comes with insight. All this getting and spending that she saw about her conveyed to her a sense of tragic irony, a sense, as Miss Lewis says, "that human destiny was ultimately, and necessarily tragic."

Not many, she obviously had to realize, had the strength to withstand the pressures of social emulation, of which the amassing of material luxuries becomes a primary goal. Such striving for temporal success is illusory and futile, wasteful of energy and character, and ultimately devoid of real satisfactions. Despite their desire for wealth and property, and despite their dedication to this satanic ideal, the people so dedicated felt no great happiness and had no sense of increased power. Such faulty ambition multiplies infinitely and progressively enlarges rather than satisfies itself. Seeing that there could be no satiety, only a gnawing hunger, Miss Cather felt the frustration of a Cassandra and witnessed the self-destructiveness of these people with pity. The city they lived in—whichever it might be—is like its inhabitants "a spent thing; its chief concern is with its digestion and its little game of hide-and-seek with the undertaker. Money and office and success are the consolations of impotence." With a tongue-in-cheek indulgence, an ever-relentless Fortune "turns kind to such solid people and lets them suck their bone in peace."

But in *The Song of the Lark*, where Miss Cather made these observations, she provided the lesson to be learned. The evil, she said, is perpetuated until the destruction becomes tragic. While the greed of the moment is being nurtured, the youth, "who are the Future, and who possess the treasure of creative power," inherit the disease and are rendered incapable of true fulfillment. Here, as in "Nebraska," she was haunted by the thought of an accretion of wasteful desires leading to forms of parasitism and inanition.

The consequences of an exhausted spirit, it seemed to her very much as it had seemed to the early T. S. Eliot, must be a general depletion of will. Lacking the vigor of purposeful initiative, most Americans of the Twenties had neither capacity for nor understanding of creative action. Human energy had become channeled into minor concerns and was occupied by littleness of imagination and deed. But if moral and intellectual instincts had withered, the need for prideful self-justification still remained. Individuals thus attempted to conceal their own pettiness by proving it to be part of an established pattern and by insisting that everyone do as they do. Safety lay in stereotyped conduct and precluded divergences from the mass. The result could only be—and was—a deadening conformity.

Constant reminders of passive unanimity of this order drew Miss Cather to the discouraged conclusion that America since the first World War was a dead land, despite its frenzied, treadmill momentum. The irritation she had expressed in such novels as *The Song of the Lark, My Ántonia,* and *One of Ours* had been directed toward a localized problem, that is, the timid conservatism of small towns. But their conformity was merely symptomatic of a condition prevalent throughout the entire country, and it was this universalized apathy that she was exposing in *The Professor's House*.

Here, consequently, she was extending her field of vision so that she might look critically at an infection that seemed to have touched not only provincial manners but every aspect of American culture. *The Professor's House*, unlike any of the other novels, supports the urgency of the author's anger. Deliberately shifting her locale to a university community, she demonstrates that academic enlightenment is no guarantee of idealistic conduct. Her anxieties heightened by this damning thesis, she temporarily abandons most of the symbolic nuances which previously had supported her meliorism and states her case in a relatively forthright manner. Even the cliff remains, which had been an unfailing source of inspiration in *The Song of the Lark*, here become a crippled image, nurturing greed and shattering friendship. Thus intellectual idealism and historical purity are no more equal to the immediate challenge of materialism than is constricted parochialism. To attack a corruption from which she saw no escape at any social level, Miss Cather revealed the dilemma as explicitly as her art would permit and—except for negligible occasions—put aside symbolic suggestion as a means of laying open a pervasive condition.

Even as a high school student, she had been aware of public hostility toward independent thought and investigation. During her entire adult life she respected the right to strike out for oneself in defiance of stereotyped behavior. Hers was a revolt against an era in which virtue was being made of standardization. Anticipating a number of recent books on the order of

The Organization Man, she had complained: "We wear exactly similar clothes, drive the same make of car, live in the same part of town, in the same style of house. It's deadly." And this deadliness had become a salable commodity for advertisers who bludgeoned the mind into submission with attractive arguments for mediocrity. It was easier to copy than to go one's own way, and the great principle of selling was dictated by this unresisting attitude. In an early story, "Ardessa," Miss Cather wrote that "in America [advertising] would go all the way—as far as you wished to pay its passage. Any human countenance, plastered in three-sheet posters from sea to sea, would be revered by the American people." Again, in "Two Friends," she wrote contemptuously of "the time of efficiency and advertising and progressive methods," and "any forms of pushing or boosting."

But not only the high-pressure tactics of American advertising were responsible for the mediocre sameness to which American society willingly condemned itself. A far more important element in its creation, as she understood the problem, was the desire for respectability. For some inexplicable reason—as she makes evident in "Paul's Case"—the more respectable an area or community, the greater the demand for sameness. Respectability—when its roots were superficial or its practice superimposed upon an area—fed on the identity that created an illusion of "belonging," resulting in endless monotony. For example, Paul's street "was a highly respectable street, where all the houses were exactly alike, and where business men of moderate means begot and reared large families of children, all of whom went to Sabbath-school and learned the shorter catechism, and were interested in arithmetic; all of whom were as exactly alike as their homes, and of a piece with the monotony in which they lived."

Willa Cather, who seldom resorted to overt rhetoric, left no doubt about her discontent. For her critical purpose, at least, she had joined forces with those angry apostles who were then excoriating national dullness. Sinclair Lewis, for instance, had described this lethargic attitude as "the contentment of the quiet dead, who are scornful of the living for their restless walking. It is negation canonized as the one positive virtue. It is the prohibition of happiness. It is slavery self-sought and self-defended. It is dullness made God."

But if American thought was marked by sameness in momentary conditions, it was also marked by inconstancy and fickleness. The patterned existence could readily give way to other equally rigid designs, for the cultural mold, no matter how binding it may be at the moment, can be broken apart and cast aside. The new occasion, the mercurial fad, inspire the manufacture of fresh but not necessarily durable or consequential attitudes. It does not matter, Godfrey St. Peter is convinced, what people think. "What they think today, they'll forget tomorrow." This pervasive inconstancy of thought led inevitably to a general worship of innovation and the smug rejection of formerly acceptable values. And the new, Miss Cather harshly and rather arbitrarily believed, was always ugly, flimsy, and even dishonest. This esthetically destructive bandwagon philosophy left its mark on architecture, as she attempted to show in *The Professor's House*. The new physics building at the university where St. Peter taught was cheaply executed, thanks to a state legislature which was more concerned with the false economy of shoddy planning than it was with a building which would memorialize a noble purpose. It was no sooner completed than it required patching and repairing. St. Peter and his colleague Crane had spent fruitless weeks with the contractors and then appeared before the legislative committee "to plead for the integrity of that building." But because the worshippers of the new lacked probity, they were unable to judge their folly and St. Peter's plea became one of his many lost causes.

Miss Cather was frankly perplexed by what she regarded as the shallow wants of her contemporaries. Try as she might, she could neither understand nor justify the apparent fact that a veneration of newness was related to modern society's hope for greater ease and comfort. She enjoyed refinements in her own existence and certainly did not begrudge them to others. This we have already observed in preceding chapters. But it will be remembered that she attached significance to the comforts that were more than mere necessities; she understood them to be rewards somehow identified with successful striving. In her own day, however, she saw a disjunction between ease and expended effort. Comforts and possessions seemed to be taken for granted and had no bearing beyond emulative desire. The intelligence of mankind, forced by social insistence, must be dedicated to the creation of those baubles which for the moment at least seem to make life less laborious. The supreme irony of this dedication is summed up in the sham upholstery that ornaments coffins. "Just the equivocal American way of dealing with serious facts," St. Peter reflected. "Why pretend that it is possible to soften the last hard bed?" His sense of this ironic futility is accentuated as he compares modern man's last home with the mental image of the cliff dwellings.

Built with care, patience, and deliberation, the homes of the cliff dwellers reflect their honest hardiness just as the American coffins, conversely, are tokens of pretense and enervating love of ease. Everything about those ancient abodes "proved their patience and deliberation." From the hand-dressed cedar joists to the carefully fitted door lintels and the clay-covered stone walls, the workmanship was meticulous and durable. There was pride also in the ornamentation, so that "some of the chambers were frescoed in geometrical patterns, one colour laid on another. In one room was a painted border, little tents, like Indian tepees, in brilliant red." Complementing the creative imagination and strength of this cliff city was the awesome location in which it hung "like a bird's nest," overlooking a wide valley and "facing an ocean of clear air." Those "who had the hardihood to build there, and who lived day after day looking down upon such grandeur, who came and went by those hazardous trails, must have been . . . a fine people." Theirs, according to Miss Cather's lights, was the fineness of devotion to tradition, permanence, and beauty, a quality to which her own contemporaries could not lay claim.

ii

In the course of diagnosing the degeneration by which her world seemed to be afflicted, Miss Cather described not only its nature and progress but also its causes. She was inclined to attribute blame to three major trends which were the hallmark of the twentieth century: the impersonality of science, the aimlessness of mechanization, and the reckless use of unearned capital. All three of these tendencies were detestable to her, particularly for the havoc which they had wrought upon artistic endeavor, politics, and education.

The Professor's House contains her single attack upon science, that is, scientific principles and methods and objectives. Her immediate antipathy to science grew out of its own vaunted objectivity and amorality and heightened her innate distrust of all naturalistic concepts. Because science holds itself apart from problems of good and evil, indeed even denying their existence, its influence is such as to discourage man from the consideration of basic moral problems. This, to Miss Cather, is a tragic corruption of a ruling principle, for she has no doubt at all that the inner compulsions by which individuals have always related themselves to a higher cause are all-important. Through St. Peter, she complains that in compensation for taking our minds away from the real problems of existence science has given us a lot of ingenious toys, whose usefulness and durability are highly questionable. No wonder, she argues, that science today flourishes with godlike vigor. Mankind, its energy already sapped by love of ease and comfort, grasps at the scientific palliative which absolves the individual of responsibility for his actions.

After all, a fundamental conflict has been obliterated if we no longer need choose between right and wrong, good and evil, heaven and hell. It is easier for modern man to walk the involuntary line of amorality than to accept the consequences of self-determined actions; it is easier to blame environment for personal shortcomings than it is to question intention. Science has deprived man of a large measure of his inner crises, but it has given him nothing that is a satisfactory substitute. "Science hasn't given us any new amazements, except of the superficial kind we get from witnessing dexterity and sleight-of-hand. It hasn't given us any richer pleasures, as the Renaissance did, nor any new sins—not one!" In short, science has all but removed the importance of human conduct, and as St. Peter muses: "I don't think you help people by making their conduct of no importance—you impoverish them." As the importance of human conduct diminishes, man himself tends to lose his importance; and without the right of egoism, without the power of self-justification for both errors and triumphs, mankind loses its right to happiness. The individual has forfeited his role as "a principal in a gorgeous drama with God," in which "The King and the beggar had the same chance at miracles and great temptations and revelations." Now, however, the mystery and privacy which supply the happiness of religious experience are no longer available, and the loss is a very great one.

Along with the hostility she felt toward the incursions of the scientific age, Miss Cather viewed the growing mechanization of civilization with almost morbid alarm. Contemporary mechanization, she believed, has disturbed peace and serenity to such a degree that "the immortal repose" of the cliff dwellings would be impossible in today's society. For Miss Cather the machine is the universal token of modernity. While for the purpose of certain novels, which we have already examined, she symbolized the machine as a virtually evil device that helped destroy the incipient fineness of the second-generation pioneers even as it depersonalized them, she did not restrict her antagonism to a single social group or geographical place.

As early as 1907 she had foreseen the results to which preoccupation with mechanical contrivances would lead. In the short story "The Willing Muse" she makes a metaphorical allusion to the impending problem, identifying contemporary existence with a six-day bicycle race. Mechanization, she says, induces a purposeless, self-perpetuating, never-ending speed. "The six-day bicycle race seems to be what we've come to, and doubtless one form of it's as much worth while as another. We don't get anywhere, but we go; and that's what we're after." Her interpretation of the similitude is too overtly presented to convey the artistic force of a symbol, as she was later to develop that figure, but here for perhaps the first time she makes unmistakably plain how disaffected she was by the mechanical obsession overtaking her era.

Not only does Willa Cather object to the directionless speed generated and encouraged by mechanization, but she further objects—and perhaps even more strongly—to the ephemeral nature of machinery in which man is placing his supreme trust. The production of numberless kinds of machinery, she unhappily believed, is a sign of transience, of idolized innovation which changes as readily as the pseudo thinking of the people themselves. She who detested change in herself, in her family and social relationships, and even in the shape of the familiar countryside, was equally alienated by shifting public attitudes toward mechanical devices. She resented the fact that a machine produced for some not necessarily worthwhile utilitarian purpose was soon regarded as obsolete and cast aside in favor of another device. In short, she might have been willing to reconcile herself to an object which time and use seemed to make indispensable, but she could never adjust to a rapid succession of objects of which one was not demonstrably better than the other.

As E. K. Brown has pointed out, she observed the restless shifting back and forth of these people, the new generation, able to create only machines and alien to ideas. She felt that they had contributed nothing lasting to society except cluttering gewgaws that are no substitutes for the old valued things and that are soon discarded in the basement or the attic much as a child turns away from his toys. This is for Miss Cather a gadget civilization and she has only contempt for it.

But if she was for the most part scornful of the

inconstant public attitude toward machines, as she was in *One of Ours*, she later felt a foreboding apprehension as she began to fear their evil propensities. Thus, the theorizing of Tom Outland in *The Professor's House* is recognized as the brilliant emanation of a brilliant mind as long as it is unapplied speculation and formulae. When converted into complicated machines by individuals who do not share Outland's idealistic imagination, then the theorizing becomes an instrument of evil, corrupting or destroying all—no matter how innocent—who come in contact with it. No doubt Miss Cather was extreme almost to the point of obsession in her fears of mechanical productions, but her fears were certainly not without basis. As it turned out, she became something of a prophet in anticipation of the atomic era, whose beginnings she lived to see. Although her arguments were necessarily set in another, nonpolitical context, she had the same concerns, which have grown infinitely larger and more significant today, for humane, responsible control of mechanical productions.

Moreover, the terrible speed generated by the use of machinery allows no time for self-analysis and introspection. Even emotions and individual reactions must in time become mechanized until man conducts himself by rote. Miss Cather protested in a lecture at Omaha in October, 1921: "We have music by machines, we travel by machines—the American people are so submerged in them that sometimes I think they can only be made to laugh and cry by machinery." Of course, she had to agree in the article "Joseph and his Brothers," mechanization made for accuracy. But what was the good of an accuracy without apparent human volition? To what end was the product of "the relentless mechanical gear which directs every movement of modern life toward accuracy." It was an accuracy without purpose and function, just as the speed created by machines had no direction.

It was indeed ironical to Miss Cather that with all this speed and accuracy men have not gone on to better things. In her own more theoretical way, she was rebelling against the same civilized complexities to which Thoreau had taken practical exception. Like Thoreau, she subscribed to the values of "simplicity, independence, magnanimity, and trust." These are individualized values which a mechanized order tends to slight. The position which she took could be called stubborn resistance to progress, or it could be called old-fashioned, even anachronistic reaction. But right or wrong, terms such as these do not take into account her courageous independence even before she had earned the security of fame and income, and her profound conviction of the need for a return to good purpose. That she believed as she did makes all the more credible her wistful backward glance to the peaceful stillness of the cliff remains as the condition most remote from modern acceleration. There, as she described it in *The Professor's House*, was "the calmness of eternity," a spiritual silence that would last long after successive waves of frenzied mechanization had disappeared.

Among other deteriorating forces of American culture, Willa Cather criticized the reckless use of unearned, inherited wealth, that is, money now in the hands of people who have created nothing in return for the privilege of its possession. One of the reasons for her detestation of the self-gratifying generation who were her contemporaries, E. K. Brown points out, is that they lived indulgently on what they had inherited without providing anything for the present or future except their gadgets. Of course, she did not expend her wrath and sadness only against the users of unearned capital. With bitterness, though also with a certain resignation, she reproached anyone who placed a greater importance upon property than upon human values and dignity and life. Miss Cather well realized that the veneration accorded to wealth and its possessors was not an individual thing; all of civilization with its instruments and agencies was geared toward the preservation of property, thinking too much of tangible goods as a standard of being. As she complains in *Shadows on the Rock,* "a couple of brass pots, an old saddle, are reckoned worth more than a poor man's life." Thus, if she was totally inimical to a philosophy in which ownership was its own end, she had no illusions that it was a strictly modern concept. The principle, she was forced to acknowledge, was probably as old as human nature.

While Miss Cather intimated that she was suspicious of "capital and enterprise," as in "The Willing Muse," she held her fears of its corrupting influence in check. Despite her qualms about the ultimate power which corporate interests or any other vast business venture might exercise, she was moderately reconciled to them if for no other reason than that those who controlled the capital had also created it. On the other hand, her condemnatory attitude toward the use of unearned capital left no room for reservations and was neither faltering nor evasive. Such wealth, she felt, could only contaminate. Its users, spoiled and soft and slothful, were incapable of putting it to creative use. Few human weaknesses were as grievous to Willa Cather as inert acceptance of another's toil. According to her spokesman, Godfrey St. Peter, if Tom Outland could have lived to see the base disposition of his fertile effort, he would have said unqualifiedly as did Mark Antony, "My fortunes have corrupted honest men." Who is to redeem the high-minded initiator when, through no fault of his own, his creativity is subverted?

St. Peter, constantly aware of this dilemma, is reminded "of that curiously bitter burst from the barytone in Brahms's Requiem, attending the words, '*He heapeth up riches and cannot tell who shall scatter them!*'" Miss Cather is not directly concerned with the source of this wealth, good or bad. Origination, she would argue, is of limited consequence, since it is in the nature of all inherited wealth to be made evil by virtue of its later uncreative use. Indeed, the more worthy and creative the beginnings of this wealth, the greater the tragedy involved; it would seem to her that the disjunction between lofty principle and base end must magnify the loss of that principle. No wonder then that Miss Cather was deeply impressed by Shakespeare's ninety-fourth sonnet. With the poet she would argue that a good has suffered "base infection" which in its turn has started a destructive cancer. "Lilies that fester smell far worse than weeds." The inherent irony of such disillusion becomes the more grave when it is the attitude of one not easily given to irony.

The Professor's House contains Willa Cather's most vehement denunciation of the corrupting influence of unearned capital. That it can breed ostentatious pride, among other vices, is obvious in the incident of the birthday festival given for Rosamond by her husband Louis, both of them recipients of Outland's wealth. The party was lavishly arranged in a Chicago hotel to take place after St. Peter had given a public lecture. Not satisfied with a family celebration, Louis invited some of the professor's colleagues whom he wished to impress. "They accepted—when was a professor known to refuse a good dinner." Louis showed off Rosamond richly bedecked with her birthday emeralds, "and, as St. Peter afterward observed to his wife, practically all the guests in the dining-room were participants in the happy event." His main objection to public magnificence was that "it seems to show everybody up in the worst possible light."

That unearned capital can, further, create petty cruelty and jealousy is evident from the change which occurs between the two sisters, Rosamond and the less fortunate Kathleen. What had once been sisterly love between them has now become scorn on one's part and gnawing envy on the other's. As St. Peter became aware of this radical change in the personalities and values of his daughters, "A sharp pain clutched his heart. Was it for this the light in Outland's laboratory used to burn so far into the night!"

Another of Miss Cather's complaints against the use of unearned capital was that it does not carry along with it a proportionate sense of individual responsibility, a willing obligation which should be attendant upon the possession of large sums of money. Captain Forrester, in *A Lost Lady*, was certainly aware of this responsibility when out of his own dwindling fortune he made good to the depositors of a failed bank the sums they had entrusted. Rosamond, on the other hand, has none of this compunction. When Augusta, the family's seamstress, loses money in worthless stock speculation, Rosamond refuses to help make up her loss, justifying her attitude by hypocritical sophistry. Having made the investment despite the better judgment of experts, Augusta—as though she were a foolish child—must now be made to learn her lesson. "Rosamond said they would do something for Augusta later, but she didn't say what." St. Peter, when he hears of Rosamond's rationalized callousness, becomes indignant and accuses her of being "altogether too blind to responsibilities of that kind."

In short, Miss Cather assumes, large sums of unearned wealth vulgarize and debase its users, distort their values, and ultimately destroy what moral vitality they once might have possessed. St. Peter is sensitive to this kind of destructiveness when he unequivocally rejects for himself the offer of some of Outland's money. He reasons that there could be no question of money between himself and Tom Outland. He tells Rosamond, who has made the offer: "I can't explain just how I feel about it, but it would somehow damage my recollections of him, would make that episode in my life commonplace like everything else. And that would be a great loss to me. I'm purely selfish in refusing your offer; my friendship with Outland is the one thing I will not have translated into the vulgar tongue." St. Peter's reproach is double edged, for he is simultaneously casting out the spurious concept that personal loyalties and affections may be held together with material ties and he is impugning the assumed right of Rosamond to make casual expenditures of money which is hers by legal rather than moral right.

iii

It becomes apparent, then, that while Willa Cather's attacks upon modern society were generalized, her subjective analyses of the causes of society's decline were rather detailed. Even of her attacks, moreover, the generalized quality tended to disappear when she discussed those matters which she felt to be most profoundly affected by the paralysis of social values. The institutions particularly susceptible to the negative influence of mass rigidity, in her opinion, were education, politics, and the arts. These three areas of endeavor earned her close and often acidulous attention because of their challenge to individualism and, conversely, because of their responsiveness to passing trends. In education, politics, and the arts, thus, she recognized activities which demanded a creative energy emanating from the strong and daring individual; but she also saw in them a sometimes dangerous pliability which made them bend before the unreliable winds of prevailing mass attitudes.

As a matter of active participation, Miss Cather was rarely concerned with politics. The artist, she felt, must preserve himself aloof from political squabbles and causes. Believing as did the Neo-Humanists of the Twenties and Thirties that reform of any kind must proceed from within, activated by an individual, introspective compulsion, and believing further that correction is properly to be directed toward another individual rather than toward a group or mass, she anathematized the professional humanitarian and reformer. She declined to join societies, no matter by whom she was asked or what their aim. This political indifference must by no means be interpreted as an absence of warm, personal regard for human beings in trouble. Indeed, Miss Cather was capable of sympathy and spontaneous response to another's dilemma.

Miss Lewis tells of just such a situation which arose when Miss Cather learned that a faithful servant, whose husband had recently died, had become unbalanced by her loss. Relatives committed the woman to an institution, whereupon the novelist devoted herself energetically to the numerous details required for getting a release; she eventually restored the woman to a useful and normal existence. "It was not benevolence or a sense of duty," according to Miss Lewis, "it was a flash of purely personal feeling that moved Willa Cather then, as always in all such acts; . . ." In personal relations, as in her writing, Miss Cather was a creature of instinct, measuring her conduct not by the calculations of reason but by the needs inspired in her.

Although she rarely discussed political theory, much

less specific political situations, she developed a highly caustic attitude toward the New Deal, which she came to regard as the political summation of the debility threatening all of modern America. "The New Deal," says Brown, "seemed to her to threaten the free activity of the strong individual by the kind of restrictive influence that seemed to her the worst of all, restriction by government." But even before the advent of the New Deal she had tended to equate American democracy with bureaucracy, and bureaucracy as far as she was concerned destroyed by its pettiness natural human freedom. Therefore, in *The Professor's House*, Outland's futile visit to Washington is drawn as an attack on the meanness, ignorance, and stupidity of modern bureaucracy. Represented with unusual bluntness, Miss Cather's meaning is too plain to be mistaken. "If you want to get attention from anybody in Washin'ton," a knowledgeable stenographer advises the frustrated Outland, "ask them to lunch. People here will do almost anything for a good lunch."

Actually, her assault on modern political institutions, including the New Deal, is focused on governmental reliance upon civil servants, the "little black-coated men pouring out of white buildings." Apparently Miss Cather could not contain her annoyance, and she amplified her impressions of these machine-like figures until they became mere caricatures. To her these people were the dross of their time, dreary, aimless men who delighted to thwart those who had energy, daring, originality, who had, in short, accomplished something. Outland carries away from Washington the depressed memory of their petty, slavish lives. The couple with whom he lodged asked him not to mention the fact that he paid rent, for even in their minor social circumstances it would have been humiliating to them if their equally underpaid government friends knew they had a tenant. "It was like that in everything; they spent their lives trying to keep up appearances, and to make his salary do more than it could." Their conversation was as gossipy as that of Miss Cather's small-town characters, and there is in fact a marked resemblance between these government workers and her second-generation pioneers. Their talk seemed always to be without consequence, revolving about the latest promotions, the salaries of other clerks, and the wardrobes of other wives. The chief struggle of their puny ambitions was for social recognition, and receipt of a coveted invitation to dinner or tea became a major triumph.

As time went on, Willa Cather's political attitudes became increasingly dogmatic, crystallizing finally in a kind of bitter conservatism. To be sure, she was vainly resisting the collapse of an era which held her richest memories. And she was stunned by the horrors of the second World War. Because she rarely discussed the war itself, many people mistakenly thought she was "not interested" in it. According to Miss Lewis, however, "she felt it too much to make it the subject of casual conversation. When the French army surrendered [in 1940], she wrote in her 'Line-a-day,' 'There seems to be no future at all for people of my generation.' " The obliteration of warmly remembered scenes in Europe and the agitation in America which attended preparations for total war seemed to her the death of everything she had held dear. All of Western civilization was being threatened because of a dictator's madness, and a free society was finding itself shackled by the regimentation of militaristic necessity. As was so often true of Miss Cather, she weighed large issues in terms of their personal impact and consequence. Thus, she had the rather egoistic notion that a younger generation than hers could hardly be expected to be as hard hit by the war as her own. Having never known a serene past, now vanished forever, they had no regrets to store up and need only concern themselves with a harsh present.

Just as government tended to stifle individual initiative, Miss Cather believed, so education held no challenge for those capable of original thought. Like life itself, education was being cheapened by the overwhelming spread of commercialism. "Both [Crane and St. Peter], with all their might, had resisted the new commercialism, the aim to 'show results' that was undermining and vulgarizing education." Education today, according to Miss Cather, particularly in the large state universities, was dedicated to the acquisition of mechanical skills and the making of money—not to an examination of moral values and the traditional liberal arts which expressed the human spirit and the human lot on earth. In connection with *The Professor's House* (and similarly in "Nebraska") "The State Legislature and the board of regents seemed determined to make a trade school of the university. Candidates for the degree of Bachelor of Arts were allowed credits for commercial studies; courses in bookkeeping, experimental farming, domestic science, dress-making, and what not. Every year the regents tried to diminish the number of credits required in science and the humanities. The liberal appropriations, the promotions and increases in salary, all went to the professors who worked with the regents to abolish the purely cultural studies."

Although close experience with university affairs, which Miss Cather did not have, would indicate she was exaggerating, there is no denying a limited validity to her argument. It is, in fact, a dispute still prevalent —and likely to continue indefinitely—in both state and private universities. She also contended that education as it was constituted in her day was interested in preserving only a surface culture. And actually, as she interpreted the problem, in the minds of most educators culture was equated not with a principled way of life but with manners pure and simple. Miss Cather illustrates this attitude toward education in her delineation of Professor Langtry in *The Professor's House*. Despite his early unpopularity, "Of late years, for reasons that had not much to do with his lectures, Langtry had prospered better. To the new generations of country and village boys now pouring into the university in such large numbers, Langtry had become, in a curious way, an instructor in manners—what is called an 'influence.' To the football-playing farmer boy who had a good allowance but didn't know how to dress or what to say, Langtry looked like a short cut. He had several times taken parties of undergraduates to London for the summer, and they had come back wonderfully brushed up." The depth and inspiration he lacked in the classroom he made up for by the sophistication he brought to fraternity and sorority lounges, where he was always a welcome guest.

Even education, the last refuge of traditional values, had no reverence for the past. In the universities the emphasis was placed decidedly on contemporary activities; a growing indifference to the notable achievements of the past was plainly manifest. And in the secondary schools attention to the classics was probably even more perfunctory. Once Miss Cather was asked why, during her teaching years in Pittsburgh and Allegheny high schools, she had for a while taught Latin as well as English. She realized with a shock that her questioner could not understand that she had done so as a matter of preference, that she happened to like the Latin language and literature and this was a good enough reason. The stress upon contemporaneity evident in higher education struck her as one more example of the veneration with which technology was being greeted in her country. She was disturbed, consequently, that practical thinking should result in a widespread willingness to place a monetary value upon certain kinds of academic training.

But it was not only for the administration and practical curricula of universities that Miss Cather harbored contempt. Even more significantly, she implied that there had been a betrayal of principle at the very source of what should have been educational inspiration. For American teachers—concerning their motives and even their ability—she had little respect. As early as 1913, when she published the essay "Training for the Ballet," she stated her belief that "America has long been the paradise of poor teachers. A man who can do nothing else in the world can teach pretty much anything—and make a living by it—in America." Again, it is plain enough that Willa Cather's subjective biases had led her into extravagant claims; but it is equally plain that her disaffection was as usual precipitated by a fundamental cultural weakness in society and was therefore at least partially defensible. Although her attack upon teachers was to become even more specific, if the characterization of Professor Langtry may be taken as a test, her estimate of American teaching did not change perceptibly. The ordinary university professor, she argued, was utilitarian, political, and self-interested. His activities in the university were unhappily motivated by the same mundane ends which existed elsewhere, in the commercialism of business and industry—the purchasable values of self-promotion and advancement. Material recognition for worthy effort, as she had also contended for the pioneers and artists, should certainly be the reward of devoted teachers. But the high cause to be furthered by devotion should be its own end, and the rewards which could follow should be incidental or secondary.

Miss Cather had even less respect for the students at the universities than for their professors, willing though she was to concede that the young people were victims of prevailing currents rather than deliberate sinners. She deplored the fact that many of them felt impelled to go to college because a college degree was negotiable in dollars and cents. She deplored even further the fact that so many of them felt socially obligated to enter one of the professions. The fallacies implicit in such unthinking conformity were shocking to her. Young people, she believed, should enter the occupations for which they were best fitted by training and talent—whether carpentry or law. She regarded as a grievous sin the compulsion to make a social and economic necessity of a college degree. The consequences were similarly regrettable, for she saw the colleges crowded with students who were academic misfits, who were incapable of profiting from the academic discipline, and who would probably be much happier in some other environment.

She is reported as saying in 1925: "One sad feature of modern education is that the hand is so little trained among the people who have to earn their daily bread, and the head so superficially and poorly educated. The one education which amounts to anything is learning how to do something well whether it is to make a bookcase or write a book. If I could find a carpenter to make me some good bookcases, I would have as much respect for him as I have for those people whose books I want to put on them. Making something well is the principal end of education. I wish we could go back, but I am afraid we are only going to become more and more mechanical." The attentive and imaginative care which workers in the handicrafts had once been capable of applying seemed infinitely more desirable to her than the mediocre, time-watching evasions of many modern professional people. And the blame for their negligence was chargeable to both misapplied talents and faulty education.

Willa Cather was no less sparing of a decline which she witnessed in the arts. As in politics and education, what frightened Miss Cather most thoroughly about the declension of art and then revolted her was a seemingly uncheckable spread of commercialism and mediocrity. The love of ease, the desire for the short cut, the reliance on a comfortable level of sameness and conformity could only lead to destruction of genuine artistic impulse. To an interviewer in New York she once explained how, in her opinion, the degeneration of American life, which was a concrete reality for her, must soon and inevitably lead to a deterioration in art. Such deterioration must be a logical outcome of American "restlessness" and "success," she argued, because these last two qualities destroy "beauty." And without beauty the painter cannot paint, the writer cannot write, the musician cannot create. She went on to accuse America of an absence of the traditional virtues of "good cookery, cottages that are homes, not playthings; gardens, repose," all signs of an inner beauty without which there can be no encouragement of great art. "These are first-rate things, and out of first-rate stuff art is made. It is possible that machinery has finished us as far as this is concerned. Nobody stays at home any more; nobody makes anything beautiful any more."

If the reasoning of Miss Cather's argument appears elusive, this cannot be said of her further explanations for the deterioration of the American arts. The large middle class—upon which ultimately the artist is dependent for economic patronage—is hostile to the artist and his achievement by nature and design. Both groups, artists and those who are not uniquely endowed, are for obvious reasons inimical to one another; the standards of each group are tacitly a repudiation of the other's. The artist's strenuous capacity for work, his sense of the illimitable continuity of the past, his indifference to material rewards, his hatred of ugliness and his veneration of truth—both objective and subjective—all these qualities lead to middle-class suspicion and ultimate rejection. And while a truly dedicated artist may and does produce in defiance of such barriers, he requires a climate of appreciation for the fulfillment of his greatest powers. In such a climate there is a reciprocity, for the appreciation which stimulates maximum achievement is rewarded by the enrichment which that achievement brings to individual lives.

On occasion, Miss Cather realized with biting cynicism, society forced itself to adopt a passive tolerance toward the artist; indeed, it sometimes went so far as to endorse a given artist. But such approval was inevitably given to the inferior artist or to the auspicious artist who, like Geraldine Farrar (one of the singers discussed in the essay "Three American Singers"), in her personal life epitomized the "American success story." Here the enchanting realization of a myth becomes a glamorized standard of public acceptance.

But Miss Cather was willing to accept the cleavage between the artist and society; she even came to regard this separation as a necessary stimulus to artistic success, as a challenge which spurred one toward proving himself. However, her acceptance of this situation made all the more intense her censure of those social pressures which caused the potentially serious artist to succumb—either through need or weakness—to encompassing middle-class virtues. For the loss of such an artist and his latent contribution, she held society alone responsible. The deprivation of even one artist out of the creative community was an irreplaceable loss to be mourned by all who possessed a moral and esthetic sense.

iv

Troubled by such a dark view of American life and obviously unwilling as well as unequipped to undertake reformist action, Willa Cather had but one means of enduring problems she detested, and that was retreat. When she said in 1925 that she liked horses better than automobiles, she was synthesizing a pattern of thought that had been developing consciously for the last few years and that was to intensify itself throughout the rest of her life. And yet, though she tended to date her self-imposed social isolation from 1922—the year in which she imagined her civilization crumbling around her—her urge to withdraw had begun much earlier than that. In "The Willing Muse," for instance, she created an artist-hero who complains about materialistic encroachments upon his sanctuary, in this case a small college town. The solution he seeks is characteristic, for in the face of threats to his personal values, he yearns for possible retreats, "where a man can take a book or two and drop behind the procession for an hour."

Once Miss Cather understood her need for retreat, she sought for it earnestly, almost ardently; and ultimately she found it in the past itself. It is this somewhat hermitic outlook which has given rise to the charge that she was either an escapist or an antiquarian or both. The criticism is understandable but, except in a superficial way, not justifiable. Miss Cather's past was not academic, static history; rather, it was a living record whose organic nature was mainly reflected intangibly as a never vanished afflatus. If it did not have the immediacy of present affairs, it had at least a benign influence which "protected and cherished" and which afforded "sanctuary from the noisy push of the present." For this reason Miss Cather enjoyed staying at the home of Mrs. Fields at 148 Charles Street in Boston. Here was salutary retreat where "the ugliness of the world, all possibility of wrenches and jars and wounding contacts, seemed securely shut out. It was indeed the peace of the past, where the tawdry and cheap have been eliminated and the enduring things have taken their proper, happy places." Miss Cather had a remarkable knack for inverting the fabric of existence, so to speak, and seeing a pattern which was not commonly visible. Although that pattern admittedly had limited applicability, it served her profoundly.

Her idealization of the past was affected directly by a hatred of change so tenacious as to prompt her once to remark, "An old house built in miserable taste is more beautiful than a new house built and furnished in correct taste." Although she knew well enough that the past was not without its perplexities and dilemmas, she felt free to reject what was not satisfying to her. But her view was carefully discriminating, shading the past with a roseate haze until it seemed unruffled by any disturbing alterations. She had to look backward, for to look ahead meant the unwilling acceptance of trivia, so-called "progress," ephemera, and the inevitable passage of time. To look ahead meant the realization of her own advancing years and a fearful acknowledgment that they must culminate in death. Thus, toward the close of her life, in *My Mortal Enemy*, there is a poignant immediacy as well as a profound truth about the reflection that "In age we lose everything; even the power to love." And again, in the posthumous story "The Old Beauty," that "It's curious how the world runs away from one, slips by without one's realizing it." This understandable reluctance to face the prospect of growing old was characteristic of Miss Cather even when she was a much younger woman. Her fictional self of *My Ántonia*, Jim Burden, dreads that after twenty years he will find Ántonia "aged and broken." Consequently, any visible proof that the ravages of age could be warded off filled her with a sense of jubilation and victory as though a great wrong had been prevented.

So, for example, she rejoiced in Mrs. Fields' "little triumphs over colour-destroying age and its infirmities, as at the play one rejoices in the escape of the beautiful and frail from the pursuit of things powerful and evil. It was a drama in which the heroine must be sacrificed in the end: but for how long did she make the outward voyage delightful, with how many a *divertissement* and bright scene did she illumine the respite and the long wait at Aulis!" Whether Miss Cather was speaking of her friends or her created beings, she treated their onrushing years as a personal crisis.

Triumphs such as Mrs. Fields' were too rare in Willa Cather's experience, and she came to venerate youth—in memory and in actuality—as a glorious if temporary antidote to the decay which comes with age. The mature musician of *Lucy Gayheart*, Sebastian, is made to "love young ardour, young fire." And Godfrey St. Peter comparably "loved youth—he was weak to it, it kindled him." His admiration for youthful enthusiasm and curiosity had never been staled by time. Miss Cather equated youth, as in the apprentice story "A Singer's Romance," with an "unsatisfied spirit" of seeking and yearning. One becomes aware, furthermore, of the consistent physical attractiveness of her young heroines, who are almost invariably blonde as though she associated yellow or golden hair with springtime and growth.

For her own inner serenity, therefore, Miss Cather had to search back to where there had been only youth and high hopes and bright beginning. That retrospective vision magnified the pleasures of the past, she had no doubt. But they were pleasures that depended for appreciation upon perspective and time, and she was not inclined to quibble about specific realities that lay behind her. "Nobody ever recognizes a period until it has gone by," she wrote in "The Old Beauty," and "until it lies behind one it is merely everyday life." She shared Sebastian's feeling that youth, like love and hope, is transient, but that it can be immortalized in the memory, which defies change. Despite the frequent hardness of her life, Alexandra in O *Pioneers!* loved to look back toward her youth as a time of expectation and enchanted desire. She particularly liked to recall a day long ago when she and her brother, Emil, drove far out into the country and stopped alongside a river to eat their lunch. There, in what now had the magic of an idyllic setting, "No living thing had ever seemed to Alexandra as beautiful" as a wild duck frolicking along the water. "Years afterward she thought of the duck as still there, swimming and diving all by herself in the sunlight, a kind of enchanted bird that did not know age or change."

For all the brilliance of memories of the past, however, their recollection is sometimes disquieting when they do not succeed in ameliorating the anguish of present problems. An anachronistic dreamer such as Claude Wheeler, for instance, is so at odds with the present that an impossible return to his carefree years seems to him his only solution. In his obvious frustration he can only be depleted. "The desire to live again sang in his veins while his frame was unsteady. Waves of youth swept over him and left him exhausted." This futile nostalgia is complemented by Jim Burden's wish to be a boy again and remain such. He steeps himself in "the melancholy reflection that, in the lives of mortals, the best days are the first to flee. '*Optima dies . . . prima fugit.*'" Subsequently, when he thinks back to his happy youth, the line from Virgil—significantly also the motto of *My Ántonia*—comes to mind as a mournful reminder that the reality of the past is gone. But there is a certain compensation in his belief that "some memories are realities, and are better than anything that can ever happen to one again." In *Lucy Gayheart*, also, Sebastian recalls his past days as his "good days," even though the memory is followed by the brooding thought "that when people spoke of their dead youth they were not using a figure of speech."

By and large, however, the past was for Miss Cather a relief, if only temporarily, from the abrasions of the real present. It was the closest approximation to peace and permanence. Her memories, intimated in *Alexander's Bridge*, conveyed an intrinsic beauty and tranquillity, a "harmony . . . without obtrusions of ugliness or change." Believing this, she necessarily felt, as in the conclusion of *My Ántonia*, that the dearest possession that people could have was "the precious, the incommunicable past." Out of the best experiences which can be remembered, the individual derives a hopeful courage to continue searching for meaning in his existence.

If the past could give Miss Cather a personal sense of timelessness, it could also provide her with a knowledge of heroic men, daring planners, and bold executors. The pioneers were all such men. Her physical description of Trueman, one of the "Two Friends,"

synthesizes her attitude toward these men. "His countenance was . . . unmistakably American . . . but
American of that period, not of this. He did not belong to the time of efficiency and advertising and
progressive methods. For any form of pushing or boosting he had a cold, unqualified contempt." He inspired
others through "an entire absence of anything mean or
small," and through his "easy carelessness, courage . . .
high sense of honour." And in a gentler fashion, but
possessing comparable qualities were the two ladies,
Mrs. Fields and Madame Grout, both of whom epitomized for Miss Cather the glory of a former age. In
Madame Grout, described in "A Chance Meeting,"
there was "a kind of large enlightenment" growing out
of "poise, great good sense, and a love of fairness and
justice." Mrs. Fields she characterized in "148 Charles
Street" as having an admirable tenacity of purpose
which enabled her "to meet a fine performance always
—to the end. At eighty she could still entertain new
people, new ideas, new forms of art." Rich in memories
and experience, Mrs. Fields enriched the new with the
positive gleanings of her long life.

In addition, the past gave substance to Willa
Cather's instinct for clarity and order, qualities that
she feared were generally lost in the speeding present.
Her devotion to regularity was a potent force in her
life. She would argue that just as the natural universe
betokened a harmonious perfection, so man's life must
be ordered. For this reason her pioneers are all imbued
with this regulatory sense—from Alexandra, who ar-
ranges her flower garden so that "you feel again the
order and fine arrangement manifest all over this great
farm," to the nuns at the Hôtel-Dieu (in *Shadows on
the Rock*), safe in their cloistered, systematic universe.
Even Godfrey St. Peter, born too late to be a pioneer,

strives after a harmonious order in his own life, as symbolized by the loving care which he lavishes upon his formal eighteenth-century garden.

But if Miss Cather had to live within her memory and her devotion to the past as "her armour against a world concerned with insignificant matters" (as did Madame Grout of "A Chance Meeting"), she had to pay a dear price indeed for this sanctuary. In writing "The Old Beauty" Miss Cather was clearly identifying herself with Gabrielle Longstreet (who, along with Godfrey St. Peter, is Miss Cather's most nearly autobiographical figure). Significantly, we are introduced to Gabrielle Longstreet in the critical year 1922; and significantly she is made a tragic character. Vainly believing that "once the war was over, the world would be just as it used to be," she learned otherwise. Her knowledge, however, did not help her to adjust to the present order, one to which she was "antagonistic . . . indifferent, at least." The result, even for one who "had outfaced so many changes of fortune," was an ever-widening sense of isolation which suffocated while it widened so that she could weep and say, "I think one should go out with one's time."

Sadly feeling that she was apart from her times, that she had lived "through a storm to which the French Revolution, which used to be our standard of horrors, was merely a breeze," Miss Cather suffered from a futility that no withdrawal could wholly alleviate. Like St. Peter, she could not admit that withdrawal from normal social concerns had made her any happier. Yet once begun the retreat must continue. As the professor explains his dilemma: "It's the feeling that I've put a great deal behind me, where I can't go back to it again. . . . The way would be too long and fatiguing." Obviously, then, the partial tragedy of Willa Cather was not her voluntary withdrawal from a society which she scorned, but her realization that her separateness meant only an uneasy truce before she must be engulfed by an incompatible force.

But that realization was not the sole cause of the pessimistic strain in her nature. Again, *The Professor's House* offers a clue. Regardless of the age in which one lived, whether it be salutary or degenerate, for the individual there remained only all-consuming death. Since death must be the victor, one could hope only for an easy end. With this knowledge of her feeling, it is perhaps easier to understand why she envied Mrs. Fields her time of death. "But Mrs. Fields never entered this strange twilight [of modernity]. She rounded out her period, from Dickens and Thackeray and Tennyson, through Hardy and Meredith to the Great War, with her standard unshaken. For her there was no revaluation. She died with her world . . . unchallenged." With the world she fondly remembered vanished, Miss Cather felt intolerably alone. Her own memories and those of a far more distant past brought her a degree of solace, but they did not restore to the living present the graciousness and idealism by which she set her course.

4 THE ARTISTIC "CHAIN OF HUMAN ENDEAVOR"

REFLECTION UPON the multiplicity of human affairs solidified Willa Cather's belief in a kind of "similitude in dissimilitude." Variety, as far as she is concerned, is a token of unification rather than of contrariety. All experiences, no matter how disparate their outer form, are interrelated by a very few moral strands, each of which is the emanation of a central being or a superior cause. Since one of her chief purposes is always to celebrate man's place in the cosmos, but only as it reveals a harmony with the workings of an ordered infinity, she accents rather than proliferates the few themes which best serve her. The constantly changing shape of events merely reconfirms her belief that each is a restatement of one of a limited number of timeless principles. Specifically, her many novels and short stories show that for her there were only three major themes, all bound together by a common esthetic-moral tie. Two of these themes, which we have already explored in the preceding chapters, have to do with the inspiration of the pioneer experience and, because of material considerations, the corruption of that experience.

The third, which is the subject of the present chapter, concerns the artist. Like the pioneer, he undergoes the crises of self-discovery, struggle, and ultimate spiritual triumph. As Miss Cather understood the aims and compulsions of the artistic principle—and this was even more a part of her experiential life than was the pioneer story—the artist and the frontiersman share kindred motivations. The successful artist achieves his desire through a dedicated spirit which acknowledges obstacles only to transcend them; and the mediocre artist fails of attainment because the spirit is turned aside by adversity, or because the will is not in harmony with the incentive. Throughout her life Miss Cather was intrigued by the image of the artist and the need to portray him. In her earliest stories, including even those produced while she was an undergraduate at the University of Nebraska, she often wrote analytically about artistic genius. Although her analyses were not profound, they expressed a sensitivity and enthusiasm alternating between awe and hostility. At *McClure's*, for which she worked as an editor, her most important articles were those in which she interpreted the personal histories of the great productive artists of the early twentieth century. Her first collection of short stories, *The Troll Garden*, is primarily an extended colloquy between the artist as hero and a personified middle-class society as the villain. And in her more lasting accomplishments—*The Song of the Lark, Lucy Gayheart,* and *Youth and the Bright Medusa*— she devoted herself exclusively to the thematic development of the artist as an individual.

The artists in Willa Cather's spiritual hierarchy— whether fictional or real—are given a fitting eminence for their greatness of cause. Endowing them with remarkable sanctity of purpose, she insists almost fiercely that they are pilgrims of imagination, driven by a single mission. All of her artists are urged forward by their inner need to seek and find a direction of life, their art being the instrument by which they guide themselves. Without externalized pressures, her seekers thrust irrevocably toward an esthetic ideal, or perhaps vision, that blossoms into creative power rich in both imagination and spiritual values. Creativeness, she says in *The Professor's House,* is a "magical element" born of the inner quest. Serving as the prototype of her own fictional artists, Miss Cather denies that genuine artistry may be diluted. Ruled by personality and ability "uncommon, in a common, common world," as Thea Kronborg is described in *The Song of the Lark,* the artist will refuse to compromise with a spiritually denuded reality or meretricious physical power. Even the ultimate rewards of the artist are intangible. For that matter, Miss Cather is not sure that the rewards which count are ever definable as anything more than a vague sense of exultation after a long and arduous adventure.

Her attitude bears comparison with the reaction described by Proust after he had composed his first successful page: "At the moment when . . . I had finished writing it, I found such a state of happiness, felt that it had so entirely relieved my mind of an obsession . . . that, as though I myself were a hen and had just laid an egg, I began to sing at the top of my voice." If Miss Cather and her artists were less fanciful in explaining the pleasures of their creative efforts, they were at least as jubilant.

"The eternal mind," as Proust called the continuity of art, becomes the controlling urge for Miss Cather's creative seekers. Because there is no end to art and no beginning, only an organic continuum, each artist represents a link with those who have gone before him and with those who are yet to come. The idea of a unifying creative aspiration among artists has been attractive to many writers. That Henry James, for instance, was drawn to this concept is evident in such essays as "The Future of the Novel" and "Émile

Zola." For James the link between artists was forged in the "eternal desire for more experience and . . . the restless desire to represent truth."

Especially in *The Song of the Lark* Miss Cather eulogizes art as a transcendent voice which baffles a grubby reality. The desire which precedes and complements artistic creation and fulfillment is a refraction of infinity, obsessive in its need "to imprison for a moment the shining, elusive element which is life itself,— life hurrying past us and running away, too strong to stop, too sweet to lose." At the moment of her artistic awakening, which is also her moment of pure dedication, Thea Kronborg beholds the clay vessels of the ancient cliff dwellers. Suffused by the magic of memories, conscious and unconscious, she allows herself an extravagant metaphor. "In singing, one made a vessel of one's throat and nostrils and held it in one's breath, caught the stream in a scale of natural intervals." Despite the strain of the analogy, there is no questioning the singleness of her feeling. Emotionally and intellectually responsive to an ineffable longing stirred by these relics, she identifies herself with the unbreakable continuity of art. She feels herself a part of the ancient dream which had brought "some promise to the sadness of the savage. In their own way, these people had felt the beginnings of what was to come. These potsherds were like fetters that bound one to a long chain of human endeavor." But the restrictions these artifacts impose—otherworldly and unifying—are without relation to that daily conformity which starves the spirit. They provide, rather, a comfortable association with values that are desirable for the very reason that they are values. Through her fictional artists, Miss Cather exalted the historical sense which underlies the creation of mature art, for meaningful creativity is grounded in the realization that no artist is an entity

in and of himself. Willa Cather's concern on this score
is comparable with T. S. Eliot's conviction that "the
artist's significance, his appreciation is the appreciation
of his relation to the dead poets and artists."

Perhaps it was because of an acute consciousness of
specific artistic personalities that Miss Cather now for-
sook massive symbolic devices which she had used to
objectify her attitudes toward the frontier. Although
most of her pioneers and their descendants have certain individualized traits, they do not have characteristically human dimensions. This we have already
observed in the range of characters from Alexandra
Bergson and Ántonia Shimerda to Marian Forrester
and Claude Wheeler. It is biographically true that
they were drawn in the image of people whom Miss
Cather had known or heard about. But their physical
lineaments were mainly expedients for depicting large
issues to which they helped give proportion and stability. Thus, while Miss Cather is talking about a particular character, she sees in him a fusion of pioneer or
antipioneer motivations which she relates to the land
or the machine as the controlling symbolic quality.

Now, broadly speaking, she also endows her artists
with symbolic properties through which she may concretize certain abstractions. But for reasons that apparently are useful to her, she identifies the symbols
so closely with personality that the artist becomes
more nearly an individual character than the somewhat allegorized pioneer. The reasons are not self-
evident, but one may speculate. Temperamentally and
occupationally, Willa Cather was an artist rather than
a pioneer. That is, she admired the frontier spirit but,
except for the accident of residence, she was more the
sympathizer or critic than the participant. The concrete symbol, therefore, was an engrossing substitute
for the more immediate condition of sensate experi-

ence. As an artist, however, she could draw more fully and authoritatively from her own being. And all of her major associations were with artists whose aspirations and accomplishments were akin to her own. It is not surprising, consequently, that in writing of artists she should give primary attention to the individuals— despite the limitations which she regarded as integral to the artistic personality—rather than to symbolic manifestations of their personalities.

Symbolism in the stories of artists is thus corollary or elaborative. The ancient remains of the cliff dwellers, for example, for all their disciplined representation, are as obviously emblematic of Thea's artistically reaching spirit as they are of Tom Outland's morally reaching spirit. In this sense, with regard to the artists' stories, the remains become virtually a stock device brought in for exemplification of meaning or for a token of self-recognition. Phenomenal beauties have already been alluded to as an important aspect of the land symbol. They occur in the tales of artists also, but in view of the individual's primacy they almost automatically take on the secondary function of showing the artist's heightened responsiveness to the colors and sounds and shapes of nature.

In at least one important instance, however, a nature symbol serves in both a primary (that is, as an emblem of greater moral significance than the individual) and a secondary (or as an emblem of lesser narrative significance than the individual) capacity. It occurs in *Lucy Gayheart*, with Lucy in a sleigh which "was such a tiny moving spot on that still white country settling into shadow and silence." Although the novel is drawn as a tragic love story rather than as a story of artistic endeavor and accomplishment, the heroine is the incipient artist and her responses are shaped by this inner quality. Suddenly Lucy Gayheart sees the first star in the darkening sky. "That point of silver light spoke to her like a signal, released another kind of life and feeling which did not belong here. It overpowered her. With a mere thought she had reached that star and it had answered, recognition had flashed between. Something knew, then, in the unknowing waste: something had always known, forever! That joy of saluting what is far above one was an eternal thing, not merely something that had happened to her ignorance and her foolish heart."

Now this simple exploitation of a lovely natural phenomenon has its echoes in the frontier novels. It is perhaps most reminiscent of the plough magnified in the sun and then diminished, in *My Ántonia*. In this context the star is revelatory of microcosmic man pinpointed in infinity; it is also the link between human striving and supernal inviolability as well as condescension. But it is also a means of showing Lucy's self-recognition even as the remains are Thea's signal. For the most part, however, Miss Cather avoids equivocal or multiple symbols of this kind in her stories about artists. The individuals themselves carry the double burden of symbolic representation and of furthering narrative credibility.

ii

Without permitting herself to become involved in scientific, rationalistic explanations, Willa Cather always tried to understand the artist's psychological development. Although she had an almost reverential interest in mature accomplishment, she was fascinated by the entire process of growth from the seed. Indeed, she has even given some evidence of dissatisfaction with her own work because of a feeling that she should have accented more than she did the years of emergent powers that precede the pinnacle of artistic success. In a candid preface she wrote that the chief fault of *The Song of the Lark* "is that it describes a descending curve; the life of a successful artist in the full tide of achievement is not so interesting as the life of a talented young girl 'fighting her way,' as we say." Thea's story, she felt, was of dramatic interest only during her "awakening and struggle; her floundering escape from a smug, domestic, self-satisfied provincial world of utter ignorance." As Thea's imaginative life became enriched and as her various conflicts receded, her personal life became commensurately paler. What Miss Cather admitted caring about was the girl's contention against a set of hostile circumstances which made possible her liberation from commonness. What followed her escape, inevitable triumph and reward, was good; but the excitement of conflict had ended and success was anticlimax.

Miss Cather yearned to know and understand the creative essence which lodged itself within an arbitrarily chosen body and refused to be denied. Between 1896 and 1901, while she was living in Pittsburgh, she frequently made the long, uncomfortable trip to New York to hear the great singers of that era—Melba, Nordica, Schumann-Heink, Sembrich, Calve, Campanari, the de Reszkes—and, perhaps unconsciously, to crystallize in her mind the certainty that the creative being is rare, that he is one of the elect. These singers had a profound interest for her, of course, as performers of exquisite ability; but even more, they interested her as artists who had succeeded after long effort and strength of vision, like her own later heroines—Thea, or Cressida Garnet, or Kitty Ayrshire—despite every conceivable obstacle. In one form or another, Miss Cather constantly stressed that to be a great singer or a great artist of any kind one had to be a great personality.

Miss Cather was always able to recognize individual artistic genius as an incontrovertible fact. But in the definition of genius and its origins she wavered. Negatively, at least, she had the certitude that creative genius is never an environmental or an inherited quality. Unwilling to commit herself positively, she nevertheless hinted at a belief in divine or miraculous origin. As a result, in "The Sculptor's Funeral" she looks to the artist's genius as part of the "inscrutable wisdom of God." In another early short story, "The Treasure of Far Island," she calls it one of the "dark things" ordered by a "dread Providence." Her concern for the source of genius emerged early out of the confident awareness of her own artistic strength and her groping development. Later, increasingly assured by her growing powers, she ceased to speculate about the inception of this gift. Like her classical and Renaissance predecessors, she acknowledged an ineffable origin and rejoiced in it.

Little though she deliberated about the source of innate genius, her beliefs are clear enough. The artist's physical birth is important only because it provides the housing, the material center, for his intangible genius. Impelled by the creative mystery which is peculiarly his own, the artist emerges from his own begetting. Esthetically self-sufficient, he creates himself, his imaginative life having little to do with physical being and processes. The stages from germination through delivery are long and difficult. "Every artist makes himself born," Miss Cather states in *The Song of the Lark*. "It is very much harder than the other time and longer." Genius, uniquely possessed by the individual, can be brought into the world only by himself. This process of self-creation, moreover, gives to the artist a sense of his independence which is denied to other human be-

ings. Generally hostile to the notion of social obligation, the artist likes to keep himself exultantly free to
express that which he alone can express. In short, "if
one became an artist one had to be born again, and
. . . one owed nothing to anybody."

For her own secular purposes, Miss Cather has virtually paraphrased the Gospel according to St. John on
the necessity of regeneration: "Except a man be born
again he cannot see the kingdom of God" (3:3), and
"Ye must be born again" (3:7). To "become" an
artist means to fulfill that capacity which one already
has. According to Miss Cather's creed, he who pos-
sesses this intuitive faculty must understand himself
and recognize the prize of which he is guardian. There
is no quarrel here over the relative merits of various
kinds of art. That is, the painter is not regarded as of
lesser or greater importance than the sculptor; nor is
the singer pitted against the poet; and so forth. Any
mode of expression which deserves inclusion among
the creative faculties shares the respect given to a common noble cause. Like the Greek *poietes*, Miss Cather's
"artist" belongs to an exceedingly small fraternity of
creators or makers, each of whom happens to be gifted
in a particular mode of making, and each of whom
must commit himself to unsparing discipline for the
loftiest expression of his genius. But even though there
is no qualitative separation among the arts, there is no
communion among them either, except for the vaguely
tutelary bonds of a sympathetic kinship. Each artist
enjoys and endures an almost impenetrable isolation
from his fellow artists and, even more, from the society
which attempts to claim him. Solitary, he must recast
his communal values in order to justify his aloneness.
Objectively, Miss Cather must be reproached for the
faults of egoism and aloofness. Yet she would condone

these traits as necessarily inseparable from the nature of the artist. This is why she charges the artist "to be born again."

The artist, further, is as little responsible to his environment as he is to heritage of birth. The splendid fact that creative genius is innate cancels any possible debt to physical surroundings. Miss Cather actually holds that environment is a constant impediment, and that part of the miracle of genius inheres in the artist's ability to transcend physical limitations. For this reason, Miss Cather projects her artists against a background which is sometimes almost malevolently hostile. In some of the early short stories which make up *The Troll Garden*, for instance, she uses this notion of a social antipathy. And it is a notion, incidentally, which she had developed even before she had an intimate knowledge of serious artists. She deplored the failure of the artist's family and society, in "The Sculptor's Funeral," to understand him as ruinous to his personal life and even to his talent.

Sir Hugh Treffinger, the painter of the "Marriage of Phaedra," poses another side of this same exacerbating condition. The son of a small English tobacconist, he grows up in an underprivileged environment "idle, lawless, and practically letterless" until he discovers his talent for painting. He leaves one inimical society only to enter another when he marries the well-favored Lady Ellen and discovers his bold experimentation collides with conventional taste. Yet the pressures of conformity are not sufficient to prevent the undertaking of his astonishingly inspired canvas, "Marriage of Phaedra," which is incomplete at the time of his death. Ironically, the only one to understand Treffinger's aim is his cockney servant, who vainly attempts to prevent capital being made of his genius, even as at another level and in another context Professor St.

Peter would attempt to withstand Outland's parasites. Environmental conflict similarly engages the hero of "The Treasure of Far Island," who reflects on the chance that makes "a hard-headed, money-saving real estate man . . . the father of a white-fingered playwright."

As Willa Cather became the friend of such people as the singer Olive Fremstad and the actor George Arliss, she discovered that she had underestimated the artistic temperament. Realization of the artist's toughness and resilience brought her to the knowledge that his talent need not be destroyed and his life embittered just because shrewd scoundrels exploited him or ignorant people thought him a fool. Superficially abrasive though the effects of external environment might be, Miss Cather did not minimize or palliate them. The sculptor is born into the ugliness of a tamed prairie, a "place of hatred and bitter waters" likened to a dung heap. Thea Kronborg and Lucy Gayheart are born into the provincial aridity of the "bitter, dead little Western town." Paul grows up in the comparable tastelessness and esthetic barrenness of the middle-class city. Treffinger must fight his way out of the brutalizing atmosphere of the London streets. Prairie farm, Western village, Eastern city, English metropolis—all are dissimilar in appearance yet alike in their automatic rejection of the artistic challenge.

Acutely aware that the nature of genius is too individual to lend itself to ready definition, Miss Cather generalized from her intuitive responses to particular instances. Consistently, she traced the creative propensity and its strength to inner sources. She concluded that the artist feeds upon himself, that inspiration and fulfillment come from within. Considering the greatness of Madame Fremstad for an article, "Three American Singers," in *McClure's* (De-

cember, 1913), she observed that the singer "gets very
little from people; she does not catch ideas or suggestions from what she sees or hears; everything comes
from within herself." The relief that some people
seek in exterior recreation was not for her. Interested
only in the beauty afforded by her art, she required no
diversion which was not related to her music. Miss
Cather would have said that creative genius is a
compound of heart and brain, emotion and mind,
undissipated and concentrated in its ability to translate
the objectivity of truth into terms of highly subjective
response. Or as she put it in *The Song of the Lark*,
there is in the voice—apart from its beauty and individuality—an ineffable something that vibrates
instantaneously, almost without consciousness, in harmony with "every shade of thought and feeling."

This rare attribute, the true singer's possession from
birth, is "almost like another gift—the rarest of all.
The voice simply is the mind and is the heart. It can't
go wrong in interpretation, because it has in it the
thing that makes all interpretation." Genius thus seen
is an eternally self-replenishing spring. In all art forms,
indeed, Miss Cather was convinced that highly individual talent requires no formula that cannot be
drawn from inner being. "The great dancer," she wrote
in the *McClure's* essay "Training for the Ballet" (October, 1913), "is made, like any other artist, of two
things: of a universal human impulse, and a very
special and individual experience of it. That this very
special experience creates ambition, devotion, very special skill, goes without saying. This is true in any art."

As artistic genius must be self-sustaining in all other
respects, so must it be responsible for its own psychological stimulus. Manifold in nature and complex in
function, this stimulus is summed up by Miss Cather
in the term "desire." Fundamentally the same inner

force as that which moved the pioneers, it incited the artists even more powerfully to action expressive of that quality. The very nature of the artist, if it is to fulfill itself, commands a degree of articulateness or outpouring that is foreign to many of the pioneers. That is not to say that they are necessarily less sensitive, but most of them lack the equipment—the spontaneous verbal gestures, plastic skills, and the like—which distinguish highly responsive artists.

The psychological aspect of desire is notable because it promotes esthetic action; and it is more notable in artists than in others because it promotes esthetic action that extends participation beyond the individual. For all its psychological properties, the concept of desire is virtually metaphysical in that it embraces a reverent attitude of perfectibility, and it is toward this effect that Miss Cather generally employs it in her fiction. Despite her individual manipulation and interpretation of the concept, the source is undoubtedly Platonic. Desire, Plato reported Socrates as arguing in *Cratylus*, is stronger than necessity, and it has the power of luring one inexorably toward unseen goals. With its origin in the soul, according to the point made in *Philebus*, desire unites pleasure and pain, "pleasure in hope and pain in vacuity." These are precisely the impressions Miss Cather strives to make.

Desire, as she interprets it in her short story "The Garden Lodge," is "a sort of mystic worship of things distant, intangible and unattainable." The mere recognition of the desire within oneself brings with it an eternal joy. In the summer of 1902, when she was experiencing vague stirrings of her own artistic desire, she watched from the terrace of a hotel in Dieppe "a little boy . . . flying a red and green kite, quite the most magnificent kite I have ever seen, and it went up famously, up and up until his string ran short and of a truth one's heart went just as high." With time, this kite became a symbol of her own Daedalian yearning never to be forgotten. In an illustration which we had occasion to use a few pages earlier in this chapter, the kite transformed by Miss Cather into a winter star becomes a critical episode in Lucy Gayheart's life. Thirty-three years after the original occurrence, Lucy, as unknowing of her artistic future as was the young Willa Cather, is made to experience a similar vision of eternity and hope. Desire is an inseparable part of the totality of creative genius, a stimulus for creation and self-revelation that dwarfs every other need. "Nothing is far and nothing is near," Miss Cather writes in *The Song of the Lark*, "if one desires. The world is little, people are little, human life is little. There is only one big thing—desire." Before this final urge, "when it is big, all is little." Translated into achievement, desire becomes the "glorious striving of human art."

Paradoxically, though desire is at its inception and source individual, it may be universal in its manifestations, unlimited by time and place, and indestructible. The cliff dwellers in *The Song of the Lark* have become a "vanished race." But everywhere that Thea looks she sees "fragments of their desire," in the glittering remains of their pottery and in the country which bears the mute testimony of their having been there. Standing among the ruins, Thea miraculously absorbs the spirit of these aboriginal people, and she fuses their ambition and effort with her own.

In a more immediate identification, Kitty Ayrshire, the artist in "A Gold Slipper," proclaims that desire may even be transmitted from one individual to another. She acknowledges a certain responsibility to society and to family. The pleasure and financial assist-

ance which she can provide, however, are merely superficial tokens. The passing emotions and tangible goods
which she can contribute are but a small part of the
obligations she has assumed. "I give money and time
and effort to talented students. Oh, I give something
more than that! . . . I give to the really gifted one, my
wish, my desire, my light, if I have any; and that . . .
is like giving one's blood!" That this power can be
transferred only to the gifted by the gifted is true because desire itself is the artist's passionate, undeviating
devotion to an ideal. Receptivity to this power cannot
be simulated and, Miss Cather asserts in *The Song of
the Lark*, "like heroism it [is] inimitable in cheap
materials." And, finally, it is in the nature of desire
to be tumultuous or to cause tumult, to be radical or
to cause radicalism. Its possession compels the artist
like Thea to reject the secure and the conventional.
Since genius insists on expression, "the old highroad
of life, worn safe and easy, hugging the sunny slopes,"
must be abandoned for the new and daring and infinitely more difficult.

The creative force—its possession and the desire to
express it—is coexistent with the awakening within the
artist to his creative self. This rousing may seem to
happen for some, as it did for Thea, in "the play of
blind chance." Yet Miss Cather would find it hard to
believe that the artist is controlled by a capricious
destiny. To persons of Thea's "vitality and honesty,
fortunate accidents will always happen." The occurrence might be something as simple as the song of
the lark after which the novel was named. Correcting
an erroneous impression that Thea's song was "of the
skylark order," Miss Cather explains: "The book was
named for a rather second-rate French painting in the
Chicago Art Institute; a picture in which a little
peasant girl, on her way to work in the fields at early

morning, stops and looks up to listen to a lark. The title was meant to suggest a young girl's awakening to something beautiful. I wanted to call the story 'Artist's Youth,' but my publisher discouraged me, wisely enough."

The awakening then, from whatever source, is inevitable; and like the full disclosure of artistic power, it is often a gradual one which carries its own gratification. At first the artist becomes aware of only gleams of promise, which seem almost foreign and temporarily elusive. Lucy Gayheart often had "run out on a spring morning, into the orchard, down the street, in pursuit of something she could not see, but knew!" Enchanted in childlike wonder, she senses the attraction everywhere of her tutelary divinity. "It was there, in the breeze, in the sun; it hid behind the blooming apple boughs, raced before her through the neighbour's gardens, but she could never catch up with it." Even before the climb to unknown heights begins, the augury conveys a large measure of the artist's happiness.

From this irrationally conceived insight grows a confident courage to strive for and capture the "fugitive gleam." As the artist's awakening becomes more pronounced, the essence of his talents becomes clearer to him. With a truthful certainty that should not be affected by conventional standards of modesty, he realizes that he is unlike other people, that he is possessed by a friendly demon which is part of himself. From these moments of understanding are born the artist's happiness. Thea Kronborg communicated with her demon which "came and went, she never knew why," and was rewarded. "Sometimes she hunted for it and could not find it; again, she lifted her eyes from a book or stepped out of doors, or wakened in the morning, and it was there,—under her cheek, it usually seemed

to be, or over her breast,—a kind of warm sureness."
Her moments of perception illuminated even her
physical surroundings and the people about her. With
the final stages of his awakening, the artist achieves
a certainty about his mission, if about nothing else.
Distrustful of most exterior things, he has no doubts
about his work. "He was sure enough there," we are
told in "The Sculptor's Funeral."

The recognition of artistic strength brings its own
sense of responsibility, which can be asserted only
through discipline. Like every other aspect of creativeness, the need for discipline arises from an inner
awareness. As a "power of application" or a "rugged
will," this kind of regulatory control is superficially
negative, for it serves to isolate the artist from the
concerns of the material world about him. Observing
the puritanical austerity with which Thea confines
herself to her music, Professor Wunsch concludes that
through her discipline the artist had repudiated the
expedient, comfortable standards of ordinary life, the
economic Darwinism of early twentieth-century America. Determination such as hers seemed extraordinary
"among people whose sole ambition was to get something for nothing," and he was reminded of "standards, ambitions, a society long forgot." Thus a good
deal of Thea's struggle is involved with her need to
free herself from the pernicious influences surrounding
her, which are not so much evils of action as they are
of inaction. From the apathetic indifference of the
"vague, easy-going world" of Moonstone, Thea must
find her way "into a life of disciplined endeavor."
Once again it was Madame Fremstad who underscored
for Miss Cather the force of the artist's self-discipline.
Because her work was all that interested her, the singer
maintained that "To know how to work is the most
valuable thing in the world, and there are very few

people indeed who know what real work is." Like all her artists, fanciful and real, Miss Cather was unsparing of herself in the acquisition of craftsmanship. Only through flawless technique, she believed, could the gift of expression be fully and supremely rendered. Work thus demands a great price but it offers a great reward.

As the artist recognizes the power within him, and as he disciplines and channels this power, he achieves his growth, which is both esthetic and moral, through "a refining of the sense of truthfulness" from within. This growth does not come easily, for the acquisition of truth is not easy. As the novelist writes in *The Song of the Lark*, "The stupid believe that to be truthful is easy; only the artist, the great artist, knows how difficult it is." Despite difficulty of attainment, truth constitutes the only real justification for the artist.

The precise nature of Miss Cather's artistic truth is not definable, for it has to do with visionary properties and is directed to sublime ends. I. A. Richards, the English critic, has examined the psychological constituents of this question, in his *Principles of Literary Criticism*, and his remarks seem applicable here. Artistic truth, as he understands it, "is equivalent to 'internal necessity' or rightness. That is 'true' or 'internally necessary' which completes or accords with the rest of experience." As applied to a work of art, then, truth is a matter of inner congruity, but it has nothing to do with objective fact or accuracy. It is apart from scientific truth, for instance, which insists on a correlation with "reality" or "real experiences." As Richards puts it: "The 'Truth' of *Robinson Crusoe* is the acceptability of the things we are told, their acceptability in the interests of the effects of the narrative, not their correspondence with any actual facts involving Alexander Selkirk or another." But Eliseo Vivas, concerned (in *Creation and Discovery*) with the esthetic relationship between truth and art, illuminates the problem still more by advancing beyond psychological, experiential tests. Believing with Franz Kafka, whom he quotes with approval, that "art consists of being dazzled by Truth," Vivas looks to an inner, esthetic condition. The light perceived by Vivas through Kafka is a form of revelation, then, and outer substance is but a distortion of that verity.

Miss Cather, both in her personal attitude toward truth and in that which she entrusts to her characters, would probably accept these evaluations, without restricting herself to Richards' psychologism or surrendering as completely as Kafka did to mystic revelation. For the artist, supernatural effects are related to the psychological ones. In those moments of illumination which even for the artist are rare, there comes an exalted sense of fullness or totality. It is what in her story "Namesake" (*McClure's*, March, 1907) Miss Cather calls a "feeling of . . . being glad that we have lived." Or, as Jim Burden in the throes of a comparable experience was to put it, "That is happiness; to be dissolved into something complete and great." Generally introspective and even egocentric, the artist becomes absorbed at his triumphant moment into a supernal creative force which supersedes all egoism and all individualism. Through the act of projecting the self in a search for the "impersonality" of ultimate truth, the artist arrives at personal happiness.

These instances of exaltation, durable in memory but infrequent in occurrence, are attained only after struggle and suffering. Whether in esthetic philosophy or in narration, Miss Cather was magnetized by the struggle and its consequences. "Success," she believed, "is never so interesting as struggle—not even to the successful, not even to the most mercenary forms of ambition." The rarity of visionary moments has made philosophically inevitable the perpetual striving which precedes the flashes of illumination. Struggle is inseparable from the conception and fruition of art.

But the artist's struggle is more than a philosophical one. It begins with his birth; because he is driven by an unquenchable desire for expression, and because all normal human relationships and ordinary virtues become subordinate to his desire, the artist is ostracized and made to suffer. Writing of Olive Fremstad, Miss Cather said: "Circumstances have never helped [her]. She grew up in a new, crude country where there was neither artistic stimulus nor discriminating taste. She was poor, and always had to earn her own living and pay for her music lessons out of her earnings. She fought her own way toward the intellectual centers of the world." Even after the world recognizes the greatness of an artist, the struggle continues. When Madame Fremstad reached the great art centers and her genius was appreciated, the cities themselves were "to be in a manner, her antagonist, the scene of her fiercest struggle and greatest conquests."

Similarly, Cressida Garnet, the successful artist in "The Diamond Mine," had for twenty years "been plunged in struggle; fighting for her life at first, then for a beginning, for growth, and at last for eminence and perfection; fighting in the dark, and afterward in the light, . . ." Conflict does not always result in such fortunate issue, however, as we are reminded in "A Death in the Desert." Katharine fought her way to Chicago and New York and Europe, "where she went up like lightning, and got a taste for it all, and now she's dying here like a rat in a hole, out of her own world, and she can't fall back into ours."

Highly sensitive to the disappointments often inherent in artistic aspiration, Miss Cather once wrote an essay about Katherine Mansfield, whom she depicted as the artist struggling alone, challenging the universe. Of Katherine Mansfield's return to New Zealand after four years in London, we are told: "There is no homesickness and no hunger so unbearable. Many a young artist would sell his future, all his chances, simply to get back to the world where other people are doing the only things that, to his inexperience, seem worth doing at all." The struggle becomes in time habitual, inextricably related to the artist's work, his personality, his life, and even his death. Thus, Willa Cather states that in the face of the dead sculptor there was none of the "repose we expect to find in the faces of the dead. . . . It was as though the strain of life had been so sharp and bitter that death could not at once relax the tension and smooth the countenance into perfect peace—as though he were still guarding something precious, which might even yet be wrested from him." Although the frustration recorded in the sculptor's face may be considered extreme for Miss Cather, it does not violate her thesis of the necessity of struggle. The artist is compulsively dynamic, and if he has dedication of spirit and purpose not even defeats can halt creative activity.

Even suffering, nevertheless, has its compensation, and the most notable aspect of this for the artist—as for the pioneer—is his occasional feat of wresting victory from adversity and of thus realizing the gloriousness of the quest. Writing in "Three American Singers," Miss Cather remembered "Wagner once said that the bigger the bell, the more difficult it is to release its tone." While a sleigh-bell will respond to the slightest tap, a great bell must be sounded with a hammer. "Goethe said: 'There are many kinds of garlands; some of them may be easily gathered on a morning's walk.'" Others have never been attained and never will. "But the pursuit of them is one of the most glorious forms of human activity."

The same seeking which held such compulsive attraction for the pioneers, in spite of dangers and difficulty, insists that the artist go ahead regardless of the odds and momentary failures. Paradoxically, the suffering depicted in art is transformed into a source of delight for the beholder, even as tragic drama conveys pleasure through the delineation of pain. To be able to transform one's own suffering into joy for another is a godlike gift. Miss Cather had no doubt that the artist so endowed belongs at the apex of a spiritual hierarchy. And she believed (as she said in *The Professor's House*) that art and religion, the same thing in the end, "have given man the only happiness he has ever had." Her virtual identification of art with religion is significant, for, regarding both as forms of consecration, she felt they made comparable demands on the individual and offered comparable rewards. The suffering which teaches compassion to the devout man induces sympathy in the artist. In each instance, devotion is severely exacting and yet illuminates all that it touches. The artist, even unconscious of the individuals upon whom he is bestowing his gifts, is the bearer of a happiness which his own suffering has made possible. Although she was orthodox enough in her religious views, Willa Cather paid special homage to the private spirit that she regarded as the unique heritage of all creative people, artists or priests or pioneers.

iii

Granting the artist his spiritual eminence, Miss Cather nevertheless had no illusions about his human failings. She recognized that frequently he is an incomplete individual and socially maladjusted. And yet his limitations, she believed, are essentials of artistic development and progress, the negative traits making the positive all the more commendable and desirable. Moreover, she argued, all artists possess certain characteristics which are almost professional trade-marks. When in "A Death in the Desert" she speaks of the "madness" of the artist, she ironically turns the popular misconception against society. She understands well enough that the artist is by necessity a nonconformist who cannot yield to arbitrary social pressures and conventions.

At the same time, she has no doubts about the normative reactions to unprecedented behavior. Society in self-justification—perhaps out of a mass feeling of guilt or inadequacy, unable to comprehend or emulate or even accept singularity—chooses to regard the artist as mad. Having been conditioned for a long time to reject the unusual, the members of society take refuge behind an epithet that has no more force than that of a pejorative cliché. But it is nonetheless an opprobrious, contemptuous term to satisfy a private belief in their own superiority. Because the artist does not discharge the obligations normally expected of social beings, he is blamed for irresponsible conduct.

These complaints, of course, are rationalizations. But what, Miss Cather wanted to know, are the characteristics of the artist's personality that cause him to be branded as a deviationist and iconoclast? Analysis of the composite artist led her to conclude that he is egoistic, socially amoral, totally lacking in caution, and overwhelmingly but impersonally generous. These traits, she added, are forged by the artist's voluntary social withdrawal, his indifferent rational intelligence, and the meagerness of his personal life.

On June 5, 1890, Willa Cather had told her high school commencement audience: "It is the most sacred right of man to investigate; we paid dearly for it in Eden; we have been shedding our heart's blood for it ever since. It is ours; we have bought it with a price." Admittedly platitudinous, as such oratory has a way of being, the rebellious note is nonetheless worth remembering as the high school graduate becomes an accomplished writer. The right to investigate is also the right to break with fixed mores in the pursuit of supramundane, imaginative goals. The right becomes a compulsion to desert the safety of stodgy comforts, to give up the stability of the familiar and to seek out the exhilaration of the unknown. Miss Cather's seekers—artists and pioneers—might be called foolhardy and even rash, but they are obeying a restless instinct which carries the greatest of them to new truths. What is common to all artists, she says in the article "Three American Singers," is "an absence of caution; they are not afraid to say today what may be quoted against them tomorrow." This trait perhaps more than any other sets the artist apart from the social world which Miss Cather saw timorously dedicated to security; and it is a trait which inheres in "all people of really first-rate ability."

Fearful of social reproach, the average individual exhausts himself in evasions "to propitiate the tongue of gossip." In the prosperous small towns of the early twentieth century, as we have heard Miss Cather say in an earlier chapter, "people's speech, like their voices, their very glances, became furtive and repressed. Every individual taste, every natural appetite, was bridled by caution." Barren of purpose and productivity, Miss Cather writes in *My Ántonia*, the legacy of such empty lives is a residue of waste. But the timidity of inaction is not confined to the small town, for it attenuates the entire social structure of the country. For example, the artist in "A Gold Slipper," confronting a prosperous business man, can say ac-

cusingly: "You are . . . oh, so cautious! You are naturally afraid of everything new, just as I naturally want
to try everything: new people, new religions—new
miseries, even. . . . But you, my friend, would be
afraid to try a new shaving soap." The stabilizing force
of the world is not gravitation, she charges, but "the
lazy obese cowardice of the people in it." From the
very beginning, it is thus obvious, Miss Cather had an
intense distaste for the philosophy of caution. The
precocious, even arrogant, words she had uttered from
the platform of her Red Cloud high school were the
center of a maturing esthetic philosophy.

Whether in philosophical speculation or in action,
the artist's only recourse to the doctrine of caution is
instant rejection. Timidity is incompatible with the
struggle that leads to artistic achievement; the search
for truth is nullified by the fear to investigate. In
short, the artist's lack of caution is basic and vital to
his art. Thea Kronborg vehemently expresses a heroically human *amor fati*. Her courage and her scorn of
cautious compromise are seen in her love of the Grieg
song "Tak for Ditt Rad": "Thanks for your advice!
But I prefer to steer my boat into the din of roaring
breakers. Even if the journey is my last, I may find
what I have never found before." Her passionate out-
burst carries her forward to a statement of her yearning for the struggle, which she symptomizes in a longing to fight her way through the angry waves of the
wild sea, "and to see how far, and how long I can
make them carry me." Having such a long road to
travel and such talent to fulfill, Miss Cather's im-
petuous artist has neither energy nor time for caution.

Despite the mutual antagonism, or at least indifference, between society and the artist, the artist is generously inclined toward all individuals. The paradox
is one which Miss Cather makes no attempt to evalu-

ate; she merely accepts the situation, as she illustrates in "A Death in the Desert." The dying artist, separated from the world, her family, even from the small clique who once appreciated her, never loses her ability to give to others. The generosity is mirrored in her eyes, "which possessed a warm, life-giving quality like the sunlight: generous, fearless eyes, which glowed with sympathy and good cheer for all living things, a sort of perpetual *salutat* to the world." Although the artist is indeed impersonal and aloof, he has a capacity for generosity because of his sympathy for human drabness, littleness, and suffering. If Miss Cather does not analyze the paradox, her artists frequently demonstrate it. They can alleviate human boredom or torment momentarily by crystallizing an ideal of life, and by setting before the timid and the cautious the transfigured beauty of artistic endeavor and hope.

For this reason Dr. Archie in *The Song of the Lark*, meditating upon his small accomplishments and disappointments, realized that his existence had meaning only when it impinged on that of Thea. From association with her he acquired some of her vivacity and was spared for brief instances the stultifying tedium of his life. Memories of the ordinary events of his life seemed faded and dispirited. Memories of Thea, however, "always seemed humorous, gay, with a little thrill of anticipation and mystery about them." Why these memories of Thea should differ from others, Dr. Archie was not quite sure, except that "nearer than anything else they corresponded to what he had hoped to find in the world, and had not found." In the midst of a random reflection he suddenly understood Thea's great gift to him, for she alone symbolized those things "which in some way met our original want; the desire which formed in us in early youth, undirected, and of its own accord." To this giving of Thea's—which was as much a part of her spirit as was her breathing—Dr. Archie became indebted for any meaning in his life. Similarly Harry Gordon recalls his long-past association with Lucy Gayheart "as the best thing he had to remember." Despite the misery he had suffered on her account, she was the only person who had ever brought freshness into his life. The inner distinction between artists and ordinary mortals is pithily summed up in the thought that "All the other men and women he had known were more or less like himself." A "gift of nature," alien to himself but irresistible, enriched his dull life long after Lucy had died. Only in retrospect did he appreciate the gift. He recalled how his own body, like hers, had grown "marvellously free and light" and how her vitality had transmitted itself to him.

Association with many artists, especially Geraldine Farrar, confirmed Miss Cather's belief that generosity is a demanding gift. Frightened by the toll which Miss Farrar's artistic liberality exacted, the novelist hoped that her friend would "train up a duller self to serve her for dull purposes." Yet she also knew that the singer, who "would rather live ten years thick than twenty thin," was not likely to spare herself. As Miss Farrar is quoted in "Three American Singers": "Why should I want to string it out twenty, thirty years? . . . I want to give it out all in a lump. I want to go hard while I'm at it!"

An artistic gift is a totality which cannot be parceled out like samples in a confectionery store. The full power is what matters, and to conserve or apportion that power is to devitalize it and render it mediocre at best. The same abundance which gave Miss Farrar a sense of mission is characteristic of the artist Kitty Ayrshire in "A Gold Slipper." Unsparing of her vitality, she dedicates her talent to mankind. Like Geraldine Farrar, she "wouldn't live on any terms but the very generous ones she had always known. She wasn't going to hoard her vitality." She insisted upon the availability of her spark with the same firmness that she would insist upon the availability of any of her limbs when she required them. If she chose to put an excessive strain upon her talents, she was prepared to accept the consequences; "she would be ill for a while and pay the piper." But she refused to be systematically prudent and parsimonious with her resources. Generosity and lack of caution are innately and inextricably united, according to Miss Cather's severe artistic creed. Without the one the other is impossible.

What amounts to the self-annihilation of his private life is the artist's indisputable proof of liberality. This destruction he willingly accomplishes by releasing all of his talent and energy and, in the process, ignoring the self. Because art is infinite, its development long and arduous, and life short, the artist must virtually deny himself the luxury of private intimacies and pleasures. He comes to see that he can justify his existence only in the wholehearted translation of his genius. The artist who realizes the meagerness of his social life accepts his condition as an inevitable one. When Thea Kronborg is asked about her nonprofessional life, she answers that she has none, that her work is all. She goes on to describe devotion to art as a kind of gigantic web from which you cannot pull away "because all your little tendrils are woven into the picture." Artistic labor "takes you up, and uses you, and spins you out; and that is your life. Not much else can happen to you." The creative passion stated here bears a close resemblance to themes developed by Henry James in such short stories as "The Real Thing" and "The Middle Years." The similarity is especially pronounced in the latter tale where Dencombe con-

cludes: "We work in the dark—we do what we can—
we give what we have. Our doubt is our passion and
our passion is our task. The rest is the madness of
art." Extreme singleness of purpose charges Willa
Cather's artists with such an inner fire that the act
of creation becomes a sweet torture, irresistibly necessary.

A subject of this racking pleasure, the operatic
singer Tradutorri of the story "Nanette: An Aside"
(*Home Monthly*, August, 1896), has given herself to
her art wholly, "without one reservation, without one
regret." Her passion is so intense that she is unaware her
art is using her up both physically and emotionally.
Thus she comes from a great performance on "one
of those eventful nights when the audience catches
fire and drives a singer to her best, drives her beyond
herself until she is greater than she knows or means to
be." This is the ultimate generosity of unselfish giving.
Willa Cather herself sees the life of one who has
succeeded in yielding himself completely to his art as
a *Picture of Dorian Gray* in reverse. Discussing Thea's
problem in her preface to *The Song of the Lark*, Miss
Cather approves that her public, artistic life should
become "more interesting to her than her own life."
Thea's "artistic life is the only one in which she is
happy, or free, or even very real. It is the reverse of
Wilde's story; the harassed, susceptible human creature comes and goes, subject to colds, brokers, dress-
makers, managers. But the free creature, who retains
her youth and beauty and warm imagination, is kept
shut up in the closet, along with the scores and wigs."
Seen through Miss Cather's eyes, the nature of the
artist betokens an implicit pathetic irony; for as the
imaginative life becomes richer the private life becomes more impoverished.

Egoism and indifferent intelligence are further vestiges of the inconsistency of the creative disposition. Almost priest-like in his office, the artist can surrender his gift only after profound, introspective searching, for his calling is a lonely one. But less ideally, he is jealous of his isolation; he needs to insulate himself against exterior complexities and inferior demands. In no terms, however, may the contradiction be reduced to simple formulae; and Miss Cather herself, both in her art and life, illustrates her perplexity. Thea Kronborg, therefore, engrossed in the progress of her career, refused to come home to see her dying mother. Miss Cather does not judge Thea's conduct, even though in "A Death in the Desert" she had insisted "there is a sacred and dignified selfishness which properly belongs to art and religion." Because he is several cuts above ordinary people, the artist must be willing to be preoccupied wholly with himself.

Exposed to personal circumstances similar to Thea's, however, Miss Cather acted in a manner that was directly contrary. While working on the manuscript of *Shadows on the Rock*, she learned that her mother, in California, had suffered a paralytic stroke. She went to her mother at once and stayed with her for extensive periods of time. Obviously, her emotional attachments were such that she could not bring theory and practice into convergence. Furthermore, at the time Miss Cather wrote *The Song of the Lark*, Thea's dilemma had been a purely conjectural one without any personal implications to engage her; hence, the author had been able to maintain an attitude of sympathetic objectivity toward her heroine's conduct. In the abstract, at least, she believed the artist must allow nothing to impede his development. Miss Cather hints that it is unjust to accuse of selfishness the person whose life is an epitome of impersonality. Thea, indeed, might have found her position less trying had she followed the course conventionally dictated as "a daughter's duty to her mother." Miss Cather sees no easy answer, but consistently within her writings she advises the suspension of all judgments on the artist's personal and moral life. An Aristotelian for this immediate purpose, she accepts the premise that "virtue is concerned with action; art with production." The standards of behavior expected of the patriot, the philanthropist, and the statesman are not applicable to the artist. As we learn in the essay "148 Charles Street," Miss Cather can forgive in the artist vanity, selfishness, hypersensitivity, and indecision on the grounds that "With a great gift . . . we must be willing to bear greatly, because it has already greatly borne."

In a narrow generality that is credible only as long as it is limited to her own characterizations, Miss Cather concedes that a superior rational intelligence is not a necessary part of the artist's natural endowments. Formal learning she believes plays no large part in the artist's life, and he need have no concern with philosophical or analytical abstractions. "A child's normal attitude toward the world," we are told in "The Treasure of Far Island," "is that of the artist, pure and simple. The rest of us have to do with the solids of this world, whereas only their form and color exist" for the artist. And in *The Song of the Lark* she repeats that the "child's attitude toward everything is an artist's attitude."

To most of her artists, moreover, the grasp of an idea comes slowly and even with difficulty. Characteristically, Thea Kronborg struggled to understand an intellectual concept. And as her teacher said, the effort was arduous, for "in spite of being so talented, she's not quick. But," he added, "when she does get an idea, it fills her up to the eyes." The artist himself is generally aware of his intellectual limitations and, indeed, is somewhat ashamed of them. For example, Cressida Garnet in "The Diamond Mine" is not even "musically intelligent." And yet she has a great musical talent. She is depressed by "her stupidities and inconsistencies," well knowing that the brilliance of her voice is mismated with her shallowness of intellect. Her deficiency makes her sensitive to the "knowledge of what a wretchedly faulty thing any productive faculty is." In the sum total of the artist's accomplishment, however, this particular frailty does not disable or even seriously hinder him. It is merely a reminder of mortality and a challenge to gain superiority which is within his means.

iv

As viewed by Miss Cather, the artist is essentially a tragic figure. Voluntarily dedicated to his life of struggle, he can hope for only rare acknowledgment from the world which she characterized in "The Sculptor's Funeral" as a new, ugly, and sordid desert. Nothing can be more destructive to the soul and mind and latent desire, Miss Cather implies, than to have constant effort meet with equally constant disinterest. From the very beginning, then, she says in "A Death in the Desert," the artist is faced with "the tragedy of effort and failure, the thing Keats called hell." And since the artist gives himself over to his art with selfless sympathy—physically, emotionally, and intellectually—his hell is an all-encompassing one. Destroying his own life in his desire to create beauty for a world which has no active wish to receive it, the artist seldom achieves personal happiness outside of his art. Miss Cather is forced to wonder, in "A Death in the Desert," "whether all the gift-bearers, all the sons of genius, broke what they touched and blighted what they caressed thus!"

The ruined, living body of Katharine Gaylord in the same story becomes the personification of the artist's self-immolation, the kind of sacrifice to an ideal, it will be remembered, that Marian Forrester of *A Lost Lady* spurned. The sacrificial motif was never far distant from the creative mind of Willa Cather, who was attracted to the often iterated concept that love and destruction of that love are collateral truths. The idea is stated baldly in the short story "The Dance at Chevalier's" (*The Library*, April 28, 1900) by the Signor who tells his sweetheart, "I like to kill the things I love." This is an extreme, even melodramatic, instance of course, but one that is related to the artist's intuition. Creative people such as Tradutorri, Roux (of "Flavia and her Artists"), Treffinger, the gifted children (of "The Prodigies"), Selma Schumann (of "A Singer's Romance"), all experience the unhappiness of being socially separate. All are denied happy personal lives outside of their art because the totality of their giving makes them enigmas to "normal," ungenerous individuals. Even the titles of some of the stories—"The Sculptor's Funeral" and "A Death in the Desert"—suggest the self-destructive element both physically and spiritually.

Much of the artist's tragedy derives from the mutual suspicion which exists between himself and society. The artist in his dealings with the social world goes through various degrees of hostility. Early in his career he realizes that there is a wide chasm separating the artistic individual from the community. Miss Cather made this discovery for herself while she was yet a college undergraduate; and she was sufficiently brash to ignore the pain inherent in this situation. "The further the world advances," she wrote in the *Nebraska State Journal*, "the more it becomes evident that an author's only safe course is to cling to the skirts of his art, forsaking all others, and keep unto her as long as they two shall live."

As far as the young Willa Cather was concerned, the artist must dissociate himself from ordinary human affairs and "lift himself into the clear firmament of creation where the world is not. He should be among men but not of them, in the world but not of the world." Stimulated by her own Byronic bravado, she assigned to artists a creative imperative which would have nothing to do with daily reality.

For Miss Cather and her fictional artists, this youthful swagger was in time to grow until it became an open declaration against the world of mediocrity. The realization came to Thea Kronborg, thus, that all these things and people constituting middle-class society "were no longer remote and negligible; they had to be met, they were lined up against her, they were there to take something from her." Determined that they should never destroy her desire for achievement, she vowed: "They might trample her to death, but they should never have it. As long as she lived that ecstasy was going to be hers. She would live for it, work for it, die for it; but she was going to have it, time after time, height after height."

This avowed hostility between the artist and society gave her the subject for an undergraduate theme, which was published in the *State Journal,* on Thomas Carlyle's fierce withdrawal from social concerns. Later, in "A Death in the Desert," she further alluded to the alienation as a "long warfare" so futile and enervating that it can only distract the artist's attention from his singular purpose. So, in the same story, the artist is made to conclude that only through withdrawal—complete and voluntary—may self-preservation be achieved. "The footlights had seemed a hard, glittering line drawn sharply between their life and hers, a circle

of flame set about those splendid children of genius."
She enjoyed a "passion for perfect expression" and a
sense of accomplishment that "were like a rosy mist
veiling her such as the goddesses of the elder days
wrapped about themselves when they vanished from
the arms of men." The isolation of the artist fascinated
Willa Cather, whether it was the real one of an Olive
Fremstad or the imagined one of principals in "The
Diamond Mine," "The Sculptor's Funeral," and
others.

Yet none of the artists whom Miss Cather knew
or invented retreated from the world any more completely than she did herself. Often accused of being
a recluse or an artistic snob, she was unremitting in
her withdrawal. Difficult though the situation was for
her, she felt that it was her only opportunity "to preserve the integrity of her life as an artist, its necessary
detachment and freedom." If withdrawal for her was
not the same fierce obsession that it was for, say,
Proust's Elstir, it nevertheless meant for her a resolute
exercise of her own will against that of the public. As
Miss Lewis says, "it was not disdain for the tributes
people wished to pay her, or a feeling of superiority
or indifference, that caused her to withdraw more and
more from the world. It was self-preservation."

Willa Cather, to be sure, responded more generously
than most of her artists to obligations imposed on her
by ties of friendship and family. But she confined these
loyalties rigorously and very nearly achieved the detachment that she idealized in her artists of fact and
fancy. She likewise, whenever she could, refined almost
out of existence the world of material affairs and sub-
stituted the intangible values of perfectibility. Her
literary success and tranquillity were won with perhaps less struggle than those of most artists; and one,
consequently, is not readily inclined to condone her

hostility to a society which gratefully accepted her talents. Similarly, she may be questioned for the sometimes dangerously generalized, always unproportioned view of the artist's social needs and commitments. The fact is, however, that she believed in these principles devoutly. She would have acceded to Eliot's premise, that "the more perfect the artist, the more completely separate in him will be the man who suffers and the mind which creates." Though it is not easy to sympathize with the plea for isolation or to agree that the suffering of the artist is of a variety superior to that of the more commonplace individual, Miss Cather cannot fail to win respect for her consistently, esthetically realized devotion to an ideal.

LIKE MOST SERIOUS NOVELISTS, Willa Cather frequently theorized about the nature, function, and processes of her art. But because she was not interested in a formal critical codification, and because each of the theories she uttered was in effect a description of some part of her own practice, her hypothesizing obviously has limited relevance. To be sure, she has influenced the techniques and even themes of other writers, and she has shaped the literary tastes of many readers. Her influence, however, has grown steadily out of the fiction she produced over a period of some three decades rather than out of her own explanations of that fiction. This is as it should be, but her self-critiques must still be considered carefully in the totality of her fictional purpose. Such criticism as she wrote provides a remarkable insight into the creative disposition of an individual author and goes far toward explaining the sources of her unique power.

The process of literary criticism, it seemed to her, must grow from the same lonely, subjective conditions as art itself. Abhorring proscription as alien to the free spirit which creates, she never doubted that an author must write with intuitive fluidity and that the critic must judge with an assurance that knows no dictum but the good taste of instinct. From the very beginnings of her literary interests she rebelled against all

restrictive measures which she thought fixed a responsibility upon the writer to set down his materials in
any given fashion or upon the critic to observe formal
rules.

The first test of her belief that literary criticism is
a way of subjective expression came while she was a
student of Professor Lucius A. Sherman at the University of Nebraska. The more Professor Sherman de-
fended objectivity and codification, the more firmly
she reacted against his teachings. As she insisted in the
Nebraska State Journal (March 4, 1894), "the supreme virtue in art is soul . . . the only thing which
gives art the right to be." Even a few years earlier,
when she was only eighteen, she could demand in the
Journal (November 1 and 8, 1891) that criticism be
affective or the product of inner response.

Youthfully fervid and arrogant, she spurned the
popular theories of intentionalism which were being
applied to *Hamlet* and gave the drama her own interpretation by equating her manner of literary inspiration with that of Shakespeare. Setting forth probably
for the first time her theory of "sympathetic" creation,
she boldly doubted that Shakespeare had any specific
purpose in the writing of his drama. "It was not like
him to write a play that should be a puzzle for all
time to come. He probably read the legend, felt sorry
for the young prince, and as an expression of his sympathy wrote about him." She guessed that Shakespeare,
perhaps affected by outer pressures, let his wrought up
feelings and individuality creep into a drama which
happened to be engaging him at this time.

The conjecture is undoubtedly an oversimplification
and is certainly not grounded in good scholarly
method, but it is revealing. It not only shows the intelligent self-assurance of the adolescent reviewer, but
it also shrewdly foretells her own future literary in-

centives. *O Pioneers!*, for instance, was a novel which she wrote "without any special reason" other than the desire to recapture scenes and people of her childhood in Nebraska. It grew out of leisurely reflection and is the mirror of her "feeling and individuality." In 1900 in *Cosmopolitan* she published "Eric Hermannson's Soul," which contains one of her earliest statements on esthetic apprehension. Even then she was absorbed by the notion that awareness comes with a profound impact, like a shock of recognition that is for the recipient "as a flash of white light, in which one cannot distinguish color because all colors are there."

The statement is critical as well as creative, explaining as it does Miss Cather's testament of her inner state and her comparable expectations of other serious artists. Awareness and appreciation she regarded as synonymous qualities which came instinctively, without warning, as a complete and perfect mystic revelation. One cannot help being reminded of Shelley's lines in *Adonais*:

> *Life, like a dome of many-coloured glass,*
> *Stains the white radiance of Eternity.*

Miss Cather, like Shelley, was exploring an image which would neutralize temporal concerns and exalt an ineffable radiance. In a critical statement which she was unable to complete before her death, the emotionalism of her esthetic becomes more pronounced. The artist, she felt, can at best create only a minutely subjective impression for the initiate and project "the thrill of his own poor little nerve," exciting and delighting only those people "who have an ear for it or an eye for it."

This somewhat nebulous statement, drawn from the essay "Light on Adobe Walls," has a more concrete parallel in "The Novel Démeublé." Here she argued for artistic indirection, even as James frequently did, feeling that any form of creativity derives high quality from subtle intimation and mood rather than from open statement, which is the flaw of an impoverished imagination. Thea Kronborg had precisely this condition in mind when she tried to explain the nature of art to an appreciative friend. "You see, Doctor Archie," she said, "what one really strives for in art is not the sort of thing you are likely to find when you drop in for a performance at the opera. What one strives for is so far away, so beautiful . . . that there's nothing one can say about it." On another occasion she spoke of artistic intuition as "an animal sort of feeling."

Miss Cather was no more vexed than her heroine by the inability of the artist to articulate feelings, for feelings by their very nature are profoundly intimate. By the same token, the artist himself is completely detached from a need for rational explanations. Professor St. Peter, historian though he is, derives artistic solace from the inner meanings of ancient records and uses facts only as they contribute to that comfort. He sees the evolution of his monumental study of the Spaniards in America as one of almost spiritual inexorability. "The design of his book unfolded in the air above him, just as definitely as the mountain ranges themselves. And the design was sound. He had accepted it as inevitable, had never meddled with it, and it had seen him through." This is true for St. Peter because of his sympathetic understanding. Miss Cather's view of "real" experience, thus, is a romanticized one in which reason and logic have value only in so far as they are refined by emotional and even religious responsiveness.

Critics and practitioners of the novel may of course take exception to a concept which places such stringent demands upon the writer that his own personality must be absorbed in each work of art, that his own being becomes virtually husk and texture of the novel. Once Miss Jewett reproached her friend gently for standing "right in the middle of each [story] when you write, without having the standpoint of the looker-on who takes them each in their relations to letters, to the world." Most novelists could not give of themselves endlessly and selflessly, at least not without succumbing to tedious repetitions. A basic element of Miss Cather's great talent, however, was the perception of infinite variations of human mood and aspiration. To enunciate such perception she had no choice but to participate in each novel, not so much through authorial commentary as through sharing in the feelings of her central characters.

Because she unconsciously violated her own premise and denied her own sensitivity, she was unable to make a successful novel of *Alexander's Bridge*. When she discovered her flaw in judgment, she went ahead to the writing of O *Pioneers!* This novel, she said, "interested me tremendously, because it had to do with a kind of country I loved, because it was about old neighbors, once very dear, whom I had almost forgotten in the hurry and excitement of growing up and finding out what the world was like and trying to get on in it." Here for Miss Cather was "a different process altogether. Here there was no arranging or 'inventing'; everything was spontaneous and took its own place, right or wrong. This was like taking a ride through a familiar country on a horse that knew the way, on a fine morning when you felt like riding. The other was like riding in a park, with some one not altogether congenial, to whom you had to be talking all the time." Writing with such exuberance and self-commitment, Miss Cather made each novel a quiet adventure in which she was thoroughly engaged. The very success of her particular method of composition, indeed, lay in the fact that she had to be a participant and that she could not be a spectator.

Miss Cather's distaste for invention should not be interpreted as anything other than impatience with deliberate contrivance that outrages credulity. Although she relied heavily upon remembered incidents and persons for the frameworks of her novels, she eschewed literal renderings as much as possible. And in the interest of dynamic presentation she even made occasional use of melodramatic episodes, such as the villainy of Wick Cutter in *My Ántonia*, or the gruesome suicide of Shimerda. But if we may substitute the term *imagination* for *invention*, then it becomes possible to demonstrate how she released herself from conventional responsibilities of structure while yet maintaining a flexibly disciplined control over her materials. Her liberation is best revealed in experimental forms, whose culmination is undoubtedly *Death Comes for the Archbishop*. Since she herself has drawn attention to her most conscious effort, *The Professor's House*, a brief view of her observations on that novel is useful.

When I wrote *The Professor's House*, I wished to try two experiments in form. The first is the device often used by the early French and Spanish novelists; that of inserting the *Novelle* into the *Roman.* . . .

But the experiment which interested me was something a little more vague, and was very much akin to the arrangement followed in sonatas in which the academic form was handled somewhat freely.

In my book I tried to make Professor St. Peter's house rather overcrowded and stuffy with new things; American proprieties, clothes, furs, petty ambitions, quivering jealousies—until one got rather stifled. Then I wanted to open the square window and let in the fresh air that blew off the Blue Mesa, and the fine disregard of trivialities which was in Tom Outland's face and in his behaviour.

Like any innovator, Miss Cather hazarded public misunderstanding and displeasure. St. Peter, to whom she attributed the same dilemma, brooded inwardly: "Nobody saw that he was trying to do something quite different—they merely thought he was trying to do the usual thing, and had not succeeded very well." But neither the Professor nor his creator were willing to compromise with mass judgment.

Determined to essay the musical analogy, Miss Cather organized *The Professor's House* into three sections as an approximation of the three movements of the sonata. The first section of the novel—as in the sonata —is the exposition, in which two themes are presented successively and in conjunction: St. Peter is in conflict with his family, their sophistication, greed and worldly concerns discordant to his philosophical breadth and selflessness. Against this background, the memory of Outland is a hovering essence meaningful to St. Peter as an idealistic solace and to the other members of the family as an intimate and genius whose benefactions stir discontent.

The sharply conflicting attitudes toward Outland are brought into dramatic harmony by St. Peter's elegant son-in-law, Louis, who typifies the mercenary world while generously paying homage to Outland's idealistic genius. The expository themes, then, are contrasted through the aggressiveness of St. Peter's family which violates the ideal conditions sought by the Professor and Outland; and they are complemented through the subtle lyricism which defines the friendship between the Professor and Outland.

Between the first, expository section and the second,

developmental section there is an abrupt but essential division. Miss Cather not only transfers her point of view from the St. Peter family to Outland, but she also reconstructs the element of time, giving it a two-fold significance. Now she presents the young inventor as a living being rather than as a controversial shade. She tells the story of his wanderings, his discovery of the Indian remains, and of his frustrated ideals, so that he becomes a total personality before the fateful meeting with St. Peter and his family. The time, then, has a dramatic significance of a biographical sort, bringing the reader to a full knowledge of Outland's activities. But it also has a spiritualized significance, for through his discovery of the Ácoma relics he learns to revere values that transcend mere historical time.

The section of development thus provides a *rapprochement* with the section of exposition and places the materials in their true perspective, the crucial shift from the St. Peters giving Outland the narrative completeness which makes him the essential if not necessarily the dramatic center. The second section, furthermore, has its links with the first; it equates Outland's visionary qualities with that of the professor, and the materialistic cynicism of Outland's partner with that of St. Peter's family. Technically speaking, Miss Cather's exposition is disproportionately long, by comparison with the development, but she justified this usage by allowing herself a free adaptation of the sonata form.

The third section is a recapitulation, returning to the central themes of the first section. Here we discover again the isolation of the professor which was stressed in the exposition and a final awareness of Outland's salutary influence. Thinking of Beethoven's mastery of form, Miss Cather permits the shape of the structure to be determined by the themes themselves.

In the novel again, as in the sonata, mood is a controlling link. Once the mood is established in the exposition, it is usually carried out all the way, a device fulfilled significantly in *The Professor's House* by the autumnal opening and close. A suggestive parallel may be found in Beethoven's Opus 31, No. 2, whose moods, like those of Miss Cather, are first despairing, then delicately rhapsodical, and then poignantly muted. The result of Miss Cather's deliberate, intensive focus on structure is one of her most successful novels.

Anyone familiar with her philosophical attitude toward the writing of a novel might be puzzled by the seeming disparity between her belief and her occasional practice. Philosophically, as we shall see, she held to a doctrine of what might be called esthetic determinism. That is, she saw structure as a natural, inevitable outcome of ideas which had long preceded the created fabric.

Yet she left the way open for experimentation with form, a condition which enabled her to select the most adroit casing, as it were, for intangible thoughts. No matter how skillfully shaped, the novel is an arrangement of symbols contrived for the representation of ideational properties. How the concept may best be framed is the choice of the novelist, even as the poet must choose between sonnet or lyric, between blank verse and *terza rima*; or as the painter must choose between oils and water colors, for instance. The novelist may choose among the traditional forms, which once were innovations in their own right, or he may develop a new structure most suitable to his particular expression. The point is, that properly executed the chosen structure will be the best possible one.

Under these circumstances, therefore, innovation is not only defensible but its attempt is artistically mandatory. Distinguishing between "honest" experimenta-

tion and "egocentric" desire for novelty, Willa Cather
frequently urged young writers to strike out for themselves and create as their inner consciousness dictated.
Her novel *Death Comes for the Archbishop*, like *The
Professor's House*, illustrates the fact that deliberate
experimentation can effectively bring about a harmonious integration of content and structure, what
Miss Cather called "composition." The technique of
the *Archbishop* will be fully considered in a subsequent chapter, so summation of its experimental
nature is not pertinent here. But the conclusion may
be restated, that what could have been a purely artificial structural design, a stylistic *tour de force*, becomes through astonishingly right fusion of material
and form the greatest of her novels.

Despite this careful exploitation of structure, Willa
Cather refused to envisage a novel as a kind of scaffold-
ing upon which the novelist could drape his images and
ideas. Nor, for that matter, did she attach primary significance to the story proper or to "interesting" characters. Architectonics, plot, and character, all these had
their special uses for the author; but they were the
machinery for attaining the ultimate goal, sensitized
means to an uncompromising end. Standing squarely
within his own creation, the artist must infuse it with
his most subjective sympathy, which he seeks to inter-
twine with that of his reader. For Miss Cather there was
only one justification for all art, the evocation of emotion, which she summed up plainly in the belief "that
in novels, as in poetry, the facts are nothing, the feeling is everything."

Yet she did not throw up a barrier between feelings
and ideas. Far from indicating hostility toward intellectual content, she persistently illustrated that there
can be no novel without idea or theme, no matter
what symbolic turns the author gives to the idea.

Seeking the means of expressing an inevitable reconciliation between the superficially disparate elements of reason and imagination, she came to subscribe to a useful artistic logic. The idea of a novel is the mature culmination of experience, growing out of and conditioned by the emotional needs of personality.

There is, therefore, a reciprocity, but one that becomes meaningful only through the intense fulfillment of personal response. The idea must become vivified, elevated and transfigured as it were, so that it blends imperceptibly with the mood which gives it being. When Willa Cather says that "artistic experiences are always mental experiences," she has in effect subsumed the second under the first. Sweeping away the division between intellect and emotion, she concludes that the artist must let the two qualities flow together as a unique experience or as a "great moment." And this "great moment" can always be reproduced by the instrument of one's art.

At first glance, the concept might suggest the crystallization of lesser moments, of seriate incidents mounting in dramatic tension to a point of maximum splendor. It might suggest, further, heroic finality of deed or decision. But there is in fact no place in Miss Cather's esthetic for classical heroism nor for the exaltation of one moment at the expense of another. Each moment that witnessed the abundance of life or the acknowledgment of a supernal will was for her a great moment. Incident must succeed incident with an equality of purpose, each containing its own seed of divinity and each contributing to an ineffable will. Inspiration in the literal sense—the breath of life—was her creative *raison d'être*, and for her symbolic construction she turned frequently to the operations of nature.

Attuned to the changing seasons, Miss Cather tran-

scribed them in literary form paralleled by few writers
in the English language. Directly and without complexity, she imaged her plains and mountains in impressionistic detail, isolating the awesome, filtering out
the ordinary, encompassing her own vision of greatness. The recurrence of such moments makes analysis
almost superfluous. The point, however, may be typified through a passage from *My Ántonia*:

> The windy springs and the blazing summers, one after
> another, had enriched and mellowed that flat table-
> land; all the human effort that had gone into it was
> coming back in long, sweeping lines of fertility. The
> changes seemed beautiful and harmonious to me; it was
> like watching the growth of a great man or of a great
> idea. I recognized every tree and sandbank and rugged
> draw. I found that I remembered the conformation of
> the land as one remembers the modeling of human
> faces.

Nothing is extraneous, nothing is unrelated. Environment evokes an awareness of apocalyptic miracles,
producing respect without the strain of self-conscious
groping. The identification of self with eternity is
gracefully moving. A complementary instance of a
great moment may be derived from *Death Comes for
the Archbishop*, when the priest unintentionally becomes witness to the mystic reverence of his Indian
guide.

> He did waken, and the fire was still giving off a rich
> glow of light in that lofty Gothic chamber. But there
> against the wall was his guide, standing on some
> invisible foothold, his arms outstretched against the
> rock, his body flattened against it, his ear over that
> patch of fresh mud, listening; listening with super-
> sensual ear, it seemed, and he looked to be supported
> against the rock by the intensity of his solicitude. The

Bishop closed his eyes without making a sound and wondered why he had supposed he could catch his guide asleep.

This is another side of the same coin, the central difference inhering in the profoundly direct ritualistic observance of the savage. In each passage Miss Cather makes the point that the religiously sensitive individual, sophisticate or savage, participating indirectly or directly, achieves the paradoxically simple greatness of the living moment. And in each moment the erasure of time brings about a coalescence of universal design.

Like a semitransparent envelope, to borrow the term Virginia Woolf used in her essay on "Modern Fiction," emotion defines the individual's world and establishes his oneness or integrity. Opaque without yet lucent within, emotion never quite bars externalized passions and always affords the assurance of being to the possessor. Emotional depth is a dimension of personality which may be transformed into depth of literary structure, making it both lambent and intense. This is what constitutes the synthesizing property of true reality. Reality of the naturalistic or documentary kind is an incomplete portrayal of experience, denying the deep cadences so necessary to the fulfillment of character, action, and setting. That Miss Cather could not create this kind of realism any more than she could believe in it is rather forcibly demonstrated in *One of Ours*, specifically in the concluding battle scenes. She was not only uncomfortable in her need to reproduce exact or literal details, but she also lacked the ability to identify herself with a war situation. Writing from such emotional distance, she could not achieve credibility.

In a letter to Edmund Wilson in 1923, the year following publication of the novel, Ernest Hemingway pungently noted the deficiency as it appeared to him. Deploring public apathy to E. E. Cummings' *The Enormous Room* (which also appeared in 1922) while *One of Ours* was achieving a commercial triumph, Hemingway suggested *The Birth of a Nation* as Miss Cather's source of realism. "Poor woman," he added, "she had to get her war experience somewhere." Hemingway, of course, is expressing his customary distrust of those who write about war without having experienced it.

Lacking a taste for harsh realism and rarely willing to practice it herself, Miss Cather tended to be hostile to those who found it their appropriate milieu. One of those whom she criticized severely was Daniel Defoe. Because she believed his work revealed a schism between realistic details and the essential ingredients of vision necessary to the highest order of fiction, she read his novels with moral and esthetic repugnance. In discussing *Roxanna*, she analyzed how he failed for her as a novelist and, inextricably, as a human being.

"Here we have the novel," she said, "stripped to its bare bones; and what have we? It happens to be much easier to say what we have not." As far as she was concerned, Defoe was inventive but unimaginative, impersonal. Although she acknowledged his skill as a smooth, convincing narrator and as a writer of strong, plain English, she looked in vain for something more satisfying—"a change of tempo . . . a modulation of voice . . . a quickening of sympathy." She expected "scenes" and found only "episodes" that never rise above the mundane. "The 'scene' in fiction is not a mere matter of construction, any more than it is in life. When we have a vivid experience in social intercourse, pleasant or unpleasant, it records itself in our memory in the form of a scene; and when it flashes back to us, all sorts of apparently unimportant details are flashed back with it." The kind of writer Miss Cather admired and the kind she aspired to become unconsciously created scenes to represent those strong or revelatory experiences in which he participated with his characters. Episodic writing, of the nature she attributed to Defoe, was barren of emotional and imaginative insight, and it suggested distance between the author and his subject.

Only scenic writing, as she described it, could produce pictorial depth. Defoe's inability to establish a third dimension, his reliance on objective episodes, deprived his work of "warm and satisfying moments" and gave it a barren quality. This criticism of Defoe is a Wordsworthian argument for the association of "ideas in a state of excitement," and it expresses Willa Cather's conviction that literary incident should be determined by the prior condition of emotion. The novelist who does not measure up to her self-imposed standards Miss Cather assesses as the novelist *manqué*. Because Defoe, in her opinion, possessed neither humor nor idealism, romance nor geniality, these traits had of necessity to be absent from his writing; and without these traits the work of art is a failure even as is the individual who attempts its creation.

Although Willa Cather was never a formal critic, she had rigid enough critical standards. Additionally, once she had become convinced of the rightness of her own literary approach she was intolerant of other methods and concepts. Having liberated herself from conventional concerns of plot and structure, she could not accept any kind of formalized art, denying in fact that prescription could foster art.

Since she resorted characteristically to the nostalgic flux of personal memory, she was obliged to repudiate Defoe, whom she considered objective and impersonal, as safe as "sterilized gauze." She acknowledged his power of observation as she allowed any artist an empiric involvement with life. Observation, she went so far as to admit in *The Song of the Lark*, is perhaps one of "the chief requisites in a good story-teller."

But she agreed with Sarah Orne Jewett that there is a danger of confusing insight with observation. When Lucy Gayheart, as we witnessed in another chapter, combines acute inner satisfaction with sensuous pleasure upon suddenly viewing a wintry star, she is Miss Cather's instrument of true perception. The star may be physically visible always, but only in rare circumstances does it communicate its symbolically essential meaning to the soul. As on another occasion Lucy discovers that words have "value aside from their direct meaning," she here apprehends in near mystic fashion that phenomena communicate more than tangible wonder.

As a kind of vestigial proof that mere visual seeing is not enough, Miss Cather alluded to an obvious fact that the most trivial of writers frequently had the most highly developed powers of observation. Taking superficial notice of lives and worlds which were foreign to one's experiences and interests could lead only to esthetic aridity, for creation depends upon profound, instinctive identification of the author with his rich imaginings. *Alexander's Bridge* always remained with her as a rueful reminder that she had begun with a failure, because that shallow novel, externally motivated, lacked a center; it had no vitality to draw from the author's personal commitment. She realized her artistic strength, as she later told the painter Grant Reynard, only after she "remembered the little Bohemian maid . . . who had befriended her in her early youth out in Nebraska, and . . . wrote in a flood of feeling about those times and days." The story of the little Bohemian maid is, of course, *My Ántonia*, the writing of which determined irrevocably the direction of her genius.

By 1921, when she was in her middle years and perhaps at the crest of her maturity, Willa Cather could look back upon her shaping influences and analyze the relation between her experiences and art. She concluded that the "years from eight to fifteen are the formative period in a writer's life, when he unconsciously gathers basic material. He may acquire a great many interesting and vivid impressions in his mature years but his thematic material he acquires under fifteen years of age." Dorothy Canfield Fisher, her close friend, judged this intensification of attitude to be a peculiarly personal trait, contrary to the opinion of many novelists that feeling and insight expand continuously with the passage of years. Disputable though Mrs. Fisher's distinction may be, she attributed her friend's feeling to the fact that she was essentially a poet rather than a prose writer. Faith in an unconscious association of ideas at any rate gives Miss Cather a decided kinship with the Romantic poets, as well as an informal connection with Freudian psychology, which she would not have acknowledged.

And she is not unlike Proust who, in writing of the successful novelist in *The Past Recaptured*, maintains: "It is not the cleverest nor the most learned man nor the one with the best social connections who becomes a Bergotte, but the one who knows how to become a mirror and thus is able to reflect his life, however mediocre." A life as rich as Miss Cather's could not justly be called mediocre; but it was ordinary in the sense that it was humane, and respect for human virtues is an epitome of her art.

Her introspective need to write of situations closely allied to her own life grew out of a further cognizance of the writer's limitations. "To note an artist's limita-

tions is but to define his genius. A reporter can write
equally well about everything that is presented to his
view, but a creative writer can do his best only with
what lies within the range and character of his talent."
This is but another way of saying that the author can
claim no creative freedom other than that which is
urged by his inner self, for talent and experience come
to the same thing. Limitation, thus, is vital rather than
enervating, contributing to the depth which gives
shape and flavor to the literary personality. Too personal and nebulous to admit of definition, the literary
personality envisaged by Miss Cather (as by Pater, to
whom she was indebted for the notion) is a nameless
vibrancy, an ineffable echo distinguishing the particular novelist from all other novelists. But while she
speculated that enduring mood and ideation are fixed
early in life, she had no rash faith in a kind of um-
bilical sensitivity and wisdom.

The wholesome discovery of restrictiveness must be
gradual before it can be translated into creative expression. The recognition must come slowly, only after
many mistakes, paralleling the self as it unfolds toward
maturity. "It is not always easy," she remarked in an
introduction to *Alexander's Bridge* "for the inexperi-
enced writer to distinguish between his own material
and that which he would like to make his own." Because the novice tends to be intrigued by that which
is newly discovered rather than by that which is deeply
experienced, he often overlooks the vitality of familiar
events and memories. In the excitement of discovering
unexpected ideas or sensations, he may take for granted
his best known things. The thrill they can afford him
are too often unrealized, lying "at the bottom of his
consciousness, whether he is aware of it or no, and they
continue to feed him, but they do not stimulate him."

Miss Cather, moreover, was convinced that the

artist's knowledge of his inner focus inevitably opened outward in conjunction with a developing intellectual liberation which allowed him to reject the conventional editorial point of view, as she phrased it. Writing, she insisted, should be either the production of fiction as a marketable commodity, or it should be an art "for which there is no market demand." That is to say, the writing of fiction may be regarded as a perfectly safe and commendable business for which there happens to be purchasers—if they can be satisfied. Or it may be regarded as a constant search for "something new and untried, where the values are intrinsic and have nothing to do with standardized values. The courage to go on without compromise does not come to a writer all at once—nor does the ability. Both are phases of natural development." Miss Cather knew when she wrote *O Pioneers!* that she was violating every accepted standard of fiction writing. In the slowly paced story which she was essaying, as she conceded, there was no "action," no "humor," no "hero." Hers was an account of dull farming folk in Nebraska, which, as she wryly described it, was *declassé*. By now, of course, *O Pioneers!* is the affectionately acknowledged archetype of its own tradition, and the braveness of its innovation is but a dim memory, if that. And yet, that it was once associated with a radical break from convention becomes apparent with the remembrance that in 1913, when Miss Cather brought forth the novel, Henry James and Edith Wharton provided the measure by which literary taste was judged, and that the so-called "novel of the soil" was still to come into its own.

Dedicated to lasting values, impatiently brushing aside the temporal, Miss Cather's ideal author is infused with paradoxical aims. His office is priestlike, for he stands apart while bringing comfort to others, and at the same time he is the communicant in the lonely quest for his own solace. His self-imposed duties are unalterably his own; they combine the rigors of urgent discipline and the emollient action of fulfillment. The novelist not only must be immersed in his inner limitations but, as Miss Cather once said in a lecture at the Bread Loaf School of English, he must also "be so in love with his subject that he forgets 'self' in his passion."

Somehow, it would thus appear, the novelist must establish with his characters and materials an identification so intense that in its ultimate transmutation it becomes the essence of impersonality. In the very act of expressing self, he performs his loftiest esthetic function, the almost total abnegation of self. The idealistic writer—and Miss Cather never wishes to be otherwise—communicates those truths which are most intimate while jealously guarding their deeply personal quality. Only the poet qua poet confesses in his own name, rightly assuming that anything less than maximum candor, symbolically veiled though it be, is alien to his particular art.

The fictionalized expectations of the novel, however, demand at least the semblance of invention. Even Joyce or Proust "invent" characters and situations that are not overtly confessional, that project a kind of esthetic coloration whose imaginative appeal draws attention away from the purely autobiographical elements. In the same tradition, Miss Cather almost always disguises her authorial self. The convenient mask of a Jim Burden or a Niel Herbert affords her the means of indirection by which she is able to reveal her soul and mind. And the "I" who appears as a childish spectator in the epilogue of *Sapphira and the Slave Girl* is no more intrusive. The voices are always those of Willa Cather, but their modulations are such that her physical presence is never obtrusive.

Miss Cather's ideal novelist embraces anomalous extremes of withdrawal and compassion, of absorbing sensitivity and understanding humanity. He "fades away into the land and people of his heart," she says, and like the phoenix, "he dies of love only to be born again." But the seeming polarity is harmonized as the uniquely self-contained individual depletes himself in order that he may enjoy constant surges of replenishment. Imbued with the ability to love selflessly, the writer has a "gift of sympathy," which is of all his talents the only one of genuinely perpetual significance. The most cohesive of all human needs, sympathy is the link between the author and mankind and unselfishly enunciated it can bring to the work of art classic immortality.

Miss Cather's thesis of impersonality is seemingly paradoxical, but in fact it is the appanage of her conviction that a novel has a life of its own. From this esthetic certitude she concluded that the characters of a novel, like all people, must be allowed to work out their lives without interference from outside forces. Miss Cather in this way imposes a stringent prohibition upon the novelist, denying him an authoritarian power to manipulate the lives and activities of his own literary creations. Control that in any sense thwarts or alters the ultimate moral design is the compounding of literary sham. Realism, according to Miss Cather's definition in "The Novel Démeublé," is "an attitude of mind on the part of the writer toward his material, a vague indication of the sympathy and candour with which he accepts, rather than chooses, his theme." Renunciation of self is the universal rule in great art; therefore egoism is the cause of much bad art. The

artist must coax and guide his materials along the way
that is apparent to his acute consciousness; but he
must not force them into any track other than that
which is natural and inevitable.

The challenge of these many creative responsibilities
is pleasurably imminent, constantly taxing the novelist's resources. Since they are inseparable from each
other they must be discharged simultaneously, or at
any rate they must levy equally upon his imaginative
capabilities. Only the individual novelist, indeed, could
begin to understand the causative demands of his art,
and not even he could allot degrees of value to them.
Though they may perhaps be discussed as entities, in
their application they are so fluidly interdependent
that they lose all meaningful individuation.

Once the distinctions have been suggested, they can
be considered only as a total, virtually metaphysical
operation. And the vitality of this operation—the literary manifestation—can be measured only by the intensity of the artist's controlling urge. Terms such as
"urge" or "drive" are intangible enough to make really
satisfactory classification unlikely. As might be expected, Miss Cather resorts to subjective, partial explanations rather than to prescriptive analysis. Sometimes
she calls the artist's motivating drive "passion," sometimes a refined "sense of truthfulness," sometimes a
"devotion to an ideal." But most often she alludes to
it as "desire," probably feeling this term to be the least
ambiguous and most readily communicable or accurate
transference of constantly experienced impulse.

Essentially, it is a desire for self-expression so individually compelling that it must find its natural outlet.
As she demonstrated repeatedly in her fiction—especially in *The Song of the Lark*, *Lucy Gayheart*, and the
short stories in *Youth and the Bright Medusa*—for the
miraculously emergent condition of desire the artist

will suffer any hardship, will make any sacrifice, and will court social and intellectual isolation. Realizing this difficult fact even as an undergraduate, she said: "Art of every kind is an exacting master, more so even than Jehovah—He says only 'Thou shalt have no other gods before me.' Art, Science and Letters cry, 'Thou shalt have no other gods at all.' They accept only human sacrifices."

The propitiatory claims of art ingrained themselves more acutely and demonstrably through her friendship with Olive Fremstad, the model for Thea Kronborg and the young Willa Cather's living symbol of the great artist. From Madame Fremstad she learned that the artist is born alone, makes his way alone, and dies alone; solitary he pursues his quest and even the enjoyment of the highest rewards of that quest. Devotional in his aspirations, the artist for Miss Cather stood apart from the tenets of conventional morality, yet, vibrantly moral, always prepared to immolate himself in the fires of his own "desire." She expected no more of her fictional artists than she did of their flesh-and-blood counterparts. If not always well-rounded or balanced, the artist compensated for his deficiencies by enjoying the exultation of undeviating allegiance to a single purpose.

ii

Despite the thematic and emotional continua which bound her novels together in a common purpose, Miss Cather never felt that any one of her works depended on the one that preceded or followed it. As is true of any serious novelist, she worked toward broad relationships among her novels and she tended to limit her field of vision to achieve that purpose. But she nonetheless subscribed literally to an organic theory, recording the people and events of each novel as unique experiences without sequential concerns. The needs of each novel provided their own laws and enforcement. Miss Cather's creative desires were of such profundity that she once likened the pleasures and anguish of literary fulfillment to parturition. She could feel the presence of the novel in the front of her head, where it grew steadily larger as does the foetus developing in its mother's womb. After long nurturing it reached the back of the head, where it lay painfully heavy awaiting delivery. This was for her the most afflictive stage of the novel's genesis, for it was during this period that she would be consumed by a nameless terror that somehow she would not be able to bring her child-novel to external life.

Like life itself, a novel without purpose is meaningless; the end of the work engages the novelist, as Ellen Glasgow says in her preface to *The Sheltered Life*, like "the solitary fixed star above the flux of creation." This fictively ideal end will determine—directly and indirectly, technically and conceptually—the molding of the material. Thus Miss Cather held that when the novelist deals with substance deeply related to his conscious and unconscious being, the choice of its molding is not really up to him, for it already has a form which needs only to be expressed. "If he tries to meddle with its vague outline, to twist it into some categorical shape, above all if he tries to adapt or modify its mood, he destroys its value." Contrived literary devices, he discovers, have little bearing on the artistic rendering of this material except in a negative way.

For the most part indifferent to formal critical theorizing, Miss Cather made statements such as these to describe her own practice rather than to propound dogmas. Her working methods were the actualization of her beliefs. Beginning a novel with only theme and direction fixed firmly in mind, she rarely plotted in advance scenes and incidents, alterations and complexities. Although she improvised as she went along, she always obeyed the consistent demands of the underlying principle to which instinct had impelled her. To those in whom she confided she often admitted that when she sat down to write, particulars were never in her mind. Rather, she relied upon the strength of her theme to carry along the story and to inspire the construction of her pattern. This does not mean that she approached composition as a purely extemporaneous affair. As reported by Miss Lewis, when Willa Cather was not writing "she was very much preoccupied with the past out of which her story sprang." Without engaging in active creativity, she would let submerged memories, impressions, and experiences rise to that level of consciousness which would make them accessible later as part of her narrative theme.

Transformation of raw experiences into the symbolic artistic pattern was a lengthy process in which actual composition was only a final stage. With Miss Cather as with her admired predecessor Henry James, the facts of experience sank into the "well" of the unconscious mind, the alchemy of her art ultimately bringing them forth altered yet recognizable. But between empiric actuality and transformed symbol she required a long meditative period. From Stephen Crane, whom she met in 1895, she learned that "the detail of a thing has to filter through my blood, and then it comes out like a native product, but it takes forever." The writer, Miss Cather insists, must have a mind like Limbo, inhabited by spectres for which he must find physical forms. Such a ghost, albeit a beautiful one, was *A Lost Lady*, which she confessed haunted her for twenty years before it could be written. "All the lovely emotions that one has had some day appear with bodies,

and it isn't as if one found ideas suddenly. Before this
the memories of these experiences and emotions have
been like a perfume." Esthetically cautious in her
selection of materials for a novel, Miss Cather rejects
the immediate situation, the immediate impression.
Only those shapes and scenes which have persisted,
survived, and recurred within the author's mind, as she
explains her own concerns; only those situations and
characters which have "teased" the imagination for
years are suitable materials for the novel.

With creative expression the fruit of such sustained
intensity and such disciplined spontaneity, we may
take Miss Lewis' word that writing for this author was
an effortless "unmixed pleasure." Quietly certain of
her purpose, "she never changed the fundamental design of a book, except in the case of O Pioneers! In
all her other novels the idea came to her as a whole,
the end as well as the beginning, and writing the novel
was simply an attempt to realize her first vision of it."

Engaged privately by the apprehension and then by
the exposition of each of her novels, Miss Cather cherished the physical action of writing as one of her
subjective rewards. As though reluctant to release her
creation until the last possible moment, she composed
her first draft rapidly by hand. She wrote steadily for
several hours at a time, without pausing to alter the
words and phrases that had virtually become a part of
her. But Miss Cather was also a good critic, sensitive
to economical phraseology and poetic connotation.
Following the first, manuscript version of a story, she
would transcribe it on the typewriter, zealously making changes and omissions that she thought appropriate. Still only a working copy, this would go to her
secretary for re-transcription and subsequent further
editing. The process of revision continued until she
was satisfied for the moment; but it went on even in

the printed proofs, which she read carefully. After paying almost $150 for additional proof corrections on *My Ántonia*, however, she learned to be more provident and confined most of her alterations thereafter to the manuscripts. Statements put down in the heat of composition, she well knew, were frequently inconsistent with precise intention and art.

She admired Robert Louis Stevenson, who had given Mr. McClure license to edit his *Letters from the South Seas* as he saw fit. By contrast with this willingness of first-rate writers to be edited, young writers seemed to her stubbornly unknowing in the way in which they guarded their phrases once they were set down, as if there were "a mystic power in a certain order of words." She was experienced enough to believe that only limited, inferior writers would resist judicious manuscript changes. "To a man of large creative powers, the idea is the thing; the decoration of phrase is a very secondary matter. . . . If his story is loose and runs thin, he is glad to tighten it. If it is congested, and he has tried to bring out too many points, he will cut. He can afford to spare a few ideas; if he has plenty." Like any apprentice writer, the youthful Willa Cather had stumbled frequently before coming to the wisdom of these observations. The early short stories are dynamic proof of the need for judicious pruning and intensified statement.

Rigorous self-criticism became as much a sign of her maturing powers as the innate sympathy which takes shape as her artistic triumph. Although she valued the *mot juste* as a means of projecting theme and enforcing structure, she detested mere rhetorical panoply. Likewise, she subordinated narrative details to her controlling ideas and emotions, while recognizing a certain interdependence. She virtually summed up her philosophy of fiction in the statement, "the design is the story, and the story is the design." Broadly considered, the subject matter is but a means to an end, for the writer must understand that he can do little even with great natural forces or elemental emotions in their bare but pure form, and that he can only "approach the major forces of life through comparatively trivial incidents." Magnitude of subject matter, indeed, had no necessary relationship to her art. "An idyll of Theocritus, concerned with sheep and goats and shade and pasture, is today as much alive as the most dramatic passages out of the *Iliad*—stirs the reader's feeling, quite as much, perhaps, if the reader is a poet."

Believing that simple lives and actions convey their own kind of drama, she worked toward the proper coalescence of all ingredients, convinced that architectonics is an inevitable if not automatic result once the theme of a work of art is honestly fixed. The Jamesian echoes are strong here. In "The Art of Fiction" we are told, "A Novel is a living thing, all one and continuous, like any other organism." And this notion is supported metaphorically. "The story and the novel, the idea and the form, are the needle and the thread, and I never heard of a guild of tailors who recommended the use of thread without the needle, or the needle without the thread."

Writing a critique of the Arnold Bennett-Edward Knoblauch play *Milestones* for *McClure's*, Miss Cather alluded to the organic fusion of all parts in a comparable figure of speech: structure is "like a spiral spring," and once it is released by the theme, "it will go its length without any prodding." Later she came to believe that the essential matter of the story, that is, the theme and all of its symbolical details of structure, is apprehended in enlightening "flashes that are as unreasoning, often as unreasonable as life itself."

Criticism of her own work was a process which engaged her not only during actual composition but sometimes long after the publication of a work. As forthright in the recognition of her faults as of her virtues, she brought to her work all the searching candor of a perfectionist. With a zeal characteristic of one who feels a consecration of purpose, she directed her energies toward approximating an indefectible artistic mission. An eclectic principle anterior to her function as a self-critic enabled her to select constantly and judiciously and to dispose of all materials extraneous to the achievement of her desired ends. Such devoted singleness of purpose led Miss Cather to its necessary consequence, a passionate respect for artistic simplicity. By avoiding excesses in all forms, she hoped to aim directly toward her goal, shunning ornate and secondary matters which might obscure her vision. Simplification was her technical means of harmoniously subordinating the parts to the whole. "Too much detail," she said, "is apt, like any other form of extravagance, to become slightly vulgar; and it quite destroys in a book a very satisfying element analogous to what painters call 'composition.'"

Resolved that literature is destroyed by tasteless amplitude, she distinguishes between the novel as a form of imaginative art and as a form of journalism. To preclude the latter danger, novelists "must select the eternal material of art." Rightly motivated, they must strive "to interpret imaginatively the material and social investiture of their characters; to present their scene by suggestion rather than by enumeration." This must be done because the "higher processes of art are all processes of simplification."

But the ability to simplify is not easily acquired, for it comes only with time and a stringent determination to cast out everything that does not contribute toward preserving the spirit of the whole. Somehow, and on this point Miss Cather is more than usually vague, excision and compression must be accomplished in such a way "that all that one has suppressed and cut away is there to the reader's consciousness as much as if it were in type on the page." If, however, she fails to codify a doctrine of action for other writers, she gives admirable evidence of her own talent for actualizing this theory.

But even during the early part of her career, while she was already being acknowledged as one of America's gifted writers, she knew that she was still short of her goal. The gem-like fastidiousness of novels like *The Professor's House* and *Death Comes for the Archbishop* had not been attained in *The Song of the Lark* or the prize-winning *One of Ours,* and only partially in *A Lost Lady.* The disappointing fault of *The Song of the Lark,* as she herself conceded a quarter of a century after its publication, is that it extends far beyond the dramatic point of interest. The heroine's struggle for fulfillment and escape from mundane reality, the real heart of the matter, are overshadowed by the static events which continue to be reported long after the conflict has ceased. The anti-climactic later part of the story should have been modulated and set in correct perspective through the use of suggestion. Instead, Miss Cather blunted her original conception by leaning on a traditional, nineteenth-century design of biographical completeness.

Undoubtedly, she had thwarted her own purpose by bringing in disruptive details—such as the rather extensive accounts of Fred Ottenburg and Landry—and continuing the history of Thea after the passing of its emotional climax. Only after friendly criticism and searching self-examination did she avow the conceptual error which had obscured her primary intention. William Heinemann, who had published the more compact *O Pioneers!* in England, declined *The Song of the Lark* because he thought it was erroneously constructed. "The full-blooded method," he wrote her, "which told everything about everybody" was not conducive to her genius. At the time, she disagreed with Heinemann and with the American critic Randolph Bourne, who raised substantially the same objection. "One is always on the defensive about one's last book," she admitted. "But when the next book, *My Ántonia*, came along, quite of itself with no direction from me, it took the road of *O Pioneers!*, not the road of *The Song of the Lark*."

My Ántonia consequently shows marks of her reappraisal, though she had not yet fully liberated herself from the fault of cumbersome detail. *One of Ours* is burdened by intrusive matters, such as allusions to the Virginia heritage of the illiterate Mahailey. Even *A Lost Lady*, for some time Willa Cather's nearest approach to a novel of total relevance, suffers occasionally from the meditative discursions of Niel Herbert. Nevertheless, her realization of error and her serious efforts to overcome them prepared the way for her technical masterpieces, beginning with *A Lost Lady* and culminating in *The Professor's House*, *Death Comes for the Archbishop*, and *Shadows on the Rock*.

Artistic simplicity, as Miss Cather came to practice it, means hermitic denial of mere costume, avoidance of the superficial or tangential. But her kind of simplicity requires a philosophical bolstering, one achieved by a special attitude toward the use of detail. Without much hesitation, therefore, she repudiated many of the sociological, realistic novels of the Thirties and Forties which were constructed deliberately as exact reproductions of natural and psychological phenomena. Essentially, Miss Cather felt, their authors were satisfied with overt impressions of objects rather than with truly deep and significant ones. She concluded, as Proust did in *The Past Recaptured*, that such writing "is satisfied to 'describe objects,' to give merely a miserable listing of lines and surfaces." Not only was this method inconsistent with art, she believed, but it also skirted the challenging difficulties of insight. She found support for her opinion in Mérimée's dictum: "The art of choosing among the innumerable features which nature offers us is, after all, much more difficult than that of observing them carefully and rendering them exactly." As Miss Cather grew older and saw her own work being regarded as old fashioned by the devotees of the new school of catalogue realism, she naturally became increasingly ardent about the need for external refinement. But her faith had started early, long before she felt the pressure of encroaching literary modes, and there can be no question of proprietary discontent. As early as 1913 she had written, "A great artist usually handles a difficult situation simply, but that simplicity has cost the imagination many births and deaths; it is the very flower of all the artist's powers."

The line that separated Willa Cather from most contemporary writers was enforced by her own attitude toward the nature and use of detail. It was an attitude developed out of an unconscious distinction between description and imagery. In her own novels she avoided objective description as much as possible, presumably because it is the physical, literal restatement of an actuality—and no more. Instead she relied heavily on the use of controlled imagery involving complexes of emotional and intellectual reactions, imagery conditioned by intimate participation. Imagery for her was a symbol of meaning to represent the creative force underlying the novel. Her employment of imagery is evidence of the sharpness with which she viewed the commonplace. While many an inferior writer invents experiences incredibly bizarre or morbid or sets down the mundane with stupefying dullness, the true artist uses materials which have been treated countless times. By some mysterious lighting effect of his own sensitive perception, he reveals aspects of them which we have never seen in their deeper refulgence.

Acute sensory responsiveness is in itself a source of pleasure, but to savor it as no more than a visual or tactile or any other kind of exterior sensation is to lose a substantial portion of its essence. Beauty is a quality to be felt intensively; first and perhaps most vividly, it strikes at the outer senses; then, profoundly, it registers a lasting impression, as it were, on the inner sensibilities. The second impression might be regarded as one of moral or transcendent significance, spiritually vivified. The double response is actually simultaneous, although verbal delineation obviously makes it appear to be a process, the one stage emerging from the other.

Although Willa Cather presents many instances of responses elicited from her, she does so with subtle permutations, and never more effectively than in her considerations of nature. To cite one of many possible illustrations, she achieves in *The Song of the Lark* an impressionistic harmony between the vastness of eternity and the diminished ordinary:

It was one of those still days of intense light, when every particle of mica in the soil flashed like a little mirror, and the glare from the plain below seemed more intense than the rays from above. The sand ridges ran glittering gold out to where the mirage licked them up, shining and steaming like a lake in the tropics. The sky looked like blue lava, forever incapable of clouds—a turquoise bowl that was the lid of the desert.

And yet within Mrs. Kohler's green patch the water dripped, the beds had all been hosed, and the air was fresh with rapidly evaporating moisture.

Again, in *My Ántonia,* she writes:

All those fall afternoons were the same, but I never got used to them. As far as we could see, the miles of copper-red grass were drenched in sunlight that was stronger and fiercer than at any other time of the day. The blond cornfields were red gold, the haystacks turned rosy and threw long shadows. The whole prairie was like the bush that burned with fire and was not consumed. That hour always had the exultation of victory, of triumphant ending, like a hero's death— heroes who died young and gloriously. It was a sudden transfiguration, a lifting-up of day.

The image is exalted and ethereal, establishing a relationship between a demiurge—both Biblical and mythical—and humanity. Through Claude Wheeler, of *One of Ours,* Miss Cather similarly transforms a natural event into an eternal, ritualistic experience:

He rose and went to look out, but the west windows were so plastered with snow that they were opaque. Even from the one on the south he could see nothing for a moment; then Mahailey must have carried her lamp to the kitchen window beneath, for all at once a broad yellow beam shone out into the choked air, and down it millions of snowflakes hurried like armies, an unceasing progression, moving as close as they could without forming a solid mass. . . . There was a solemnity about a storm of such magnitude; it gave one a feeling of infinity. The myriads of white particles that crossed the rays of lamplight seemed to have a quiet purpose, to be hurrying toward a definite end. A faint purity, like a fragrance almost too fine for human senses, exhaled from them.

Even in *Alexander's Bridge*, where she is much more given to formal description ("A harp-shaped elm stood stripped against the pale-colored evening sky, with ragged last-year's birds' nests in its forks, and through the bare branches the evening star quivered in the misty air.") than in her later novels, Miss Cather with Wordsworthian overtones creates this kind of imagistic affinity:

> It was one of those rare afternoons when all the thick-ness and shadow of London are changed to a kind of shining, pulsing, special atmosphere; when the smoky vapors become fluttering golden clouds, nacreous veils of pink and amber; when all that bleakness of gray stone and dullness of dirty brick trembles in aureate light, and all the roofs and spires, and one great dome, are floated in golden haze.

Willa Cather's novels derive much of their plasticity from reverential wonderment of this order. Whether she projects nature through the imagistic vision of Thea or Claude or Bishop Latour or any other of her acutely sensitized characters, she mingles the temporal with the everlasting.

This supraocular vision was a quality Miss Cather cherished in the painters of Dutch interiors and of still life, such as Vermeer. To change ordinary mate-rials into effective pictures with the aid of light and shade and patient execution is her forte as well as theirs. Reflecting on an exhibition of Dutch painters which she saw in Paris just before beginning *The Professor's House*, she wrote:

> In many of them the scene presented was a living-room warmly furnished, or a kitchen full of food and coppers. But in most of the interiors, whether drawing-room or kitchen, there was a square window, open, through

which one saw the masts of ships, or a stretch of grey sea. The feeling of the sea that one got through those square windows was remarkable, and gave me a sense of the fleets of Dutch ships that ply quietly on all the waters of the globe—to Java, etc.

A comparable distinction between literalized description and imagery determines her ultimate criticism of Balzac and Tolstoy. The novels of Balzac she finds overfurnished; reading them gives her the impression of walking into the shop of an interior decorator. His loving, lavish descriptions seem dull, so that impatiently "the eye glides over them." Tolstoy, on the other hand, devoted as much attention to physical things as did Balzac, but without unpleasant cloying. And she goes on to explain:

> But there is this determining difference: the clothes, the dishes, the haunting interiors of those old Moscow houses, are always so much a part of the emotions of the people that they are perfectly synthesized; they seem to exist, not so much in the author's mind, as in the emotional penumbra of the characters themselves. When it is fused like this, literalness ceases to be literalness—it is merely part of the experience.

Thus, Tolstoy's description is complex in method and function. He shuns the superfluous word and the adjective which do not reveal anything. Over-reaching mere representation, his description becomes imagistic, providing a sense of sudden liberation from the mundane, a sense of freedom from the limitations of space and time.

Compression and selectivity, insistence on total relevance—these became Miss Cather's stylistic and thematic tenets. Idealizing a form of literary reticence in which the hint or even the unspoken word convey the essential impression, she discovered a brilliant model in Stephen Crane. She admired one who estimated details at their true worth, making them serve his purpose and feeling no further responsibility about them. Only the relevant engaged him; "he never tried to make a faithful report of everything else within his field of vision, as if he were a conscientious salesman making out his expense-account."

Eventually she was able to achieve a power of literary selectivity which was to become a characteristic of her own style and which was to be largely responsible for her artistic fame. Fellow novelists such as Ellen Glasgow and Ford Madox Ford praised her restraint. The latter, indeed, went so far as to call her "one of the greatest novelists of the present day" perhaps because "she never does make any comment." Probably, however, Ford let his enthusiasm carry him into harmless exaggeration. While Miss Cather was less frequently guilty of authorial intrusion than most writers of her day, she did on occasion make observations in her own voice. Sometimes they were tersely revealing asides, as when she said of Ray Kennedy (in *The Song of the Lark*): "He had the lamentable American belief that 'expression' is obligatory." In the single word *lamentable* is summed up a characteristic philosophical displeasure which she never abandoned. Or in *One of Ours* she makes her criticism much more explicit, as in this paragraph which we alluded to earlier:

The farmer raised and took to market things with an intrinsic value; wheat and corn as good as could be grown anywhere in the world, hogs and cattle that were the best of their kind. In return he got manufactured articles of poor quality; showy furniture that went to pieces, carpets and draperies that faded, clothes that made a handsome man look like a clown. Most of his money was paid out for machinery,—and that, too, went to pieces. A steam thrasher didn't last long; a horse outlived three automobiles.

Elsewhere in *One of Ours,* as well as in *O Pioneers!* and *My Ántonia,* there are complementary statements of her disaffection with materialism. Omniscient expressions are not lacking in *A Lost Lady,* as when the humble Blum brothers become aware of caste distinctions: "They realized, more than their companions, that such a fortunate and privileged class was an axiomatic fact in the social order." All these comments appeared in novels that Ford could have read before he made his remark in *Return to Yesterday* (1932). But even three years later, in *Lucy Gayheart,* when Miss Cather was practicing maximum restrictiveness, she could end a section as social commentator:

> In little towns, lives roll along so close to one another; loves and hates beat about, their wings almost touching. On the sidewalks along which everybody comes and goes, you must, if you walk abroad at all, at some time pass within a few inches of the man who cheated and betrayed you, or the woman you desire more than anything else in the world. Her skirt brushes against you. You say good-morning, and go on. It is a close shave. Out in the world the escapes are not so narrow.

Although Ford Madox Ford's opinion is obviously in need of qualification, it is not completely wide of the mark. Asides such as those above are exceptional rather than the rule. But if their very infrequency causes them to stand forth, they are by no means extraneous. Occasioned only by special circumstance, they do not seriously violate Miss Cather's restrictive principle and almost always are skillfully absorbed within the narrative context. They tend, indeed, to humanize an author whose theoretical concerns, at least, are at times almost distressingly ethereal.

The dominant mode of the period in which she wrote was anything but one of reticence. The novel after the first World War aimed at comprehensive literalness, gluttonous totality, the stocking up of detail after detail in an effort to create a reportorial, photographic realism. Symptomatic of this entire trend is the "Camera's Eye" of John Dos Passos, but as far as Miss Cather was concerned, human beings "don't see what a camera would see." If, however, she was antithetical toward the fashion of relentless verisimilitude, she was even more hostile to the unalleviated thematic concerns of the twentieth-century novel. Believing that art and religion were of the same root, dealing with the same material, she was interested chiefly in moral verities. She felt that "there are only two or three human stories, and they go on repeating themselves fiercely as if they had never happened before; like the larks in this country, that have been singing the same five notes over for thousands of years."

The thematic limitations thus enunciated in *O Pioneers!* and adhered to throughout her own fiction are remarkable for their variations on a few ideas. As long as the novelist's preoccupation is with man's moral and emotional conflicts, just so long will the "two or three human stories" be reiterated. The themes of true literary creation "will be the same until all the values of human life have changed and all the strongest emotional responses have become different—which can hardly occur until the physical body itself has fundamentally changed." What Miss Cather is saying, then, is that genuine art is the product of temporal and spatial freedom. Taking for itself the subject and object of eternity, it can draw its materials from the most remote past and address itself to the most distant future. And it can do this only because in the final analysis any artistic creation is the subjective expression of a universal experience.

Unquestionably committed to such a philosophical attitude, she could feel only repugnance for the cult of fictional purpose, for writers such as Dos Passos and Steinbeck and Farrell and a host of others who, aiming to reform society through literature, "tried to make a story out of every theme that occurred to them and to get returns on every situation that suggested itself." As we have seen, she could not always divorce herself from social indignation. Her objection, indeed, was not to the occasional and creatively synthesized reproach but to the dreariness of unrelieved protest.

She was in fact opposed to the naturalistic, sociological novelist who believed that man's concern was not primarily with moral truths but with the physical urgency of remaining alive in a jungle of economic inequities. Economics as such, she felt, was not suitable material for the novelist; "industrial life has to work out its own problems." Like Proust she was skeptical of the fears of the so-called realists. To her they were only superficial and meretricious materialists who did not recognize that spiritual transfiguration of this world is the aim of literature and, indeed, of all art. Impatient with functionalism, she believed that art could serve no cause but its own and consequently rejected the widely held notion of the Thirties that literature must propagandize in the cause of social reformation. Conversely, she believed that if art could serve society, this service must always be an incidental by-product of its main purpose, which is to offer sanctuary from an affected, insincere world. The sole possibility of escape from tormenting reality lies in art.

And yet in her novels of second- and third-generation pioneers, epitomized by *A Lost Lady* and *One of*

Ours, she demonstrates clearly enough that she was not unaware of the economic problems confronting mankind. In these novels she virtually states that the spiritual individualism and idealism of the pioneer had been destroyed by the grasping, antispiritual forces of "machine-made materialism." Certainly this was a theme not foreign to Steinbeck, particularly in *The Grapes of Wrath.* But Miss Cather's treatment of the problem differs drastically from Steinbeck's both in emphasis and approach. For her the problem has little to do with the social investiture of economics, with the pyramiding of money, with the building up of powerful financial empires; nor with their correctives. She comprehends issues as purely moral. She recognized that true idealism is recurrently overrun and defeated by immoral acquisitiveness; but through a grasp of historical perspective, she envisioned idealism always rising self-regenerated, revitalized and strengthened.

Even as Miss Cather in her thematic concerns stressed the moral aspects of the human condition, so she argued that the basic satisfaction arising from literary expression grows out of moral concentration. A clue to her analysis of creative happiness may be found in the short story called "A Gold Slipper," in which she is indebted to Tolstoy for her understanding of the artist's personal fulfillment. According to Tolstoy, whom Willa Cather accepts without question, man is made up of a number of appetites which, because they are rapacious in their demand for satisfaction, are evil; and the activities into which man is driven for their satisfaction are likewise evil.

But within some miraculously chosen individuals a divine ideal is born which can be satisfied only by the starvation of all other appetites. Through the satisfaction of this new craving, actually the desire for artistic expression, comes man's greatest happiness; "for happiness lies in ceasing to be and to cause being, because the thing revealed to us is dearer than any existence our appetites can ever get for us." It is this humanistically oriented belief which lies behind the prosaic statement she made toward the end of her artistic life. "When people ask me if it has been a hard or easy road I always answer with the quotation, 'The end is nothing, the road is all.' . . . I have never faced the typewriter with the thought that one more chore had to be done." Writing, then, could never be a chore, for it represents creation and creation represents the greatest possible human happiness for the creator.

If we accept sociological and historical, analytical and psychological complexities as the indispensable tools of modern criticism, then Willa Cather is not a literary critic. She herself was actively disaffected by contemporary criticism, believing that the last of the great American critics was Henry James, and the last of the good ones W. C. Brownell and H. L. Mencken. She would deny, moreover, that criticism must be nurtured in an intellectually disciplined atmosphere. The critic, she would maintain, need have only the work of art open before him; after study, there is then established between the critic and the object of criticism either personal rapport or personal hostility.

The limitations of such a critical standard and method are self-evident. For one thing, this concept ignores the continuity binding together like works of art; it lacks historical perspective. For another thing, it tacitly rejects the tremendous impact made upon writers by the sociological and economic upheavals of the last century. Here, to be sure, the repudiation is deliberate, for Miss Cather—theoretically, at any rate— viewed literature as divorced entirely from economic and industrial forces; but the denial does not carry its own validation. Finally, she refused in her subjective quasi-criticism to employ the findings of the new school of analytical psychology fostered by Freud, Jung, and their followers. For Miss Cather, people were seldom psychologically complex; they were good or evil; they were motivated by creative "desire" or they were not. Apart from limitations of approach and method, her findings are too dependent on the particularized response of the reader. Once she arrived at a subjective critical decision, it was done and there was no room for debate. She frequently indulged in personal intentionalism, imposing her own standards and preconceptions upon a piece of literature not her own. This kind of fallacious evaluation allowed her to judge writers and even whole schools of writing in terms of her own methodology and aims of composition.

But Willa Cather's position as a critic is by no means negative. Endowed with unusual sensitivity, she read with the taste and shrewd discrimination which, after all, constitute a large part of the critic's talent. Her judgment of literary figures and even trends in modern fiction is for the most part unerring, despite the instinctive manner by which she reached her conclusions. Most salient of all, however, Miss Cather's criticism is significant for the light it throws on her own work, her methods of composition, and her ultimate aims.

It is not uncharitable to place her efforts at the end of a long line of nineteenth-century belletristic criticism, which managed to survive and perpetuate itself until the end of the first World War. Even if she arrived at her critical faith without conscious reliance on her predecessors, she becomes associated with one of the most significant theories in literary criticism, that which insists the imagination has a sympathetic capacity for identifying itself with given objects. As a concept, it had been hinted at by Aristotle and other classical theorists. But it had its modern roots in the eighteenth century and was brought to its fullest development in the nineteenth, especially by William Hazlitt with some assistance from John Keats's notion of "negative capability." And toward the end of the century, Theodor Lipps, the German esthetician, revitalized and codified it as *Einfühlung* or "empathy." She herself, whose sympathies "slid back into yesterday's seven thousand years," would not object to informal identification with that movement. At the same time she would object to the mere appellation of critic, for she said succinctly and positively at one time: "When God has made a man a creator, it is a mistake for him to turn critic. It is rather an insult to God, and certainly a very great wrong to man."

6 ON THE COMPOSITION
OF A NOVEL

EVEN WHEN Miss Cather attempted in her criticism to elucidate certain technical mannerisms or to trace creative lines which she had followed, she seemed to fall back in spite of herself upon a language of subjective response. For all the eloquence of her explanations, they frequently elude clear definition. This haziness—if such it may be called—was unavoidable, for she was reflecting rather than asserting, and her subject matter was of such private intensity that it simply did not lend itself to a critical rationale. Miss Cather, it seems to us, invited the sympathy of her readers to both her fiction and her critical explanations. She took for granted a measure of kindred feeling, assuming that in the absence of a perhaps intuitive understanding of her aims no definition or objective enlargement could instill the emotions which she portrayed and hoped to share. This is by no means a suggestion that she was indifferent to her audience, but she was well aware that neither she nor any other author could hope to reach all readers. The fact, however, that she has attained such wide circulation is rather convincing evidence that she succeeded in communicating and sharing her feelings without resort to an essentially objective rhetoric. Terms such as "desire," "yearning," and "spirit" may seem elusive when attempts are made to compress them into terse definitions. They are abundantly clear in narrative context, however, generally eliciting the response of feeling when incisive statement is inadequate.

For these reasons Willa Cather's critical attitudes must frequently be "felt," or reasoned with some difficulty, even when she sets them down in the shape of pronouncements. As an example, she once described the texture of *Shadows on the Rock* as "mainly anacoluthon," but she did not bother to connect this term specifically to her novel. She knew what she meant, and she assumed that anyone interested enough would establish the relationship for himself.

Classically, the purpose of anacoluthon was to evoke an emotional or moral effect through a temporary suspension of completeness—that is, like a series of minor suspenses—within the individual actions of the principal framework. Once identified, the term has great bearing on the working out of *Shadows*. The seeming disjunction implied by the term she attained by initiating episodes and then disclosing their resolutions in subsequent appropriate phases of the novel. It is an example of Miss Cather's critical density, her tendency to put undefined or meagerly defined theories into esthetic practice. Anacoluthon as a critical term had particular meaning for her. She suggested it as the basis of the form she used, but was not concerned with pursuing it as a critical academic matter. And it is not of any great consequence to the general reader for whom *Shadows* is primarily a warm, imaginative experience. The critic whose reading of the novel is somewhat more formal, however, seizes gladly upon the bare hint and finds his task of explication facilitated and enriched.

Occasional hints of this nature are helpful to a deeper understanding of Miss Cather's aims and accomplishments, particularly since her major novels represent unobtrusive experiments with concept and form. *The Professor's House*, as we have already seen, was cast in the approximation of the musical sonata, and other novels were worked out according to subtle patterns that might slip by unheeded without some casual word from the author. Sometimes, however, the experimentation is compounded of elements which Miss Cather has not noted directly. The wells of unconscious memory, perhaps, autobiographical incidents, former acquaintances, travel, even diligent research in libraries—all may play their part in a novel, absorbed silently and artistically into a created masterpiece. Then it becomes valuable to turn to a confidante or a chapter of biography or a historian in an effort to work out answers that may broaden one's reading. A novel such as *Death Comes for the Archbishop* is an unusually engrossing subject for detailed study, providing a synthesis of Willa Cather's attitudes—toward the frontier and the past—her moral sensitivity, and above all—at least for the purpose of this chapter—her manner of composition. To follow the delicate trail of the *Archbishop* from its unconscious beginnings to its auspicious appearance is to become aware of the summing up of a distinguished talent, mind, and moral agent.

ii

For Willa Cather as for Henri Bergson, whom she admired, literary creation—that is, the choice of subject matter and the technique enforced by it—was an "intuitive" rather than an "intellectual" process. When she stated in an introduction to *Alexander's Bridge* that the novelist dealing with material that is deeply a part of his conscious and unconscious being has "less and less power of choice about the moulding of it," she was expressing her belief in esthetic inevitability. Great art, because it centered in the moods of the self, is an outpouring of intimate associations; and because all art as Miss Cather understood it is emotively representational, it is compulsive in its need for release. Certainly in the *Archbishop* she was engaged with familiar material, or as she would say, her "own material," which she knew and lived instinctively. Yet she was incapable of rendering personal experience or emotion literally, and she always sought new ways of communicating. That is, experimentation with form was as integral to her as was the moral substance of the themes she wished to narrate.

Of all her many novels the *Archbishop* was the most candidly and deliberately experimental. Preferring the term "narrative" to that of "novel," she shaped the *Archbishop* as a legend in the medieval tradition of Christian saints' lore, and of self-imposed necessity she eschewed all obvious dramatic treatment. Instead of the rising action and complexities which propel more conventional novels, Miss Cather drew scenes of a simplicity characteristic of her general practice and gave equal stress to each. The incidents, then, she selected with exceeding care, not for the evocation of suspense but for a cumulative effect.

It was toward this end that she integrated the details of theme, plot, characterization, and mood which make up the novel. For many years, she admitted in an essay "On Death Comes for the Archbishop," she had been tantalized by the possibility of emulating a pictorial model in prose. Since her student days, when she had first seen the Puvis de Chavannes frescoes of the life of Saint Geneviève, she had hoped to write "something without accent, with none of the artificial elements of composition." As in the Golden Legend, where the commonplace events of saints' lives receive the same emphasis as their martyrdoms, she wished to show how all human experiences—noble and trivial—project from "one supreme spiritual experience . . . The essence of such writing," she said, "is not to hold the note, not to use an incident for all there is in it—but to touch and pass on." In adapting technical treatment to subject matter and in selecting locale and situation, she was affected by numerous determinants—her theory of literary genesis, her personal experiences and friendships, her readings. All these factors entered significantly into the composition of the *Archbishop*. And though we have neither space nor need to explore every condition which led to the publication of the novel, we propose to sample those most pertinent to its being.

Like all of Willa Cather's novels of the frontier, the *Archbishop* allegorizes the individual's withdrawal from cold reality toward sanctified purpose. Believing that time and space are irrelevant to the pioneer impulse, she merely extended her focus to create the two major historical novels, the *Archbishop* and *Shadows on the Rock*. And, of course, she had previously intimated the broadening of her interests in the idyllic interludes about the cliff dwellers in both *The Song of the Lark* and *The Professor's House*. In her historical imperative nothing is superfluous but that which is temporal or material. When she writes about prehistoric aborigines, seventeenth-century Canadians, or nineteenth-century priests, Mexicans, and Indians, she does not look for the surprising oddities of custom and event which distinguish particular eras but for the profundities of faith which unite all men of all time. Each frontier becomes a stronghold of private need, but it is a need which widely disparate men have experienced and satisfied. The broad thesis of Miss Cather's frontier philosophy is probably best served by the *Archbishop*, for here she was encouraged to speak out directly for religious principles that not only were hers by choice but that in their prevalence brought a beautiful purpose to a country ripe for their influence. When she wrote *Shadows on the Rock* she was in effect reiterating the judgments of the earlier *Archbishop* and had nothing essential to add to them. Through the course of her novels, it might be said, she was developing creative strength and collecting a store of knowledge as though in anticipation of the *Archbishop*.

She long cherished an affection for the Southwest and its mythology even before her first visit in 1912. Considerably before this date and undoubtedly long before the idea of the *Archbishop* came to her, she had become intrigued by a legend which tells of how a tribe of Indians, a thousand or more years ago, were isolated from their home on Katzímo, a vast New Mexican mesa-top, forbidding and impregnable to hostile Indians. This people, according to the legend, farmed the fertile desert at the foot of their *mesa encantada* or enchanted mesa. One summer while almost all the members of the tribe were harvesting, a fierce storm destroyed the sole passage leading to the summit of their island of rock. Hopelessly cut off, the tribe moved on to Ácoma mesa, where they established their now traditional home.

From these materials, Miss Cather created her short story "The Enchanted Bluff" (1909), an interesting forerunner of her spiritual interpretation of the Ácoma mesa in the *Archbishop*. Although vague in its outlines, this early story is yet significant in that it conveys some of the sense of yearning and seeking which gives tonality to the Ácoma incident in the *Archbishop*. When Miss Cather set down her story, the Katzímo legend was already something of a *cause célèbre*. The controversy over its authenticity, engaged in by Charles F. Lummis, Professor William Libbey, and Frederick Webb Hodge, had flared in newspapers, magazines, and scientific publications. That Miss Cather was familiar with the quarrel is evident from "The Enchanted Bluff," in which she has her characters prepare to scale Katzímo by a unique method used by Professor Libbey. At the same time she repudiated Libbey's skepticism, accepting the authenticity of the legend as it was proposed by Lummis and Hodge. Thus she took sides in an issue which at the time had no immediacy for her except that of imaginative curiosity; she had not seen Katzímo and was not destined to do so until 1926.

Almost from the beginning, then, Miss Cather was "teased" by the magic of the Southwest. While she and her brother Douglass were still children in Nebraska, they had talked of exploring the Southwest together, even as the youngsters in "The Enchanted Bluff" dreamed of a similar exploit. Then in 1912 she visited Douglass in Winslow, Arizona, where he was employed by the Santa Fe Railroad. Her first trip to this storied country became the realization of a childhood dream, and she was imbued with the satisfaction expressed by Father Joseph in the *Archbishop*: "To fulfill the dreams of one's youth; that is the best that can happen to a man." She remained several months and, according to Miss Lewis, "a whole new landscape—not only a physical landscape, but a landscape of the mind, peopled with wonderful imaginings, opened out before her." She visited Arizona again in 1914, although it was not until 1915 that she made her first lengthy sojourn in New Mexico, and she returned in 1916 once more.

Ardently attracted to the natural splendor of the territory and desirous of understanding people such as she had never known before, she did not concern herself with the possibilities of literary exploitation. Only after her love of the land had matured and become implanted with its significance did she put into words the *Archbishop*, her most profound and in some ways her most meaningful novel. Its technical conception came to her appropriately enough when she returned to New Mexico after a nine-year absence, and it was seemingly inevitable. In a single evening during that summer while she was stopping at Santa Fe, as she often said, the idea of the *Archbishop* emerged essentially as she afterward wrote it.

That Miss Cather should have been so long in the concrete formulation of the novel fits in admirably with her theory of literary genesis. In her ennobled view of the writer's function, as she once postulated in an essay on Sarah Orne Jewett, a merely good story is not enough and the process by which superlative art is achieved is very different from that which supports mere competence. Hard pressed as usual to define a concept, she concluded the main characteristics to be "persistence, survival, recurrence in the writer's mind." Only those things and events which have long tantalized the mind, "when they do at last get themselves rightly put down, make a very much higher order of writing, and a much more costly, than the most vivid and vigorous transfer of immediate impressions." Never one to settle consciously for the second best, Miss Cather had long given herself over to this kind of deliberate—taxing yet the most satisfying —process before she could write the *Archbishop*.

Significantly, she made the above observation just before her crucial trip to New Mexico in 1925. She returned from New Mexico to Jaffrey, New Hampshire, in the autumn of that year and, almost at a sitting it seemed to Miss Lewis, she wrote the introduction to the novel. All that winter in New York she continued to work on the *Archbishop* happily and with calm assurance. But as the novel progressed she realized that there were many things and places she needed to learn about, many details that she wished to verify. And so once more, in July of 1926, she went to her beloved New Mexico.

These trips to the Southwest not only made concrete for her the physical landscape, but they also introduced her to people and experiences invaluable for the genesis of the novel. For example, on her first trip to Arizona she met a friend of her brother, the Reverend Father T. Connolly, the Catholic priest in Winslow. Frequently Willa Cather accompanied him on his long drives to distant parishes, and they talked about the country and the people, and about the old Spanish and Indian legends that still survived. Later she met Father Haltermann, a Belgian priest, who lived with his sister in the parsonage behind the church at Santa Cruz, New Mexico. This hearty, bearded clergyman, whose duties among his eighteen Indian missions had brought him close familiarity with the native traditions, endeared himself to the novelist through his animation and intellectual acuteness.

Of these priests who devotedly served in the Southwest, Miss Lewis recalls that her friend was impressed by the "tact and good sense so many of them had with their Mexican parishioners, and the cultivation of mind that gave them a long historical perspective on the life in these remote little settlements." Indeed, from Father Haltermann and his colleagues, among others, Miss Cather learned about many of the religious and secular traditions of the area, and about the simple and yet devout Catholicism of their parishioners. Observant and retentive, in this fashion she gleaned for her book details that became almost as much a part of her as if she had experienced them at first hand. From her church friends she also discovered many of the unofficial and intimate details about the construction and financing of the Cathedral of Santa Fe which appear in the *Archbishop*.

Further details of the novel owe their realistic presentation to the author's acquaintance with several Indians native to the region. Foremost among these, Tony Luhan made an immediate impression upon Miss Cather. Her companion describes him as "a splendid figure, over six feet tall, with a noble head and a dignified carriage; there was great simplicity and kindness in his voice and manner." Arrayed in his purple blanket and silver bracelets, this commanding individual accompanied Miss Cather to some of the most remote and barely accessible Mexican villages in the Cimarrón Mountains. He revealed much to her about the country that an outsider could not have discovered alone. And though he was characteristically taciturn, his infrequent conversation was wise in content and poetic in quality. Tony in all likelihood became the model for Eusabio, the Navajo Indian portrayed in the *Archbishop* as "extremely tall . . . with a face like a Roman general's of Republican times. He . . . wore a blanket of the finest wool and design. His arms, under the loose sleeves of his shirt, were covered with silver bracelets . . ." Like Tony Luhan, Eusabio, wearing an expression of "religious" seriousness, "talked little, ate little, slept anywhere, preserved a countenance open and warm, and . . . he had unfailing good manners."

Associations of this kind reconfirmed Willa Cather's faith in human simplicity and her detestation of artfulness. The fact that in her sophisticated times such fundamental piety and natural courtesy could thrive was a further testimony of the greatness of the frontier spirit. The basic truths she had sought so long came to life for her in the desert, and the certainty that they existed enabled her to inspirit her novel.

The *Archbishop*, like her other frontier novels, was an intensely personal experience, in conception and creative growth. It was not so much a piece of fiction —a mere story—as it was her vision of life and attitude toward truth. The point at which actuality and invention merged was invisible, for except in necessary mechanical details Miss Cather herself made no such arbitrary distinction. Her experiences of life were the book and the book was her life. Like a great metaphor, the novel became a subtle evaluation of her attitudes and felt emotions.

Even as she drew upon knowledge from individuals to express a philosophy and mood, she drew also from events which she experienced in the Southwest. Every year in Santa Fe, for instance, a procession honoring the Virgin commemorated De Vargas' recapture of the city for Spain in 1692. Recorded historical details of the procession were of course available to Miss Cather, but the fact that she had witnessed the procession and reacted emotionally to its spiritual implications was even more important than her readings. In the novel she directs her focus to the image of the Virgin Mother carried through the streets by the participants. She concentrates on utterly simple elements to describe the love which the Mexicans cherished for the holy figure. Although this incident is organically inseparable from the sympathetic portrayal of religious love which is the secondary thematic concern of the novel, Miss Cather pauses briefly to inject a few lines of exposition for the fuller clarification of her meaning. She has Father Latour reflect that the poor Mexicans were expressing themselves as part of a spiritual tradition. After all, the Virgin Mother had been celebrated in great art, music, and cathedral architecture. Even "before Her years on earth, in the long twilight between the Fall and the Redemption, the pagan sculptors were always trying to achieve the image of a goddess who should yet be a woman." Concerned with the continuum of tradition, Willa Cather implies a spiritual if not a doctrinal link between heathen and Christian rites. The question she raises is not one of judgment upon idolatry, for example, but of sympathy with a universal religious need. The fulfillment of that need is basically more important than the crude manner of its fulfillment. Miss Cather no less than Latour was touched by this sign of devotion, and she translated her experience into a brilliant scene.

Other events in the *Archbishop*, such as that related in the chapter "The Lonely Road to Mora," have autobiographical bases. One of the most striking portions of the novel, the chapter describing Father Latour's introduction to Ácoma, reveals Miss Cather's typical fusion of personal experience, interpretation, and random reading. From her own visit to the mesa she stored up an impression which has been recorded by Miss Lewis: "As we passed the Mesa Encantada (the Enchanted Bluff) we stopped for a long time to look up at it. A great cloud-mesa hung over it. It looked lonely and mysterious and remote, as if it were far distant in time—thousands of years away." The same experience emerges thus in the *Archbishop*:

Ever afterward the Bishop remembered his first ride to Ácoma as his introduction to the mesa country. One thing which struck him at once was that every mesa was duplicated by a cloud mesa, like a reflection, which lay motionless above it or moved slowly up from behind it. These cloud formations seemed to be always

there, however hot and blue the sky. Sometimes they
were flat terraces, ledges of vapour; sometimes they
were dome-shaped, or fantastic, like the tops of silvery
pagodas, rising one above another, as if an oriental city
lay directly behind the rock. The great tables of granite
set down in an empty plain were inconceivable without
their attendant clouds, which were a part of them, as
the smoke is part of the censer, or the foam of the wave.

Fittingly, the sensitive priest is made to describe a
phenomenon which invites not only a poetic response
but a religious one as well. Only a person from a cul-
tured background would be aware of the exotic naturalism, and only a person of strong religious inclina-
tions would at such a time think of Catholic ritual.
Willa Cather, sharing Latour's refinement and some
of his inner repose, was able to elaborate this natural
wonder as she did.

But if much of her knowledge of Ácoma and the
nearby Mesa Encantada was informed by acute observation, it was probably derived also from historical
and quasi-literary sources. For some of her factual
details she was indebted to Charles F. Lummis' vol-
umes and to Twitchell's treatment of New Mexican
history.* From Lummis especially she derived her
references to Fray Juan Ramirez, "a great missionary,
who laboured on the Rock of Ácoma for twenty years
or more," his mule trail, "the only path by which a
burro can ascend the mesa, and which is still called
'El Camino del Padre,'" his massive church with its
beams drawn from the San Mateo Mountains. There
are further allusions—drawn from Lummis and
Twitchell—to the military invincibility of the Ácomas,
their single defeat at the hands of the Spaniards, the

* *Mesa, Cañon and Pueblo* (New York and London, 1925), pp.
264 ff.; *Some Strange Corners of Our Country* (New York, 1915),
pp. 262 ff.; Ralph Emerson Twitchell, *Leading Facts of New Mexico
History* (Cedar Rapids, Iowa, 1912), I, 199–200.

picture of St. Joseph and its magical rain-producing properties.

These real details, verifiable as they are in recorded sources, lend the novel a comfortable verisimilitude. Empowered, as it were, by the authority of history, Miss Cather could create a reasonable sense of the historical past. But the chronicle format was after all a mere convenience, since her purpose was larger than that of decoration and the reconstruction of past events. In short, although her specific details are vital to the narrative frame, they are far less important than the intuited significance of the Ácoma mesa. Her purpose, having to do with the interior essence rather than the exterior fact, is served through her particular understanding and symbolic transference of the rock in which she synthesizes everything she means by sanctuary. Latour is again granted the imaginative intelligence that makes him her spokesman:

All this plain, the Bishop gathered, had once been the scene of a periodic man-hunt; these Indians, born in fear and dying by violence for generations, had at last taken this leap away from the earth, and on that rock had found the hope of all suffering and tormented creatures—safety. They came down to the plain to hunt and to grow their crops, but there was always a place to go back to. If a band of Navajos were on the Ácoma's trail, there was still one hope; if he could reach his rock—Sanctuary! On the winding stone stairway up the cliff, a handful of men could keep off a multitude. The rock of Ácoma had never been taken by a foe but once,—by Spaniards in armour. It was very different from a mountain fastness; more lonely, more stark and grim, more appealing to the imagination. The rock, when one came to think of it, was the utmost expression of human need; even mere feeling yearned for it; it was the highest comparison of loyalty in love and friendship. Christ Himself had used that comparison for the disciple to whom He gave the Keys of His Church. And the Hebrews of the Old Testament, always being carried captive into foreign lands,—their rock was an idea of God, the only thing their conquerors could not take from them.

In the chapter as a whole she has refined and intensified a great natural phenomenon through artistry; but she has also projected a deeply personal commitment, expressing her inner state through a peculiarly apt religious symbolism, with its mingling of the pagan and the Christian. Her analysis of the symbolic meaning of the Ácoma mesa leaves no doubt in the reader's mind. Nor is it an isolated—hence eccentric—symbol, for in slightly altered form it appears repeatedly in *The Song of the Lark*, *The Professor's House*, and *Shadows on the Rock*. Consistency like this is synonymous with the "persistence, survival, recurrence in the writer's mind" that she held to be the substance of lasting art.

The genesis of the *Archbishop*, finally, appears to owe much historically and philosophically to the many source works which Miss Cather read. Michael Williams in an article for *Commonweal* rightly pointed out that in order to write her book she had read and studied a great deal. Miss Lewis, who was in a position to know, has substantiated Williams' remark with specific observations on the novelist's avid researches. Among the books she read were the Rev. J. H. Defouri's *Historical Sketch of the Catholic Church in New Mexico* (San Francisco, 1887); J. B. Salpointe's *Soldiers of the Cross* (Banning, Calif., 1898); the *Catholic Encyclopedia*; the works of Lummis; Bandelier's *The Gilded Man*; the Rev. Francis Palou's *Life of Ven. Padre Junípero Serra* (San Francisco, 1884); Twitchell's *Leading Facts of New Mexico History*; and the translation by G. P. Winship (in the 14th annual report of the Bureau of American Ethnology) of Castenada's *The Coronado Expedition.*

Although Miss Cather does not openly acknowledge her use of any of these books, her indebtedness becomes readily apparent in certain details, a character sketch or two, and casual historical allusions. To one volume, however, she was overtly indebted. This was *The Life of the Right Reverend Joseph P. Machebeuf* (Pueblo, Colorado, 1908) by William Joseph Howlett, a priest who had worked with Father Machebeuf in Denver. It was from this volume that she drew most of her biographical data about Father Latour (in real life Archbishop Lamy) and Father Joseph Vaillant (Father Machebeuf). Mrs. Bennett relates that after the publication of the *Archbishop,* when the author had forgotten to mention Father Howlett's book, the priest gently reminded her of the oversight. Contritely, Miss Cather sent an open letter to *Commonweal* explaining how she came to write the novel and crediting Father Howlett as a source. At the same time she sent him an autographed copy of the *Archbishop,* apologized for her omission, and asked his blessing. As further acknowledgment, she gave autographed copies of the book to the St. Thomas Seminary in Denver, Father Machebeuf's diocese, and again admitted her debt. Later, in her essay on the novel, she stated that in the work of Father Howlett "at last I found what I wanted to know about how the country and the people of New Mexico seemed to those first missionary priests from France." There can be no question, then, of the esteem in which she held the basic printed source of the *Archbishop.*

iii

The reading which shaped the component elements of the novel must not be confused with rigid, unimaginative paraphrase. She molded her materials rather according to artistic necessity. To achieve an aura of realism—and it must be remembered that Miss Cather's technical intention of emulating a legend allowed for no more than a peripheral reconstruction of facts—she borrowed from her reading seemingly casual historical references. To bolster her primary purpose—thematic reevocation of pioneer striving, its success and in some instances its failure— she gleaned from her reading a series of characterizations and contrasting character sketches. Her purposeful selection of characters, further, made necessary the delineation of an appropriate religious backdrop for their activities. For this end also, her reading equipped her with essential details, and it sharpened her insight. All these materials she manipulated to fuse a relatively sophisticated Catholicism with the ancient paganism of Indian rites on the one hand, and with primitive Mexican devotion to Catholicism on the other.

The least important of Willa Cather's borrowings may be found in her use of historical facts, which she characteristically subordinated to the novel's structural totality. Since reportorial accuracy was distant from her aims, she consciously developed a power of selectivity supported, as she herself admits in "The Novel Démeublé," by Mérimée's estimate of Gogol. Choosing from among the innumerable aspects of nature, the former had said, is a much more difficult literary achievement than impartial observation and literal rendering. Consequently, Miss Cather never introduces facts as such or for their own sakes. And rather than linger over them she mentions them briefly and without pedantry. Twice in the course of the *Archbishop*, for instance, she touches on the massacre of Governor Bent, which occurred in 1847. This readily verifiable event she could have encountered in any history of New Mexico.

In all likelihood, however, Miss Cather based her

account on the more familiar volume by Father Howlett. He mentioned (p. 227) a generally circulated
rumor that Father Martinez had an active part in the
uprising by Indians and Mexicans at Taos when, on
January 19, 1847, the Governor and a number of
Americans and Mexicans loyal to him were slain. Martinez "at least shared with the Indians and Mexicans
in hatred for the Americans, and, in their ignorance of
events and conditions outside their little valley, they
imagined they were but beginning a patriotic war
which would result in freeing their country from the
foreigner, who was supposed to be an enemy to their
race and to their religion."

More forthright than most of the other chroniclers
of the affair, Father Howlett was cautiously convinced
of Martinez's guilt, even though a United States tri-
bunal absolved the padre of direct complicity. Working from such unresolved hints, Miss Cather in her
first mention of the massacre is but vaguely allusive,
mentioning by name neither the Governor nor the
supposed leader of the revolt. Early in the *Archbishop*
she records dispassionately: "Only last year the Indian
pueblo of San Fernandez de Taos murdered and
scalped the American Governor and some dozen other
whites. The reason they did not scalp their Padre, was
that their Padre was one of the leaders of the rebellion and himself planned the massacre." Convinced of
the priest's guilt, she merely set the stage and then
temporarily abandoned it.

One hundred and thirty pages later, when she mentioned the affair a second time, she was like Father
Howlett much more explicit, identifying by name the
priest who engaged her attention in one of the central
incidents of the novel: "It was common talk that
Padre Martinez had instigated the revolt of the Taos
Indians five years ago, when Bent, the American Gov-

ernor, and a dozen white men were murdered and scalped. Seven of the Taos Indians had been tried before a military court and hanged for the murder, but no attempt had been made to call the plotting priest to account. Indeed, Padre Martinez had managed to profit considerably by the affair." Her first allusion broadly suggests the hazards of pioneering under the zealous but subverted state of religious belief which prevailed in New Mexico. The second allusion occurs much later, after she has introduced Father Martinez as an antagonistic character. Now, when she wishes to expose the priest's ruthless, materialistic aspirations, she makes concrete his complicity in the massacre. For her purposes, indeed, she does not allow herself even Father Howlett's charitable suspension of absolute judgment. Miss Cather, it would appear, accepted Father Howlett's suspicion, and then manipulated the evidence to conform to the shape of her novel.

Father Martinez himself acts as her spokesman in another use of historical data. Conversing with Father Latour, the renegade priest comments on the historically famous revolt of Popé in 1680, "when all the Spaniards were killed or driven out, and there was not one European left alive north of El Paso del Norte." He boasts that Popé, a San Juan Indian, operated from Taos. Once again this particular fact is common knowledge, although the fullest account of it probably available to Miss Cather appears in H. H. Bancroft's *History of New Mexico and Arizona* (San Francisco, 1889). Bancroft emphasizes, as Miss Cather does, that the revolt originated among the pueblo communities in their effort to rid themselves of foreign domination. Father Martinez's reference to the Popé rebellion is thoroughly consistent with Miss Cather's characterization of the unruly priest. By implication Popé becomes the archetype of Martinez; by indirection Father La-

tour is being warned that Martinez, likewise operating
out of Taos, will not brook foreign interference.

The threat veiled in the reference to Popé is, indeed, all the more sinister for its obliqueness, dangerously enhancing Martinez's cool warning that future
European meddling will be met with violence. He says,
"You are among barbarous people, my Frenchman,
between two savage races. The dark things forbidden
by your Church are a part of Indian religion. You cannot introduce French fashions here." Vastly effective,
this entire episode is a crucial part of the novel. The
parallel between historical reality and Miss Cather's
theme is so close that her embroidery is imperceptible
and the conflicts stand forth with dramatic rightness.

Many of her historical facts Miss Cather selected
because they convey her faith in the human longing
for sanctuary. Symbolically expressive of this kind of
yearning is her interpretation of the Navajos' struggles:
their slaughter by white troops at the supposed impregnable Cañon de Chelly, their enforced exile to the
Bosque Redondo, and their eventual return to the
lands of their fathers. As she manipulates these historical incidents, they take on a mystical, religious significance. She imagines the canyon a spiritual fortress,
where the Navajos "believed their old gods dwelt . . .
the very heart and centre of their life." The Indians'
exclusion from the fastness she sees as their tragic loss
of sanctuary, without which they must perish physically
as well as spiritually. The Navajos' ultimate return
becomes for Miss Cather a presage that genuine faith,
and this not necessarily Christian, will assert itself
against base aspirations and abuse.

No authoritative work on the religion and mythology of the Navajos supports her proposition that their
gods dwelt in the canyon. But what is apparent
is that the struggles of the Navajos have for her a mys-

tic significance comparable to those of the Ácomas. Her visit to the Cañon de Chelly in 1925, enhanced by romantic legends of its supposed inaccessibility, gave shape to her interpretation. The traditional Navajo nostalgia for homeland, poignantly stated in many of their commonly sung chants, complemented further her literary needs and spiritual bent.

Historical eras widely separated in time challenged rather than inhibited Miss Cather in her artistic constructions. Frequently this separation afforded her a basis for believing that man's problems are eternally reiterated, and that they are distinguished only by external details of history. For her only the inner meaning is the essential one, enabling her boldly to link events which had occurred centuries apart, in order that the early occurrence should serve as a parable for the later one. This is the kind of spiritual union which she achieves in recounting the decline of the Pecos tribe from the splendor it had enjoyed in the sixteenth century to its pathetic moribundity in the nineteenth.

Through the sensitive eyes of Father Latour, Miss Cather witnesses the contemporary atmosphere of death and decay—"empty houses ruined by weather and now scarcely more than piles of earth and stone." She chose to interpret the process of decay as beginning with Coronado and his men who "set forth . . . on their ill-fated search for the seven golden cities of Quivera, taking with them slaves and concubines from the Pecos people." As she frequently does, she recalls here ideas or events that have long engaged her. Her interest in Coronado and his search for the cities of Quivera had even found its way into *My Ántonia*, where she inserted an unrelated discussion of the explorer's activities. The waste begun by the white man in the sixteenth century culminated in the ravages of the modern white man, whose civilized diseases—she wrote in the *Archbishop*—"were the real causes of the shrink-age of the tribe."

Drawing her account—particularly the description of the Pecos pueblo—from several nineteenth-century sources, she establishes a series of contrasts as a *memento mori*. She offers first the contrast between the thriving Cicuyé of the sixteenth century and the dying Pecos pueblo of the nineteenth. She then places against the strong Indians of Cicuyé the yet stronger Spaniards of Coronado who in their hungry search for gold and new worlds were destroyed, as she sees it, by the dis-sipation of a noble dream into the lust of materialistic desire. Through the adroitly analogical fusion of his-torical time, Miss Cather accentuates the perpetual conflict between spiritual serenity and greedy turbu-lence. In so doing she accommodates one of her favorite themes: that sophisticated civilizations are ac-quisitive, and that materialism is a betrayal of man's spiritual wants, leading to negation and destruction. The *Archbishop* brings together and stabilizes in its most acute rendering a theme which breaks down temporal barriers. A Spaniard in armor or a modern money-lender are equally the poorer for the dislocation of inner cause; and a Tom Outland or a Father Latour are equally the richer for the reverence of ideal values. Accidents of time and place are merely sobering re-minders that in a world of seeming flux there is always one immutable point.

Characterization is of primary importance in the *Archbishop*, for Miss Cather relied strongly upon her principals to communicate the concept of the pioneer quest within the superficially simple format of the legend. Once again recorded history gave her sound, convenient models for her human portraits. But only for the outlines of events and people did she go to sources, and these outlines she enriched with her deliberate imagination. From the works of Howlett and Lummis she derived the patterns of her major characters, Latour, Joseph, Martinez, and Chavez, making each representative of a pioneer type and yet as individualized as it is possible for a type to be. All are motivated by an intangible, spiritual seeking. Fathers Latour and Joseph undergo a metamorphosis from the functional, historical treatment of Howlett's biography, where Latour (Lamy) especially is an incompletely and nebulously drawn personality. In Miss Cather's hands they are contrasted gently, even lyrically, as symbolic of the complete flowering of the pioneer type. Although Latour and Joseph are impelled by comparable spiritual motives, they are constituted differently. Father Latour, an aristocrat and philosopher, is strengthened by an introspective power of love for all individuals; in his rare moments of uncertainty he is never torn by doubts about the sanctity of his mission but rather by fears of his own capacity for love. Father Joseph complements his friend by his practicality. Lacking his superior's philosophical penetration, he drives onward by bustling activity and never-questioning acceptance of his mission and capacities. For several reasons Father Latour remains a comparatively shadowy figure throughout the novel, while Father Joseph becomes more and more realistic.

By his very nature Father Joseph is dynamic and essentially not "intellectual" as is Latour. Howlett, moreover, concentrates mainly on Joseph, and hence, it might reasonably be expected, gives Miss Cather a more tangible working model. Finally, she deliberately idealized Latour as her representation of the esthetically refined qualities of the pioneer search. As Father Joseph evaluates the life and work of the Archbishop, he reflects: "Perhaps it pleased Him to grace the beginning of a new era and a vast new diocese by a fine personality. And perhaps, after all, something would remain through the years to come; some ideal, or memory, or legend." From the mosaic of scenes through which Miss Cather achieves finally a total impression (rather, perhaps, than a portrait which connotes an exact or full reconstruction) of the man, the reader carries away the belief that for Miss Cather the memorable quality of Father Latour is the essence, and that while physical substance like Joseph's has great charm and inspiration his ultimate purpose is to carry out the beautiful designs promulgated by his Bishop.

Against these two monumental figures Miss Cather sets up Father Martinez, drawn from Howlett, and Don Manuel Chavez, from Lummis. Both characters, historically and fictionally, have a passionate desire to safeguard their pioneer frontier against the inroads of the people whom they regard as "foreigners," as despoilers of the "wild land" and the old order. But both are made to represent the pioneer of warped aims who falls short of complete realization because of the flaw which renders him incapable of love. And because both are trying to preserve the unpreservable, they must be destroyed, figuratively if not literally. As Miss Cather says of Father Martinez: "The American occupation meant the end of men like himself. He was a man of the old order . . . and his day was over." Somewhat reminiscent of Captain Forrester, at least conceptually, Martinez and Chavez are admirable dramatic foils to Latour and his positive idealism. That history could provide Miss Cather with such dynamically probable contrasts is a token of her ability to weigh human values, for discoveries such as these could come only with discrimination and with esthetic-moral sensitivity.

Without overestimating the importance of historical sources to the *Archbishop*—for, as we have repeatedly indicated, reading was no more to the author
than a rough frame is to a sculptor—Father Howlett's
biography gave a firm base to Miss Cather's creative
scheme that a comparison between the two books will
vivify. The large number of details, incidents, and
psychological qualities that she borrowed only to re-
mold may be suggested briefly in the following
catalogue:

	ARCHBISHOP	HOWLETT
Latour's shipwreck at Galveston, the loss of his worldly goods (see also Salpointe, pp. 195–96, and Defouri, p. 33).	p. 18	p. 156
Latour's trip across Texas, his fall in a jump from a wagon (cf. Defouri, p. 33; Salpointe, pp. 195–96).	18	157
Latour's entrance into Santa Fe.	19–20	164
Latour's visit to the Bishop of Durango and its results (cf. Defouri, pp. 34–5; Salpointe, p. 196).	20, 32	178
Father Joseph as a cook.	35	95
Father Joseph's theory of "rest in action."	35	29
Father Joseph's description — his nickname.	37	50, 412–13
Father Joseph's nostalgic reference to his life at Sandusky, his "alleged" hesitance at going any farther into the wilderness.	39–41	152–53
The miracle of the bell.	42 ff.	152–53
The white mules.	52 ff.	216 ff.
Reference to Father Joseph's sister Philomène.	65	*passim*
The coming of the Sisters of Loretto.	78	187
The suspension of Father Gallegos.	118	191–92
Father Joseph's illness, his nickname of "Trompe-la-Mort."	199 ff.	77, 325

	ARCHBISHOP	HOWLETT
The portrait of Padre Martinez, his biography, his excommunication along with Father Luceros (cf. Defouri, p. 125).	193 ff.	227 ff.
Father Joseph's function à fouetter les chats.	164	227 ff.
Father Joseph and the month of May.	202 ff.	22, 25, 33–35
The religious character of the Mexicans—their childishness and their faith.	206 ff.	164
Boyhood and early training of the two priests, Joseph's father as a baker, Joseph's fear of his father and his desire to join the army.	225 ff.	20–21, 26–27
Father Joseph as a beggar (cf. Salpointe, p. 231).	228	300–301
Father Joseph at Rome.	230–31	128–29
Father Latour's recall of Father Joseph from Arizona.	239	256 ff.
The Colorado territory.	246 ff.	256 ff., 286
Father Joseph's wagon.	252	286
Joseph's letters to his brother and sister just before his departure to Colorado.	255–56	286
Father Joseph's accidents.	260	290–310
The begging trip of Father Joseph.	260–63	300–301
The departure of the two young priests for America.	286 ff.	43, 46

For the most part, Miss Cather admits that she follows her basic source faithfully—but not slavishly. On a few occasions, however, she uses Father Howlett's book merely as a jumping-off point; that is, on these occasions she takes merely the kernel of an idea which was suggested by Father Howlett and develops it into a fully detailed incident. For example, one of the most terrifying episodes of the novel—the character and death of Father Lucero—grew out of the following brief statement (*Archbishop*, pp. 164–74; Howlett, p.

228) : "There was a Mexican priest, Mariano de Jesus Lucero, at Arroyo Hondo . . . whom Bishop Lamy was obliged to suspend for irregularities and schismatical tendencies, and who was a former pupil and great friend of Father Martinez. These two now joined their forces and continued their opposition to Bishop Lamy, until he was obliged . . . to pronounce upon them the sentence of excommunication." Similarly, one of the most delightful interludes in the book—"The Bishop Chez Lui"—is based on but a single sentence in a letter of Father Machebeuf to his sister, May 26, 1841: "But Necessity, the mother of invention, has taught us a little of the science of the kitchen, and I am able to give the cook a few lessons." (*Archbishop*, pp. 35 ff.; Howlett, p. 95.)

But this kind of creative expansion is rare for Miss Cather, who usually reproduces situations more closely than in the above instances. Indeed, she will sometimes carry over in an incident not only the ideas, point for point, but much of the language as well.

Archbishop (pp. 202–3):

> He smiled to remember a time long ago, when he was a young curate in Cendre . . . how he had planned a season of special devotion to the Blessed Virgin for May, and how the old priest to whom he was assistant had blasted his hopes by cold disapproval. The old man had come through the Terror, had been trained in the austerity of those days of the persecution of the clergy, and he was not untouched by Jansenism. Young Father Joseph bore his rebuke with meekness, and went sadly to his own chamber. There he took his rosary and spent the entire day in prayer. *"Not according to my desires, but if it is for thy glory, grant me this boon, O Mary, my Hope."* In the evening of that same day the old pastor sent for him, and unsolicited granted him the request he had so sternly denied in the morn-

ing. How joyfully Father Joseph had written all this to
his sister Philomène, then a pupil with the nuns of the
Visitation in their native Riom, begging her to make
him a quantity of artificial flowers for his May altar.
How richly she had responded!—and she rejoiced no
less than he that his May devotions were so largely
attended, especially by the young people of the parish,
in whom a notable increase of piety was manifest.

Howlett (pp. 33–35):

At the approach of the month of May, Father Machebeuf wished to make preparations for May devotions.
This was quite natural for him, but it was a new
departure for the old pastor. It was a novelty! an
innovation! The lingering consequences of Jansenism
were yet visible, and new forms of devotion were not
encouraged by the old pastors. Special devotions to the
Blessed Virgin were of the suspected class. The aged
priest may have partaken of this prejudice . . . but in
any case, he was old, and it is difficult to move old
men. . . .

Not discouraged, however, the young curate went to
his room, and taking his rosary, he spent the rest of
the day in prayer. He prayed, not that he might have
his own way, but that whatever was for the glory of
God might be done, and he felt confident that Mary
would arrange all things for the best.

. . . [The pastor consents to the fete.] . . .

Immediately he wrote to his young sister, who was
a pupil with the nuns of the Visitation in his native
village of Riom, expressing his lively joy and requesting
her to make up and send to him at once a supply of
artificial flowers for his May altar. This she did with
great pleasure, and she was delighted to learn and to
record the fact that the May Devotions were numer-
ously attended and resulted in a great increase of piety
in the parish of Cendre.

Most frequently Miss Cather borrows to preserve the basic situation of an incident, and then elaborates only enough to concretize it, to make it more credible. This is exactly what she has done in her depiction of Father Joseph at Rome. The matter-of-fact account in Father Howlett's book is now enlivened not only by Father Joseph's personality and humor, but by the inclusion of the procedure followed during an audience with the Pope. This last piece of information, she obtained, as she herself admits in "On Death Comes for the Archbishop," from conversations with Father Fitzgerald in Red Cloud, Nebraska.

Archbishop (p. 230):

> Joseph had stayed in Rome for three months, living on about forty cents a day and leaving nothing unseen. He several times asked Mazzucchi to secure him a private audience with the Pope. The secretary liked the missionary from Ohio; there was something abrupt and lively and naïf about him, a kind of freshness he did not often find in the priests who flocked to Rome. So he arranged an interview at which only the Holy Father and Father Vaillant and Mazzucchi were present.
>
> The missionary came in, attended by a chamberlain who carried two great black valises full of objects to be blessed—instead of one, as was customary. After his reception, Father Joseph began to pour out such a vivid account of his missions and brother missionaries, that both the Holy Father and the secretary forgot to take account of time, and the audience lasted three times as long as such interviews were supposed to last. Gregory XVI, that aristocratic and autocratic prelate, who stood so consistently on the wrong side in European politics, and was the enemy of Free Italy, had done more than any of his predecessors to propagate the Faith in remote parts of the world. And here was

a missionary after his own heart. Father Vaillant asked for blessings for himself, his fellow priests, his missions, his Bishop. He opened his big valises like pedlars' packs, full of crosses, rosaries, prayer-books, medals, breviaries, on which he begged more than the usual blessing. The astonished chamberlain had come and gone several times, and Mazzucchi at last reminded the Holy Father that he had other engagements. Father Vaillant caught up his valises himself, the chamberlain not being there at the moment, and thus laden, was bowing himself backward out of the presence, when the Pope rose from his chair and lifted his hand, not in benediction but in salutation, and called out to the departing missionary, as one man to another, *"Corraggio, Americano!"*

Howlett (pp. 128–29):

The great event of his visit was his audience with His Holiness, Pope Gregory XVI, on November 17. The Holy Father was greatly interested in his account of missions, and gave him apostolic benediction for himself and his flock, and Father Machebeuf still further remembered his flock by asking the Pontiff to bless for them the supply of rosaries, crosses and medals with which he had provided himself for the purpose and occasion.

The interview made a lasting impression upon him, and the words of the Holy Father—"Courage, American!"—were never forgotten by Father Machebeuf, who often recalled them afterwards, and always with a strengthening effect.

On another occasion Miss Cather has fused two characterizations from her original source to make up a single, complete portrait, for the fully developed study of Padre Martinez which appears in the *Archbishop* is in reality based upon the combined sketches of Fathers Martinez and Gallegos in Father Howlett's book. The biographical details of Father Martinez's life which Miss Cather presents are historically accurate, but his career as libertine, carouser, Don Juan, and dissipator was suggested rather by Father Howlett's description (pp. 191–92) of Father Gallegos, another priest whom Archbishop Lamy was forced to excommunicate.

> The Padre [Gallegos] was very popular with certain classes in the parish, and these were the rich, the politicians and business men, few of whom had any practical religion. With these he drank, gambled and danced, and was generally a good fellow. He was a man of more than ordinary talent, and on that account he received considerable respect and deference. His conduct, however, gave scandal to the good within the fold, and also to those without the fold, for it furnished them an occasion for reviling the church.

To round out the details of Father Latour's portrait, Miss Cather drew from the writing of still another churchman, Father Salpointe, who had come to the archdiocese of Santa Fe only nine years after Father Lamy. *Soldiers of the Cross* was the source of valuable factual information, particularly for details of the Archbishop's declining years. In that work (p. 275) Salpointe mentions the country place Lamy purchased in 1853, and to which he withdrew after his retirement in July, 1885. Shortly after taking possession of the land, he had a small house and chapel built; and when the burdens of age and administration dictated rest, he would seek it in this refuge. Those familiar with the *Archbishop* will readily identify a parallel situation in the description of the country house where the aged Latour spent many hours in tranquil meditation.

From Salpointe's book, too (p. 233), Miss Cather drew the inspiration for the extremely moving description of Father Joseph's funeral and the devotion of Father Raverdy, himself mortally ill, as he rushed from France "to make his report to Bishop Vaillant and die in the harness." The scene in the novel reaches poignant culmination when the "dying man, supported by the cab-driver and two priests," makes his way through the mourners and drops to his knees before Father Joseph's bier. And, finally, Miss Cather derived wholly from *Soldiers of the Cross* (p. 275) details about the Archbishop's death: his catching cold at his country house, his desire to return to Santa Fe, the nursing ministrations of the Sisters of Loretto, and his request for the Holy Viaticum.

For Chavez, the fourth of her important characterizations in the *Archbishop*, Miss Cather went to Lummis' *A New Mexico David* (New York, 1891, pp. 190–217); and this reading she substantiated through reference to Twitchell's history (II, 383–84). Chavez's derivative portrait contains such elements as his aristocratic lineage, his pride, his skill with the bow and arrow, his anti-Americanism, the murder of his brother by Navajos, his own near death when he was eighteen, his two-day march across the desert while he was wounded, his home in the San Mateo Mountains. All these matters were verifiable. But while she accepted factual details about Chavez, Miss Cather subjected them to an interpretation which would weave them into the fabric of her conceptual scheme. In her eyes Chavez was a pioneer diverted from his genuine purpose by unfortunately distorted values. Her sympathies, unlike those of Lummis, were for the Indians, not Chavez; and in altering superficial details to accommodate her inherent attitude, she acted in thorough consistency with her artistic purpose. Willa Cather measured the significance of Chavez's actions less by their place in history than by the broader, moral meaning which she could infer from them.

Because her major pioneer characters were men of faith, she was obliged to provide for them a locale which combined the frontier and profoundly contrasting religious attitudes. Her serious reliance upon contrast for the development of both background and characterization is, indeed, a notable aspect of her technique. Against the sophisticated scholarly introspection of Father Latour and the practical religious activity of Father Joseph, she sets forth the muted simplicity of Mexican faith and the barbaric continuity of Indian ritual. Finally, as a historic and symbolic parallel to the efforts of the two French priests, she recounts the arduous toil of Father Junípero Serra, the priest whom she identifies so closely with the Western missionary spirit as to make him a symbol of its heroism. All this information for her religious backdrop Miss Cather absorbed principally from her observation and interpretation of the area, as well as from conversations with informed persons. But as always her reading provided invaluable suggestions and partially developed ideas.

Among the religious elements which attracted her early in her involvement with Southwestern culture was the primitive artistry of Mexican religious images. She speculated in the *Archbishop* on the motivating force behind the creation of these images, concluding that for these simple people "who cannot read—or think" the image is "the physical form of Love!" Here, as in other aspects of her concern with the spiritual problem, she was drawn to instinctive goodness unalloyed by rational considerations. She sensed also that these images were expressions of an entire culture, individually created in the reflection of native poverty

and struggle as well as elementary devotion. Father
Latour found the wooden saints in the humble Mexican homes "much more to his taste than the factory-
made plaster images in his mission churches in Ohio
—more like the homely stone carvings on the front of
the old parish churches in Auvergne."

Although Miss Cather makes no obvious statements
about Father Latour's mild censure of the mass-
produced statuettes, her implication is sufficiently
clear: they are to be equated symbolically with the
disappearance of the frontier under the pressures of
"machine-made materialism," and they spell the attrition of individualized, emotional worship. In the New
Mexico of Father Latour's day this enervating force
was not yet at work. Later, however, in her own trips
to the Southwest Miss Cather was to see the beginnings of this same negated idealism.

Writing "On Death Comes for the Archbishop,"
she deplored the fact that "conventional factory-made
church furnishings from New York" were replacing
the traditional if homely ornamentation and images.
She feared that only after it was too late would Catholics regret the loss of these artistically and historically
valuable symbols. How much better, it seemed to her,
if "all these old paintings and images and carved doors
that have so much feeling and individuality" were to
remain in the old churches, than to be transported to
some New York or Chicago gallery where their innate
meaning would vanish. She felt this trend toward
desensitized ugliness and uniformity reflected the loss
of creative imagination which she deemed essential to
the pioneer spirit.

In juxtaposition to the gentle, simple devotion of
the Mexicans which she stresses (she devotes an entire
chapter to the history of the Shrine of our Lady of
Guadalupe, but makes only passing reference to the

fanatic piety of the Penitentes), Miss Cather represents the age-old pagan rites of the Indians. She even magnifies their barbarism and antiquity by viewing them through the agency of the fastidious Father Latour. Thrown into physically close proximity to Indian ritual, he is repelled by its antediluvian nature. Seeking shelter from a snow storm, he entered the Pecos ceremonial cave and "was struck by a reluctance, an extreme distaste for the place. The air in the cave was glacial, penetrated to the very bones, and he detected at once a fetid odour, not very strong but highly disagreeable." And though nothing remarkable happened at the time, years later the cave "flashed into his mind from time to time, and always with a shudder of repugnance quite unjustified by anything he had experienced there. It had been a hospitable shelter to him in his extremity. Yet afterward he remembered the storm itself, even his exhaustion, with a tingling sense of pleasure. But the cave, which had probably saved his life, he remembered with horror." From this concretized incident with its mere echoes of ancient ritualism, Willa Cather moves to more specific details of pagan worship. In their recording she has an opportunity to display her knowledge of Pecos religious legends, such as their year-round care of an undying fire, snake worship, and the hidden shrine in a cavern of the Pecos hills.

Treating these Indian rites and legends in evocative fashion, Miss Cather is yet purposely vague about them; again and again she points out that her sources are mainly rumor and hearsay. We may take her word, then, in assuming that common talk probably brought her attention to the notion of a sacred cave known only to the descendants of the Pecos Indians. The secret of its contents and location was supposed to have been successfully withheld from any white man.

Earle R. Forrest, for example, in *Missions and Pueblos of the Old Southwest* (Cleveland, 1929), records this information as being a popularly disseminated rumor.

Similarly, she may have derived her information about actual religious practices from common knowledge. But it is also possible that she learned of them from Lt. J. W. Abert's official report (*Executive Documents . . . of the Senate*—Washington, 1847—IV, 30–40). He alluded to one belief that immense serpents were kept in their temples, and another that a perpetual fire kindled by Montezuma and guarded by a member of the tribe was an object of worship. "As the severity of their vigils always caused the death of the watchers, in time this tribe became extinct [Miss Cather speaks of this perhaps fanciful interpretation in the *Archbishop*]. Again, I have been told that some six or eight of their people were left, and that they took the sacred fire and went to live with the Pueblos of Zuni." Lt. Abert expressed amazement at the interest in Pecos religious superstitions shown by "enlightened man."

Always, whether she treats the religious faith of the Mexicans or the mysterious ceremonies of the Indians, Miss Cather succeeds in creating an atmosphere of religious continuity which can be stifled only temporarily but never destroyed. She creates, in short, a sense of spiritual timelessness rooted in the unrecorded past and extending toward an unfathomable future. This emanation of pious continuity is symbolized in part by the fourteenth-century Spanish bell, the story of which Miss Cather borrowed directly from Howlett. For over a hundred years the bell hung in the Church of San Miguel at Santa Fe, and then lay for another hundred in a cellar from where it was once more resurrected, this time by Father Joseph. A thing of metal, the bell yet had been founded for an inspirational cause that made inevitable its restoration so that it could help celebrate an eternally true devotion. The same tones that had been heard centuries ago in the desert would continue to remind the devout that they were Christians. The same conviction of timelessness is given substance even more overtly in a single incident related in the *Archbishop* by Father Joseph:

> Down near Tucson a Pima Indian convert once asked me to go off into the desert with him, as he had something to show me. He took me into a place so wild that a man less accustomed to these things might have mistrusted and feared for his life. We descended into a terrifying canyon of black rock, and there in the depths of a cave, he showed me a golden chalice, vestments and cruets, all the paraphernalia for celebrating Mass. His ancestors had hidden these sacred objects there when the mission was sacked by Apaches, he did not know how many generations ago. The secret had been handed down in his family, and I was the first priest who had ever come to restore to God his own. To me, that is the situation in a parable. The Faith in that wild frontier, is like a buried treasure; they guard it, but they do not know how to use it to their soul's salvation. A word, a prayer, a service, is all that is needed to set free those souls in bondage. I confess I am covetous of that mission. I desire to be the man who restores these lost children to God. It will be the greatest happiness of my life.

Although Miss Cather brought to the episode a sanctified interpretation that is her own, the physical occurrence is by no means her invention; the history of the Southwest contains numerous comparable incidents. The Catholic clergy in the uncertain days of their missionary toil frequently were compelled to bury their sacred treasure in anticipation of Indian raids, and subsequent discoveries such as the novelist recounts were fairly common. She may have heard of a find like this during one of her many visits to New Mexico; and certainly she read of similar incidents, particularly in the work of Salpointe (p. 227) and in the diaries of two Army officers who visited the area in 1853 (Smithsonian Inst., 1855 *Annual Report,* pp. 296–316). Out of legend and record, she distilled the materials which make up the present scene.

Miss Cather saves for the conclusion of the *Archbishop* the story of miracles experienced by Father Junípero, augurs of piety which she employs as climactically as her legend-like construction of the novel will permit. From Palou's biography (pp. 12–13, 21–22) she selects three wonders which befell the missionary priest: the miraculous fording of the river, the "manna" in the desert, and the visitation of the Holy Family in the guise of poor Mexicans. But she develops only the last supernatural occurrence—at once the most inspirational and the most dramatic of the three—into a full-blown incident or scene. At its conclusion she meditates upon what it signifies to her:

> There is always something charming in the idea of greatness returning to simplicity—the queen making hay among the country girls—but how much more endearing was the belief that They, after so many centuries of history and glory, should return to play Their first parts, in the persons of a humble Mexican family, the lowliest of the lowly, the poorest of the poor,—in a wilderness at the end of the world, where the angels could scarcely find Them!

Through Willa Cather's presentation of the miracles she makes her complex intention most apparent. Here she concretizes the religious simplicity of her frontier locale. Here, also, she recreates Father Junípero as a figure heroically parallel to Father Latour, and in so doing she reiterates her faith in the Archbishop not only as a remarkable individual but as the representative of a hardy, sanctified breed.

And finally, she points to the ameliorations of those hardships which beset the religious missionary. This last goal she states positively by reminding her readers that "no man could know what triumphs of faith had happened there, where one white man [the early missionary] met torture and death alone among so many infidels, or what visions and revelations God may have granted to soften that brutal end." The naïveté of humble acceptance becomes an instrument of transcendent reality. Stated artlessly as an ultimate truth to which there can be no alternative, the divinity represented by miraculous intervention invites no argument from rational skeptics. The token of supernal will is there to be believed—the loss is his who somehow fails to respond.

For her deeply felt imaginative purposes, then, Willa Cather has made rich application of literary borrowing and personal experiences and observations. Surprisingly, despite manipulation of data, she never distorts information or makes serious departures from historical authenticity. She alters facts only twice, to increase dramatic impact in certain scenes, and in each instance she anticipates the reader's knowledge and probable objections. She has Father Joseph die before Father Latour, a circumstance which is not historically accurate, as she herself points out in "On Death Comes for the Archbishop." Moreover, she consciously alters the date of the abandonment of the Pecos pueblo. When dealing with rumor or common supposition, she is in most cases careful to point that out. Yet it should be abundantly evident by now that her concern is not with facts as such but, rather, with facts as they convey ethical meaning through their symbolic or metaphorical nature. Surely Coleridge's belief that "veracity does not consist in saying, but in the intention of communicating, truth" would have been most acceptable to Miss Cather as a statement of her own conviction.

And the most satisfying technical aspect of her use of factual materials is her artistic genius in molding and individualizing their diversity into an organic totality. This is her achievement of "similitude in dissimilitude." Usually charitable in her evaluations of historical figures, she feels a tremendous bond with them and their environment. Actually, it is her consistently fostered sympathy in union with discriminated historical details which has made the *Archbishop* the greatest of her novels.

Of Willa Cather it may be said, as she herself said of Sarah Orne Jewett, that she achieved a monument noble and enduring by giving herself absolutely to her material. Her great gift is that of sympathy. The artist, she said, "fades away into the land and people of his heart, he dies of love only to be born again." The lasting accomplishment is not to be won by the spurious process of "improving on his subject matter, using his 'imagination' upon it and twisting it to suit his purpose." The best that can be gained from such writing is "a brilliant sham, which . . . looks poor and shabby in a few years." For Miss Cather the things that mattered were those to which she devoted a lifetime of love and experience and which she had to represent in their true essence as she understood it. From this came the happiness of a fulfilled promise whose best qualities she brought together in the *Archbishop*.

THERE IS a steadiness about Willa Cather's fiction that defies the crosscurrents of the literary age in which she lived and wrote. Like many conscientious American writers, she was profoundly aware of the growing cleavage in her society between moral values and expedient action. Dislocations following the military and economic disasters she witnessed in her lifetime caused her to share a widespread fear that the future was bleakly uncertain, that a spiritual chaos threatened the central purpose of existence. More than most thoughtful Americans, perhaps, she was personally sensitive to devalued conduct and customs. Because she had consciously built her life upon a structure of traditions, and because she had preferred the solid virtues of an inspiriting past to the mercurial shifts of practical reality, she suspiciously resisted change. From time to time she protested against the violation of durable truths, although rarely in the clamorous voice used by many contemporary writers. Looking backward to the fixed values of a satisfying past, she reaffirmed the moral standards she cherished, thus ultimately denying they could be destroyed by temporary upheavals. In so doing, she committed herself to a pattern of continuity and became part of an exclusive but nevertheless great tradition of American writing.

Given fullest expression in the nineteenth century, the tradition is synthesized in the fiction of Cooper, Hawthorne, Melville, and James. Although they differed in their reactions to the convulsions afflicting an America in flux, they are unified by certain connections of personal responsibility. In the opinion of Marius Bewley (*The Complex Fate*, New York, 1954, pp. 3–4), these authors "form a line in American writing based on a finely critical consciousness of the national society." Although all of them drew upon America as the source of their creative purpose, they resembled each other in their awareness of national exigencies rather than in any superficial resort to a common region or even set of circumstances.

Admiring the potential greatness of their country, they at the same time recognized certain shortcomings and imperfections which menaced that greatness. Their art, which makes their union in a tradition relevant, was derived from a conflict between apprehension and conviction. Their tradition was compounded of earnest, mutual concern for the realization of an American destiny. Because they identified their fears with their hopes, they felt obliged to acknowledge that the positive advances of which their nation was capable were too frequently accompanied by attrition. In order to nullify, or at least retard, negative developments, they often spoke out against them in sharply critical fashion. Constructive criticism became one of their means of asserting optimistic conclusions.

In every essential detail, Willa Cather aspired toward the ethical and creative goals of the great tradition, consequently becoming the twentieth-century successor of these four nineteenth-century novelists. Miss Cather's novels are still relatively recent, and historical perspective may not yet permit an ultimate evaluation of her literary position. We do have standards of continuity by which we may measure her achievement, however, and if these standards have any critical validity then Miss Cather is surely in the line of succession. More notably even than Cooper, and with a moral intensity comparable to that of Hawthorne, Melville, and James, Miss Cather has represented the tensions of American existence in the late nineteenth and early twentieth century. Like her predecessors—especially the last three—she is a commentator on the prevailing American condition. Sometimes urgent in her fears but always ardent in her faith, she constantly held before herself the vision of realizable ideals. Out of inspired singleness of conviction grew a distinguished art. To a greater degree than any of the four traditionalists except James, Willa Cather was absorbed in the total identification of an esthetic with moral purpose. Great achievement in the fusion of two inalienable ideals sets her apart from her own contemporaries and fixes her in a continuity of distinguished American writing whose practitioners are few.

With the United States as a common subject, and with its frustrations and destiny as a common theme, the tradition makes comparisons inevitable. But even within the limits of an idealized cause, the writers assert their separateness, demonstrating in their respective works of fiction that individual talents must search through varieties of conscience, and of literary modes and incidents for answers to the riddles of being. The changing mask of America furthermore exacts from each writer attention to problems which, at least in an exterior fashion, are significantly focal in his age and in no other. The frontier which Cooper writes about in the first half of the nineteenth century is obviously different from that with which Willa Cather concerns herself in the twentieth. The Calvinistic or Puritanical assumptions of sin which beset Hawthorne and Mel-

ville have a theological basis which is not directly
germane to the esthetically controlled questions of
Miss Cather. Yet she is no less engaged by the meaning of the frontier than Cooper, nor any more casual
about human salvation or destiny than are Hawthorne
and Melville. The denominators are common but the
point of view is individual. The inner-directed concentration which each serious artist brings to an understanding of certain universal conditions is in a large
measure the unifying force of the tradition. Each was
driven by a need to deal earnestly and artistically with
large, pervasive issues.

At first glance, Miss Cather would appear by virtue
of her frequently used frontier subjects to be closest
to Cooper. In fact, however, the frontier provides only
a superficial resemblance, and Cooper was the writer
most distant from her in temperament even as he was
in time. That they were alike at all in aim is the result
of the fact that they were deeply engrossed in the solution of American crises, each in his own way. Yvor
Winters (*Maule's Curse*, Norfolk, Conn., 1938, p. 29)
has said of Cooper that his "concern was primarily for
public morality; it was the concern of the statesman,
or of the historian, first, and of the artist but secondar-
ily." This statement of Cooper's literary interests,
acutely defensible, it appears to us, shows the polarity
between him and Willa Cather. National morality
was, to be sure, intensely part of her fiction of the
frontier. But in Cooper's intention we find a reversed
image of Miss Cather's. She was the artist, and—more
significantly—the moral artist, first. It was only after
she had appeased her esthetic-moral sense that she
spoke as the historian, and then but to give fuller definition to her primary intention. Dealing with ethics
rather than with manners, dedicated to a personal,
nondoctrinal concept of salvation, she drew her char-

acters as moral agents, somewhat as abstractions, if more balanced in physical properties than Hawthorne's.

Sharing with Hawthorne and Melville a moral propensity that is unusual in the twentieth century, Miss Cather built her novels along allegorical lines which we have described in our opening chapter. Without engaging in tedious, inconclusive comparisons or judgments of ultimate worth, however, we suggest that the parallels, as in the case of Cooper, must be limited because of differences in concepts of the novel.

Essentially an allegorist, and hence essentially a moralist, Hawthorne deliberately restricted his artistic materials for maximum concentration upon his moralistic intention. He used the exterior circumstances of physical reality, but he made them shadowy symbols of profoundly inner necessity. His selection of details was rigorous in order that each physical moment be allowed to direct most searching attention to its moral equivalent. The seriousness with which he viewed the relationship between facts and the ultimate truths of being is apparent in the short story "Wakefield," where he described his concept of fiction. His starting point would be a private symbol in which he had discovered eternal, salutary meaning. From the symbol he would proceed to the construction of a narrative through whose constituent parts he translated the moral in terms related to the experiences of his readers. In this sense, which is consistent with his usual practice, Hawthorne's allegorized stories became processes of correlation between inner truth and outer matter. As Miss Cather observed about *The Scarlet Letter*, in "The Novel Démeublé": "The material investiture of the story is presented as if unconsciously; by the reserved, fastidious hand of an artist, not by the gaudy fingers of a showman or the mechanical industry of a department-store window-dresser."

Our examination of Miss Cather's novels reveals a concern which differs mainly in degree and intention. In her tendency to allegorize her moral searchings, she like Hawthorne never lost sight of her function as a creative artist. Indeed, she devoted herself to the notion that only through the highest expression of art could she give worthy representation to her inner desire. More specifically than Hawthorne, she cherished people as people and incidents as incidents. She softened the lines of her figures and actions, but she never clothed them in such abstractions that they lost verisimilitude. She respected the varieties of human emotions and meant them to be credible aspects of daily, familiar experience.

She was furthermore acutely conscious of artistic techniques, giving her search for esthetic perfection equality with her yearning for inner meaning. With regard to artistic credibility, she was closer to Melville than to Hawthorne, for like the former she sought a more immediate equation between physical reality and spiritual significance. As is true of Melville, she portrayed phenomenal reality and human beings in readily identifiable proportions. She made them agents of an ultimate truth but always invested them with properties which could be accounted for immediately at the conscious level of perception as well as at the somewhat mystic level of moral insight. If she was less visionary than Hawthorne and Melville, and less profound in her moral intensity, she was the more accomplished technician and consequently the more readable novelist.

But among the major writers in the tradition, Henry James undoubtedly bears the closest creative resemblance to Miss Cather. Both as an artist and as a moral realist he was the literary personality who figured most prominently among the influences shaping her artistic development. Greatly respectful of his esthetic achievements, she was attracted to his singularity of purpose, to the manner in which he made an art form cohesive with serious thematic details. James was so evidently the novelist she herself cared to be that she imitated him unsuccessfully in *Alexander's Bridge*. Her blunder, as she realized, was the attempt to capture a style in which meaning was not appropriately related to personal experience. But if James ceased to function as her model for the execution of idea and form, he left a permanent impression upon her because of the purity of aim which she always venerated as the essence of her own practice. Although they dealt with comparable themes somewhat divergently, each drawing upon his particular genius, the subtle likenesses between them make their exterior differences relatively unimportant.

What is important, in the present connection, is the attitude which they took toward their art. It is an attitude of moral sobriety, a deeply serious concern with quintessential American problems. Basic to this commitment is an esthetic sensibility which transfigures ethical responsibility into organic narrative situations. Both Henry James and Willa Cather believed that without appropriately conceived shape the novel fails to represent in true essence the inner experience which is the only justifiable substance of fiction. For each, therefore, a moral sense is powerfully one with an esthetic sense. Concept and form admit of no separation, the two growing simultaneously in the created work, inevitably and rightly. With respect to technical virtuosity, James and Miss Cather progressed beyond the earlier writers. In their fusion of moral idea and physical reality, they acknowledged to a remarkable degree the demands of their art, and then went on to fulfill the obligations to which they had committed themselves.

James and Miss Cather, furthermore, are related in the subjects they chose, although they attacked them from different angles. Yvor Winters (p. 170) has pointed out that James wrote about "the spiritual antagonism which had existed for centuries between the rising provincial civilization and the richer civilization from which it has broken away, an antagonism in which the provincial civilization met the obviously superior cultivation of the parent with a more or less typically provincial assertion of superiority." Whereas for James the antagonism lay between an ancient European culture and an upstart American culture, for Miss Cather the rift existed at times as an exclusively American phenomenon. That is, she focused her frontier novels on the divisions existing among native cultural forms. She may be said to have narrowed her view intensively, looking to the frontier first as a reaffirmation of traditional American values, and then to its development as a corruption of those values. As a further point of comparison, however, it must not be forgotten that even in the frontier novels, such as O Pioneers! and My Ántonia, she often considered with affection the traditions the first-generation pioneers had brought with them from Europe. But whether James and Willa Cather treated American themes as outgrowths of cultural divisions between nations or within the nation, they always did so with a moral responsiveness. Each brought to his novels a personal commitment which wedded feeling with insight, although Miss Cather's sympathies for America were the more immediate and direct.

As a traditionalist in an age which had no reverence for tradition, Miss Cather was a lonely figure. The moral integrity of the individual implied an exaltation of personality, even of egoism, which collided with the mass standardization and rapidly shifting values of mechanistic progress. To resist in a practical sense was, of course, vain. But the convictions of writers such as Miss Cather and James, as well as of Hawthorne and Melville, transcended practicality. Thus, Miss Cather, who formed very few intimate alliances in her lifetime, clung to a somewhat solitary position from which she idealized universal truth and frequently denounced temporization. Like Thoreau she challenged her own society, and like him she demanded a return to good purpose. "Turn to the old; return to them," he wrote in *Walden*. "Things do not change: we change."

Her attitude has implicitly the same insistence upon values which Irving Babbitt and Paul Elmer More enunciated in their doctrine of neo-humanism. They preached moderation, abhorring the excesses of both naturalism and asceticism. While they sought a mean between amoral action promoted by animal instinct and the profound introspection often attendant upon organized religion, they optimistically looked for a balance point in existence. The fulcrum, they decided, must be within the individual; it must be based upon awareness of the human condition, it must incorporate the better properties of instinct and faith, and it must be controlled judiciously and wisely by means of an inner check. Man, mature and responsible, is thus the measure of this demanding philosophy. As Stuart Sherman summed it up (*On Contemporary Literature*, New York, 1917, p. 17), the neo-humanistic position urged "the desirability of continuing to work out in the world that ideal pattern which lies in the instructed and disciplined heart."

Miss Cather did not subscribe formally to the tenets of this philosophy, which had arisen out of protests against the irritations of a prevailing naturalistic temper. But her fiction is ample evidence of her privately and esthetically derived humanism. She was consistently moderate, but she never doubted that within the cares of real human problems individuals could and should work toward positive values. To this end she identified her art with a moral realism, even as James had, which helps to clarify her distinctive contribution to literature. The kind of realism she practiced is usefully defined by Sherman (p. 101) in his sharp attack on "The Barbaric Naturalism of Theodore Dreiser." Finding Dreiser devoid of moral value and esthetic worth, Sherman proposed a separation between the naturalistic and realistic novel. "Both are representative of the life of man in contemporary or nearly contemporary society, and both are presumably composed of materials within the experience and observation of the author. But the realistic novel is a representation based upon a theory of human conduct. . . . A naturalistic novel is a representation based upon a theory of animal behavior. Since a theory of animal behavior can never be an adequate basis for a representation of the life of man in contemporary society, such a representation is an artistic blunder."

This is not an occasion for judging the naturalistic novel or the realistic novel, but Sherman's description of the latter genre is very much to the point, in that Miss Cather also drew upon her experiences and observations to formulate in fiction a theory of human conduct. Furthermore, she repudiated contemporary naturalism, artistically expressing her distaste for a theory of animal behavior applied to human beings. She was repelled not only by the premise of action determined wholly by raw instinct, but also by the relentless inclusiveness of details which was the hallmark of naturalism. Of the early naturalists, only

Stephen Crane seemed to her to be free of this creative flaw. Indeed, she admired him as "one of the first post-impressionists," as one "who never tried to make a faithful report of everything else within his field of vision, as if he were a conscientious salesman making out his expense-account." But for the naturalistic movement in general, with its divorce from humane and esthetic principles, she harbored contempt.

Although she considered certain American writers of the 1930's—notably, Hemingway, Wilder, Fitzgerald, and Lewis—to be genuine artists, she thought the fiction of that period was largely without purpose. Yet, if she was hostile to the overt tone of pessimism and cynicism which pervaded much of contemporary fiction, she was closer in spirit to this literature of harsh reality than she herself would have cared to admit. For all the external disapprobation and negativeness of such writers as Dos Passos, the early Faulkner and Steinbeck, Caldwell, Farrell, and many others, they are innately idealists. They are idealists because they imply the possibility of something better and do not lean back upon the comfortable false optimism of settled peace and contentment that could be illusory at best. The positive goal is there, but it is implicit as a reaction against those very qualities and subjects of which each author writes.

Even in the primitive, naturalistic concept the stringent sense of determinism—handed down from Crane, Norris, London, and Dreiser—does not totally conceal hope. Steinbeck, for instance, is thematically close to Miss Cather because he has a high regard for the life of simple necessity and because he shows us that despite economic disaster it is still possible for men to retain at least vestiges of their traditions, to seek a social and even spiritual well-being, and to have respect for the inherent dignity of man. And Faulkner, likewise—especially in the later phases of his career—appears to conclude that man is worthy; that he is capable of dignified and even noble action; that, in short, he will endure and prevail. Wolfe bears another kind of resemblance to Miss Cather because of his profound respect for the artistic temperament.

All the serious writers who were contemporary with her share an awareness of the brotherhood of man. The principles of Darwin, Marx, Freud, Einstein, and the new atomism have, to be sure, tended to supplant the old orthodoxies. The urgencies imposed by the mechanics of the new science, the law of survival of the fittest, biological determinism—all these have taken away much of the awe and wonder of existence and have replaced them with a fear and contempt of the finite and material. But the strong sense of mechanical determinism after all underscores rather than denies the need for values that transcend the temporal.

Because of her morally sentimental attachment to the traditional past, however, Willa Cather was less adaptable to the present than most of her contemporaries. Because the note of protest is less frequent in her writings than in those of other novelists, when it occurs its contrast with her customary tranquillity makes it all the more pronounced. One of her protests is directed against science and scientific materialism, and its major occurrence is in *The Professor's House* and *One of Ours*. Unlike most of the naturalistic writers who deal with this debilitating phenomenon through satire or the inevitable tragedy of determinism, Miss Cather speaks out with an unusual bluntness which is the testimony of her personal grievance. In this respect she is more akin to several distinguished poets, who were more inclined to voice a spiritual distress, than to the sociologically minded naturalists. E. A. Robinson, Robert Frost, and T. S. Eliot have, each in his own way, developed a thesis of the negative effect of science on modern morality, a thesis which complements Miss Cather's own displeasure (see Hyatt H. Waggoner's *The Heel of Elohim*, Norman, Okla., 1950). Here, too, is a tradition of idealistic protest which may be traced to the nineteenth century, especially to the writings of Thoreau.

But science was only one aspect of what seemed to Willa Cather to be a universally hollow condition. As far as she was willing to see, existence in her times had become spiritually devitalized and values meaningless in a wasteland of conformity and aimless enterprise. The implications were immediate enough for her, even though the notion of futility is given expression in numberless idealistic contexts. Surrender to this kind of inner exhaustion had been described by Shelley as moral death and by Arnold as philistinism. Depleted and insecure, the victims of this waste—to borrow from Thoreau—"lead lives of quiet desperation. What is called resignation is confirmed desperation."

The particular phenomenon of modern times which aroused Miss Cather to explicit statement was the rise of small towns in the wake of westward expansion. As a result—most pronounced in *My Ántonia* and in several bitter short stories—she challenged the spiritual aridity of a narrowly conformist society. Thus she takes a place alongside Sinclair Lewis and Sherwood Anderson, among others, in her attack upon smug provincialism. She was irritated by the complacent inertness of those people who accepted the material comforts handed down to them by their hard-working parents, as in the frontier novels, or by men of vision and accomplishment like Tom Outland in *The Professor's House*. Both contemptuous and grieved because of wooden acceptance, she gradually visualized it as an infection spreading even to the large, established communities of America and Europe. Her attack upon conformity at all levels of society is consistent with a widely shared theme of contemporary literature. It is reminiscent, for instance, of Marquand's more specifically contrived ridicule of New England sameness. The fact that Miss Cather's buoyant spirit generally causes an optimistic note to prevail in her fiction by no means lessens the seriousness of her inner fears.

Throughout her novels, then, Miss Cather is in the curiously ambivalent position of standing apart from her contemporaries, and yet at the same time of sharing many of the immediate moral problems which they had made their responsibility. Although she directed her vision to a traditional past, as they did not, she was nonetheless able to assess the dilemma of modern times through a conjunction of tradition with present reality. The important thing for her, of course, was that values may never be divorced from art. But it must also be acknowledged that for most serious writers of modern times moral or social responsibility must coincide with esthetic awareness. Willa Cather addresses herself most memorably to a tradition of conscience and hope; in this respect she is in the main stream of great American literary achievement. But she also addresses herself trenchantly, if in a minor key, to affairs of material reality. Eloquently joining past and present, affirmation and censure, she has memorialized herself as an American classic.